Patternmaking History and Theory

Patternmaking History and Theory

Edited by
Jennifer Grayer Moore

BLOOMSBURY VISUAL ARTS
LONDON • NEW YORK • OXFORD • NEW DELHI • SYDNEY

BLOOMSBURY VISUAL ARTS
Bloomsbury Publishing Plc
50 Bedford Square, London, WC1B 3DP, UK
1385 Broadway, New York, NY 10018, USA
29 Earlsfort Terrace, Dublin 2, Ireland

BLOOMSBURY, BLOOMSBURY VISUAL ARTS and the Diana logo are trademarks of
Bloomsbury Publishing Plc

First published in Great Britain 2020
Paperback edition published 2021

Cover design: Charlotte Daniels
Cover image: Valentino with a model in his atelier
(© Reporters Associati & Archivi/Getty Images)

A catalogue record for this book is available from the British Library.

A catalog record for this book is available from the Library of Congress.

ISBN: HB: 978-1-350-06264-1
       PB: 978-1-350-22780-4
     ePDF: 978-1-350-06265-8
    eBook: 978-1-350-06266-5

Typeset by RefineCatch Limited, Bungay, Suffolk

To find out more about our authors and books visit www.bloomsbury.com
and sign up for our newsletters.

Contents

List of Illustrations

Notes on Contributors

Fatma Baytar is an assistant professor at Cornell University, US, in the Department of Fiber Science and Apparel Design. Her research focuses on digital technologies in apparel design, particularly three-dimensional (3D) computer-aided design (CAD)/ virtual prototyping and 3D body scanning, and examining how these technologies transform apparel design processes and products. Dr. Baytar has conducted research in the areas pertaining to the accuracy of 3D virtual garment prototypes, the impact of using 3D virtual prototyping on design skills, virtual avatars and body image issues, augmented reality applications for virtual dressing rooms, functional and protective apparel product development, and digital technologies' impact on environmental sustainability. Her research findings have been disseminated in major peer-reviewed journals and presented at international conferences.

Anthony Bednall is a trained fashion designer who has a broad industry and academic background. He is presently the Associate Head of the Manchester Fashion Institute, Manchester Metropolitan University, UK. As a designer, he has shown fashion collections in London, Paris, and Tokyo. Whilst based in Beijing, he designed garments for international companies including the Hilton Hotel, Audi, Lenovo, and Sofitel, and was a regular judge at China International Fashion week. He regularly produced articles for newspapers and magazines such as *China Textiles, China Apparel*, and *China Fashion Weekly*. His research is focused on the relationship between fashion, culture and society, identity, and art, falling into two distinct categories, twentieth century Chinese fashion and sculptural artifacts. He has produced book chapters, conference papers and curated exhibitions on Chinese fashion, both nationally and internationally, with a specific interest and focus on the context, cultural capital, and visual codification of clothing as a representational and symbolic illustration of a culture trying to clarify its own existential identity through socio-political turmoil and economic change. His artifacts are constructs, made from non-traditional fashion materials such as cardboard, currency, wood, and vellum, all of which are rooted in patternmaking. The artifacts he produces interrogate fashion, the body, cultural identity, and embedded narratives, in relation to, and synergistically with, metropolitan landscapes and have been exhibited internationally.

Gozde Goncu-Berk received her PhD degree in Design with an Apparel Studies track from University of Minnesota, US. She holds an MA degree in Clothing Design and BS degree in Industrial Design from Istanbul Technical University, Turkey. Currently Dr. Goncu-Berk is an Assistant Professor at University of California-Davis, Design Department. Her research interests are new product development processes, cross-cultural aspects of design, functional apparel design and wearable products for healthcare applications.

Rebecca J. Keyel received her PHD in Design Studies at the University of Wisconsin, Madison, US. She holds an MS in Human Ecology from the University of Wisconsin, Madison, and a BA from Wellesley College. Her research interests include material culture, textile and knitting history, folklore, and home craft. Her current research project examines American women's hand knitting for servicemen during the First and Second World Wars and its relationship with labor, patriotism, and the zeitgeist of the home front.

Addie Martindale, PhD is an Assistant Professor in the School of Human Sciences, in the College of Behavioral and Social Sciences at Georgia Southern University, US. Her research focuses on the motivations and consumption practices of nontraditional apparel consumers, transformable garment design, adoption of minimal wardrobes, and apparel design and merchandising pedagogy. Dr. Martindale's creative scholarship explores sustainable apparel design methods including generating design solutions for pre-consumer and post-consumer textile waste.

Ellen McKinney is Associate Professor in Apparel, Events, and Hospitality Management at Iowa State University, US. Her primary research focuses on theory in patternmaking. Her area of specialization is apparel sizing and fit with interest in the use of technology to develop patternmaking theory for improved garment fit, how apparel consumers, retailers, and wholesalers impact and are impacted by garment fit, and teaching fitting techniques. Dr. McKinney's creative production is related to her research in apparel fit, intercultural exchange through design, and exploration of ways to creatively recycle textile products.

Jennifer Grayer Moore is an art and design historian who lectures at the Pratt Institute in New York City, US. She is a graduate of the Design Studies PhD program at the University of Wisconsin, Madison and earned an MA in Art History from Hunter College. She has taught art, design, and fashion history as well as courses pertaining to the business of fashion for the past fifteen years. Dr. Moore's research is largely focused on twentieth and twenty-first century fashion, with a special interest in the intersection between design and the business of fashion. Her most recent publications are *Fashion Fads Through American History: Fitting Clothes into Context* (2015) and *Street Style in America: An Exploration* (2017). *Patternmaking History and Theory* is her first edited volume.

Catherine Roy is a tailor, author, and curator. She received her Tailoring Technician (Honors) diploma from the Northern Alberta Institute of Technology in 1978 and her MSc in the history of dress from the University of Alberta, Canada, in 1990. She has worked as a custom tailor and a theatrical menswear cutter (1978–2000). Catherine was the Acting Curator of the Clothing and Textiles Collection at the University of Alberta from 1991–4 and a lecturer in the History of Dress. She was Assistant Curator, then Curator of the Western Canadian History Collection of the Royal Alberta Museum from 2000–16. From 2012 until her retirement in 2016, Catherine developed historical exhibitions with subject matter that ranged from the early oil industry to community theater for the new Western Canadian History Gallery, Royal Alberta Museum.

Eulanda A. Sanders is chair of the Department of Apparel, Events, and Hospitality Management at Iowa State University, US. Dr. Sanders also holds the Donna R. Danielson Professorship of Textiles and Clothing in the Apparel, Merchandising and Design program, and has taught over 300 classes in fashion and textile design at the university level for the past twenty-eight years. Dr. Sanders has worked in the industry as a patternmaker and has taught patternmaking classes for twenty-five years. Dr. Sanders is featured in the 12th annual 2018 Women Impacting ISU calendar for her outstanding leadership and advocacy for student, faculty, and staff success. She has been recognized for her outstanding work in teaching, research, and outreach by Iowa State University and Colorado State University. Dr. Sanders has a variety of published work in the area of the impact Blacks, mainly Black women, have had on the textiles and clothing industry. Dr. Sanders' research has been published and recognized in the *International Journal of Fashion Design, Technology and Education,* and *Clothing and Textiles Research Journal.*

Bingyue Wei is a PhD student in Apparel, Events, and Hospitality Management at Iowa State University, US. Her research is centered on creative fashion design, including transformational design and wearable media. Her current research focuses on building interaction between the garment and the environment. She specializes in the development of garment and pattern fit with integrated technology.

Hannah Wroe is a lecturer in fashion at the University of Lincoln, UK, where she specializes in pattern cutting. Originally trained in made-to-measure womenswear, she completed her MA at Nottingham Trent University researching pattern cutting and construction methods. Her research interests include material culture and object-based approaches to the study of dress and textile history, pattern cutting, and the history of fashion education. Since 2015, she has been committee member of The Costume Society where she currently sits on the Communications Committee.

Elli Michaela Young is currently a PhD candidate at the University of Brighton, UK. Her research focuses on the use of fashion and textiles in the production of Jamaican identities during the period of transition from colony to independent nation (1950–75). Elli studied at London Metropolitan University for her undergraduate degree in Design and Goldsmith's College for her MA in Postcolonial Cultures and Global Policy.

Preface

Much has been written to document the history of dress, both fashionable and workaday. Writers across disciplines have documented the social history of fashionable dress, the individuals who helped shape tastes and practices, and the industry in which the production of apparel and accessories has flourished. Additionally, scholars have theorized the social and psychological aspects of adorning the body. Theoretical explorations have considered human motivation for modifying the physical self with piercings and tattoos, engaging in physical regimens to tame, train, and re-shape the physical form, as well as motivations for engaging in *fashionable* dress. In the course of exploring both this history and this theory, the lion's share of ink has been expended on the end result, especially completed garments and accessories, the individuals who *designed* them, and the social context in which they were worn. Histories of individual creators often overlook the issue of patternmaking; perhaps only taking a line to note that the *créateur* was not versed in this skill set. Notably by making creators and objects the focus of study, much is gained. Our understanding of dress practices has been greatly enriched by viewing dress through the lenses of creative people responding to their social contexts and by examining the actions of people adorning themselves as a means of self-expression in the eras in which they lived.

Both the history and the theories of patternmaking are not unexplored topics, but arguably they are underexplored, underexposed, and not reasonably integrated into either the history of dress or the practical and creative practice of pattern design. This text is an effort to cast new light on the related subjects of patternmaking history and theory. It is an effort to highlight new research and also a means (by virtue of literature reviews, citations, and bibliography) to bring the attention of modern readers to incredibly important texts on these subjects.

Patterns, whether draped, drafted, or in the case of instructions for techniques such as knitting, written as lines of directions, are the meticulous, mathematical, technical specifications for the creations to which we credit makers, whether they are named designers (or their houses) or friends and family who we know. Apparel and accessories patterns are the progenitors of the objects in which we adorn ourselves. Like the finished items, the construction of which they facilitate, patterns have the ability to reveal creative impulses, qualities of the maker, aspects of cultural context, and the state of the fashion industry in a given period. Additionally, exploring patternmaking from both historical and theoretical perspectives opens up the study of fashion to include the study of a skill that is both technical and creative, and which is often the area of expertise of an unnamed creative whose efforts made actual the dreams or drawings of a customer or couturier. Thus, scholars and students who make dress the focus of their work, either in whole or in part, will benefit from exploring this rich and complex topic. Making a consideration of patterns one more aspect of the rich and complex tapestry of ideas that comprise dress studies will serve to enrich the study in its entirety.

Introduction

One afternoon in New York City, during a pause for questions at a lecture about eighteenth-century European fashion, a student asked how patterns for complex garments like the *robe a la française* were created. I thanked the student for the question and paused as I reflected on the fact that not only did I not know the answer, but truly I had not realized that this important part of the story of fashion was not a part of my repertoire. At that point I had been a student and a teacher of the subject for more than a decade, had read countless volumes about the history of Western dress, and had never encountered the subject in monographs, surveys, or scholarly articles. Could it be that the subject had not been explored?

The first step in any research project is to review the extant literature. In so doing I found there has been significant research in this area, yet it seems that much of this important scholarship has not been adequately integrated into contemporary dress studies and some seminal texts, written in the late twentieth century, and now out of print, have been overlooked by far too many scholars in the field of dress studies. This collection of essays builds on the scholarship that has already been done, strives to re-integrate it into contemporary fashion studies, and extends the exploration in several important ways. First, many of the chapters in this book provide a shift in focus from the pattern viewed primarily as an independent technology to the consideration of the pattern as a tool that is used by a person in a given context of culture, economics, craftsmanship, and experience within the arts and crafts of apparel construction. In fact, several contributions to this volume specifically engage the issue of socio-cultural context as an important factor that shapes the conceptualization and execution of a pattern. This human-centered standpoint facilitates new considerations of the technological advancements in pattern creation, distribution, and use and encourages consideration of the diversity that has existed among the individuals who make and utilize patterns for apparel design and construction. The focus on makers and users extends to chapters that focus on how new technologies have impacted the conceptualization of pattern design and the contexts in which patterns are communicated and revised.

In the introductory chapter, "A Brief History of Patternmaking," two important tasks will be accomplished. First, the chapter will provide a general overview of the history of patternmaking in Western fashion including when patterns were first used, who made them, what they were made of, the technology and materials that were implemented in their crafting, and their relation to fashion design. This introduction will provide context to better understand the chapters that follow, but importantly it will draw from several exhaustively-researched aspects of patternmaking history, and will thereby provide an extensive literature review of some of the important scholarship that has already been done. This portion of the volume will give readers a general sense of what is known and where deficits in this portion of dress history lie. It will hopefully encourage readers to seek out some of these important sources, and may also inspire inquiry into aspects of patternmaking history or theory that have yet to be adequately explored.

In the first part of the book, "Approaches to Patterning Apparel: Formal Systems and Improvisation," the essays explore ways in which patterns for apparel and accessories creation have been communicated to homemakers, home sewers, and professionals, and how these carefully-conceived blueprints may be implemented by those who use them. In this section, the emphasis on design-thinking, problem solving, innovation, and interaction with patterns is emphasized.

Many students of pattern design complete at least part of their education by following the guidelines presented in a patternmaking text. "An Education in Pattern Cutting *c.* 1950; the work of E. Sheila MacEwan" explores a pattern cutting text that was published in Great Britain in the wake of the Second World War, but which was designed for use by the home sewer who would not have had the benefit of personal tutelage. Through a close reading of the work of E. Sheila MacEwan, who first published *Your Pattern Cutting* in 1950, Hannah Wroe reveals how the author streamlined the essentials of this "craft" into a compact 128-page book packed with 263 diagrams. Wroe reveals that beyond being a manual of technical instruction, close analysis of this text offers a rich insight into the philosophies of fashion education, including precisely what was being taught, who such manuals were being written for, and how these considerations reflected and responded to the social, political, economic, and technological developments within this period. Wroe argues that an education within the "craft" of pattern cutting preserved a skill that was becoming less relevant in the post-war boom of the ready-to-wear market and offered agency to the home sewer to create and design her own fashion. The close reading of this pattern cutting text sheds light on the integration of pattern and apparel making in the industrialized world in the middle of the twentieth century, and extends our understanding of the role that patternmaking manuals can play.

Patterns used in industrial contexts such as large-scale manufactories are generally intended to be followed without deviation of any kind, thus facilitating the production of a predictably uniform product, however, how an individual maker chooses to work with her or his pattern (even a commercially produced one) is often a matter of personal taste or choice. Patterns, like recipes, may be followed line-for-line or, alternatively, they may be modified to meet a unique specification or adjusted to accommodate for an inadvertent mistake. "'Knitting Instructions': An Analysis of Red Cross Clothing Patterns" explores the patterns and instructions that were disseminated by the Red Cross in an effort to harness the labors of homemakers during the First and Second World Wars. The efforts of home knitters were required to produce apparel according to meticulous specifications: each garment produced by volunteers had to be knitted exactly as the printed pattern stated, using yarn and needles that were supplied or otherwise specifically stipulated by leaders of knitting circles at individual Red Cross chapters and through image and text in printed publications. Author Rebecca Keyel reveals that although the physicality of both the ephemeral patterns and the sweaters, caps, and socks knit from them changed over the years, taken as a whole they reflect a continued emphasis on the importance of these handmade garments to aiding both servicemen and civilians. These patterns show how the Red Cross was able to strike a balance between the unpredictability of handmade garments and the need to have a finished product that was carefully controlled. The degree of control, Keyel shows, was something that was only made possible by the publication of clear and specific patterns and specifications about the materials used to execute them. Importantly, Keyel explores the ways in which Red Cross patterns accommodated knitters of various skill levels and abilities. Without precise directions these handmade items would have been unusable by active servicemen. This analysis of knitting patterns for apparel, accessories, and other utilitarian objects from the first half of the twentieth century observes the changes in layout, paper, typeface, and written directions while demonstrating how differences in the physical form of the patterns reflect changes in the needs and values of the Red Cross and their volunteers. Ultimately, the patterns demonstrate clear and concise encouragement of volunteers to participate in a kind of handmade assembly line process. This analysis shows the importance of understanding the relationship between the patterns and producers of finished products. Additionally, it highlights the importance of patterns as an instructional tool and sheds light on the way in which a patternmaker must consider the end user of this roadmap to apparel creation.

In "Making and Mending for Victory: Pattern Creation, Distribution, Use, and the Goal of Conservation for Home Sewers During the Second World War," Jennifer Grayer Moore explores patterns used for apparel construction and renovation during the Second World War. Wartime efforts to remake, remodel, and mend old clothes as a response to fabric and apparel shortages are often highlighted as important contributions by civilian women, especially in the United States and Great Britain; however, the specific ways in which these goals were met has been overlooked. Similarly, the complexities of pattern use, alteration, or creation have been given little consideration, while the patriotic symbolism of the end product has been highlighted. This chapter begins by considering the culture of sewing and patternmaking that existed prior to the Second World War and proceeds to consider the many ways in which fabric and clothing conservation were achieved. The study then moves to a review of the ways in which home sewers accessed both physical patterns and pattern ideas including commercial patterns, government publications, pamphlets made by notions manufacturers, and sewing and patternmaking texts. The requisite pattern reading and patternmaking skills will be considered along with the complexities contributed to the process by the use of repurposed textiles. Throughout the chapter the author compares and contrasts how these efforts differed in the United States and Great Britain and considers the role of the home sewer with regards to patternmaking and pattern utilization.

In the second part of this text, "Perspectives on Technical Design and Technological Advancement in Apparel Pattern Drafting," the contributing authors explore technical aspects of patternmaking and their relationship to the greater project of apparel design. In each of these contributions, a specific technology for pattern creation and/or distribution is explored as an example of innovation and development that aided apparel production. Each approach is then connected to the individuals who utilized it. In "The Tailor's Voice: Pattern Drafting Systems and the State of the Art," Catherine Roy explores data taken from primary source materials of the tailoring trade, giving special focus to pattern drafting systems that were published between 1800 and 1920. Using these primary sources, Roy produces an analysis of these trade resources and how they fostered a transformation of the tailoring trade from a business that was primarily artisanal to a business that was organized as a factory "sectional system" of clothing manufacture with many scales of operation within the trade. Roy shows that pattern drafting systems changed dramatically over time. The early system's author assumed extensive prior knowledge on the part of the user, which included the ability to make adjustments to accommodate physical abnormalities and idiosyncrasies. Over time, the makers of systems attempted to quantify and calculate adjustments to insure a perfect fit. Roy shows that both the entrepreneurial spirit of small business owners, and improvements in printing technology led to the development of increasingly detailed written pattern drafting systems, which were sometimes connected to schools of tailoring. Through these systems, as well as through journals, tailors shared their skills, their findings about fitting the human body, and their techniques for rendering two-dimensional pattern shapes so that they would suit and (in some cases) improve the human form. The tailoring trade evolved throughout the century and mirrored the changes in both American society and industry. Roy's close examination of ninety-one published drafting systems reveals information about the strengths and weakness of individual systems, the intended purpose of the publication, the technology of patternmaking, the measurement system employed, and the sophistication of the author. This study also sheds light on the decline in the importance of the apprenticeship system, improvements in print materials, nineteenth-century entrepreneurial zeal, and the effects of a rapidly increasing appetite for fashionable dress on the apparel trades. Thus the dissemination of cutting principles gives us a window into the nineteenth-century tailor and patternmaker's working life and a uniquely human perspective on the evolution of technology and the people who applied it.

The requisite skills as well as the creative capacities of the patternmaker are evolving as technologies for designing, grading, producing, and disseminating patterns are impacted by computer hardware and software platforms. In "Computer-Aided Patternmaking: A Brief History of Technology Acceptance from 2D Pattern Drafting to 3D Modeling" Fatma Baytar and Eulanda Sanders examine the introduction and dissemination of CAD (computer-aided drafting) technologies in apparel patternmaking and their stages of development and adoption over time. The chapter begins with an examination of two-dimensional modeling systems and proceeds with an examination of the adoption of three-dimensional CAD patternmaking platforms. The authors track the history of these technologies and how they were used from the postwar period onward. The authors note that patternmaking became more effective as CAD systems allowed a speedy and accurate process of pattern manipulation from existing databases, and ease of data transmission for decision-making and production purposes. Baytar and Sanders show that during the infancy of CAD adoption, most apparel companies still preferred manual patternmaking and used software only for grading and marker making, as CAD systems were costly and most patternmakers were not trained to use the technology. However, over time, as the diffusion of CAD innovation continued throughout the apparel industry and accessibility increased, companies started integrating computers into their patternmaking processes and hiring patternmakers with CAD skills. In the twenty-first century, the gap in linking 3D designs to 2D patterns is closing fast due to powerful 3D visualization technologies, which allow patternmakers to visualize the drape of textiles as well as overall fabric appearance as they synchronously draft patterns in the 2D workspace of the CAD software. The same 3D CAD technology also allows reverse engineering, as garments can be taken apart and analyzed digitally, removing instant haptic feedback and requiring new mindsets when working in a digital environment. Thus, this contribution to the volume reveals how advanced technologies are impacting the art of pattern design, while also having profound effects on the design-thinking required to draft a pattern and thus reshaping crucial aspects of the patternmaker and his or her process.

Whether designed on paper, modeled in muslin, or created using digital technologies, most patterns for garments are designed to produce a single, fixed piece of apparel in a given size and shape. In "Patternmaking Methods for Creating Size-Adjustable Garments," Ellen McKinney and Bingyue Wei explore the phenomenon of garments that can be modified for size and fit and the aspects of pattern design that make such features possible. Using patent applications as well as garments from an apparel archive, the authors reveal the specific ways in which garments have been made adjustable. In addition, McKinney and Wei posit how these methods of adjustability could be harnessed in the current fashion landscape as a way to make garments with a more sustainable lifespan while also considering size-adjustability concepts as ways to design better-selling garments that circumvent common fit problems. Thus, McKinney and Wei explore both technologies of pattern design as well as ideologies of the pattern designer, thereby providing insight into contemporary techniques for pattern creation and contemporary issues in today's apparel economy.

Technological advancements stemming from the widespread proliferation of the internet are manifold. In particular, the use of social media and web-based platforms such as blogs and websites by today's home sewers are important issues that relate to communication of and human interaction with apparel patterns. The internet is used as a technology for dissemination as well as a place to share techniques and learn how to use patterns. In "Home Sewing Transformed: Changes in Sewing Pattern Formats and the Significance of Social Media and Web-Based Platforms in Participation" Addie Martindale addresses the communication of home sewing patterns through such digital platforms as a PDF (portable document format). Martindale reveals this pattern format allows home sewers instant access to the patterns they have selected because the tiled format can be printed on home printers along with meticulously detailed instructions, which are often accompanied with step-by-step photos. Vital to this new pattern format is the interaction and engagement of home sewers through social media and other internet-based platforms. Such interaction involves communication among sewers of varying skill levels as well as interaction with pattern designers who are also the individuals promoting and selling their patterns. Martindale reveals that pattern designers are actively involved with their customers and provide pattern support for issues and questions about their patterns through Facebook groups and other social media outlets such as Instagram. Furthermore, the success of a PDF sewing pattern is largely dependent on members of the sewing community sharing and recommending patterns through social media, sewing Facebook groups, blogs, and other web-based sewing platforms which are a vital part of a new wave of individuals teaching sewing and learning how to sew. Home sewers have built a global online community to share knowledge, find friendship, and support each other in their sewing endeavors.

Cultural perspectives impact artistic creation, the development and implementation of technologies, and approaches to design thinking. In the final part of this book, "Creative Diversity: Multicultural Approaches to Pattern Creation," patternmaking is approached through the lens of culture. How a design project is conceived, planned, and executed reflects the context in which a designer is operating. Design-thinking reflects social context as well as the availability of necessary materials. In "Creolized Patternmaking: A Jamaican Perspective," Elli Michaela Young examines Jamaica's fashion design as it is practiced by individuals grappling with social and economic hardship. The author explores the Jamaican practice known as "tek dem hand and mek fashion," which describes the ability of the Jamaican woman and man to use whatever is available to them to create something that is valuable to their daily existence. Young notes that Jamaican dress history often conceives of Jamaican dress aesthetics as a bricolage of multiple dress cultures that results in a creolized Jamaican aesthetics. Young advances this observation by examining the creolized skills used in dress production. While traditional techniques of patternmaking as well as the acquisition of commercially-prepared patterns are evident in the history of Jamaican apparel creation among individual seamstresses and the Jamaican fashion industry, it is the Jamaican "freehand patternmaking" technique that is the focus of this examination. Using archival materials and oral histories the author reveals how and why the freehand techniques are employed. Young provides a detailed analysis of the techniques of freehand Jamaican patternmaking, revealing how it is a creolized method of production, and considers how these patternmaking techniques have been utilized throughout Jamaican dress and fashion history. Using a close reading of garment cut and construction, the author shows how creole patternmaking has allowed Jamaicans to explore their creativity and create dress practices that are uniquely Jamaican.

Contemporary designers, manufacturers, retailers, and the fashion buying public routinely discuss and debate issues of sustainability in fashion in the twenty-first century. Tactics for making fashion more sustainable include the use of low-impact dyes, use of organic textiles, up-cycling of old garments and low-waste or zero-waste patternmaking. In "Re-Make, Re-Model, Re-Define: Fashioning a Nation's Identity," Anthony Bednall reveals that the interest in reducing demands on resources and the recycling and reworking of old and used garments was a topic of interest in mid-twentieth century China during a period when shortages of raw materials were pervasive. This interest in re-appropriating old textiles was the focus of a 1959 pattern cutting book produced by the Shanghai Cultural Department in conjunction with the Shanghai Textile Company, entitled *New Clothes from Old Clothes*. Bednall's chapter lays the groundwork for exploring this pattern cutting text by first introducing the reader to the cut and construction of a selection of traditional Chinese garments. This step is made in order to fully explore and understand the text's instructions for the deconstruction and re-fashioning of both traditional Chinese garments including the men's *changshan* and women's *qipao,* as well as western style suits and coats. Bednall's text considers this instructional manual and the execution of its directives as both a pragmatic exercise in recycling garments to support the conservation of limited resources as well as a complex political gesture, aimed at reinforcing political ideologies in Communist China. Bednall reviews the content of this and other key texts within the context of a century of political, social, and cultural turmoil and change in China, and considers the fashioning of clothes as expressions of national, political and gender identity.

Apparel as a reflection of cultural norms and ideals is a common theme in dress history. Textiles and embellishment are regularly considered as indicators of notions such as taste and status. In "Designed to Impress: The Ottoman Kaftan" Gozde Goncu-Berk pays keen attention to pattern design, cut, and construction details of Ottoman court dress. Goncu-Berk demonstrates that in the Ottoman Empire, dress had significant meanings associated to ranking and profession of the individual in the social system. Therefore, design details such as cut and construction, in addition to quality and embellishment of textiles, functioned as a visual language conveying meanings of status. In particular the *kaftan* functioned as a symbol indicating the power of the Emperor. In this study, patterns of *kaftan* worn in the Ottoman court are analyzed in detail focusing specifically on the cut of the silhouette, including the collar and neckline, sleeve, and pocket designs. Construction details such as seam finishes, linings, and facings are explored in addition to closure details such as buttons and buttonholes.

Taken as a whole, the essays in this book are designed to bring fresh focus to an important aspect of dress studies that has been underrepresented in recent scholarship. It is hoped that the diversity of approaches to the topic of patternmaking will both provide interesting and useful information while also exciting and enticing some readers to explore additional topics in this vein of inquiry. Incorporating more aspects of design and construction, technology and technique, and additional considerations pertaining to the challenges of making apparel can only augment the already rich and multifaceted story of apparel design.

A Brief History of Patternmaking

Jennifer Grayer Moore

This chapter provides an overview of the known history of patternmaking as well as a review of many excellent sources of information on this topic. This historical overview sets the stage for the chapters that follow by providing a broad historical context and a sense of the continuum. Given the brevity of this text relative to the breadth of topics it is likely that readers will be left wanting more. Notably, some of the topics that are included in this overview are explored in detail by other chapters or parts of chapters in this text. Tailoring systems are discussed in detail in Chapter 5, "The Tailor's Voice: Pattern Drafting Systems and the State of the Art." The topic of patternmaking books is explored in Chapter 2, "An Education in Pattern Cutting *c.* 1950; the work of E. Sheila MacEwan." The integration of computer technology is explored in detail in Chapter 6, "Computer-Aided Patternmaking: A Brief History of Technology Acceptance from 2D Pattern Drafting to 3D Modeling."

This introductory chapter is designed to provide the reader with a brief history of patternmaking, and in so doing will accomplish several tasks. First, this chapter will provide fundamental information that is not regularly or thoroughly incorporated into dress history or dress theory texts. Second, in providing a summary of the historical development of patternmaking, this chapter will help to situate the chapters that follow within this text. In that this chapter builds in part on important published works of incredible detail and complexity, it also serves as a review of seminal scholarship that will hopefully drive readers to further explore some of the topics that are summarily explored herein. While reviewing and incorporating elements of research that have been completed by other scholars, I will also strive to expand upon an important vein of inquiry that is intermittently explored in the works of scholars who have preceded me; namely an emphasis on the role of the *users* of patterns, texts, and drafting systems will be highlighted as a means of contextualizing innovations within the periods in which they were introduced and thereby providing a point of entry for the reader to understand the patterns and patternmaking technologies as they were understood in their day. By making connections to the users of patterns and the prior knowledge and skills they would have needed to effectively use each technology, I hope the reader will find continuities and make personal connections.

There is evidence of patterns for ornamental designs and narrative compositions in antiquity. For example, the precise replication of ornamental repeats such as egg-and-dart or Greek keys (meanders) across wide expanses of the Greco-Roman world is evidence of careful observation and transportation of design motifs either from physical objects in the public domain, or possibly from source materials (now lost) maintained by artists and craftsmen. The evidence of a source for replication is clear: artwork executed on items such as sarcophagi, architectural friezes, ornamental panels, and grave stele, which often included complex narratives and/or poses, were created over centuries and across geographic space with incredibly strong similarities. Additionally, compositions were modified over time to accommodate new stories (namely the shift from pagan to Christian narratives) while retaining clear references to established compositions.

The history of patternmaking for clothes does not extend as far back in time. In fact, it is well understood that there was a time when patterns for apparel were not necessary. Garments such as the ubiquitous tunic or Grecian peplos, as well as a great variety of draped accessories and outerwear garments were largely constructed from loom lengths, the proportions of which were determined in part by the weaving technologies and traditions of a given culture and the precise time period in question.[1] Most looms (especially looms in the ancient world) create rectangles of fabric and these rectangles were either woven to the size of the wearer, woven to be stitched to another panel (to create greater width), or woven to be subdivided for the creation of straps or sleeves that could be fashioned with virtually no waste. Apparel concepts that were developed in pre-industrial contexts wherein weaving was a slow and laborious process, were conceived with economy as a guiding principle. Curtailing waste meant curtailing curvilinear cutting as well as complex tailoring techniques and therefore precluded the need for pattern pieces.

The gradual advances in spinning and weaving technologies, the professionalization of apparel and textile trades, and the ongoing expansion of trade routes and partnerships in the long and complex medieval period in

Europe contributed to the development of increasingly elaborate fashionable dress. In addition, when the development of these interactions and technologies is situated within the context of increasingly mobile and interactive royal courts and developing urban landscapes in which people of varied backgrounds increasingly interacted, the scene is set for both the desire and the need to distinguish and assert oneself nonverbally and publicly. As more textiles, of increasingly greater variety and luxury became available, individuals sought ways to use the precious raw materials as declarations of affluence and status. In part, such declarations could be made through extravagant flourishes: puffed sleeves, dagged edges, peascod bellies, trains and flounces—elements far more complex in shape and concept than loom lengths. Novel approaches to apparel necessitated a plan for cutting shapes that both conformed to and elaborated upon the natural silhouette of the body.

It is implied through textual references and legal code that patterns for garment making existed in the fifteenth century. Sumptuary laws were regional and ephemeral laws designed to curtail sartorial expression among the lower classes. Restrictions on dress could be implemented by edicts that stipulated the use of color, fabric type, trim, and importantly, cut. So important was the curtailment of ostentatious cut among the lower classes that sumptuary laws sometimes ventured into detailed specificity. The careful regulation of cut in turn implies that garment makers were following specific plans for executing apparel. Additional written references to patterns can be connected to the court of Charles VII (reigned 1422–61), which sent representatives to Paris to copy patterns for apparel and embroidery.[2] To date, no fifteenth-century patternmaking documents (especially tailors' books) for apparel have been located, reviewed, and published.

A recent study of three Austrian tailoring manuals sheds important light on the early history of apparel patterns. *Drei Schnittbücher: Three Austrian Master Tailor Books of the 16th Century* reproduces pages from texts dating from as early as 1560. These tailoring books include line drawings of pattern shapes but little in the way of textual explanation or written procedure. Within these texts, the pattern shapes were illustrated on a small scale and arranged in a rectangular panel corresponding to the proportions of the requisite fabric in a fashion similar to the diagrams that accompany modern paper patterns. However, these line drawings were largely unlabeled (although sometimes numbers were used to correlate pieces) and nothing resembling a notch to align the individual pieces was implied. Notably, measurements were not included as these books were created during a period when measurements were neither standardized nor exact, with the ell (the unit of measurement used for fabric) varying from town to town. Scholars Katherine Barich and Marion McNealy, who analyzed these texts, noted that they were produced as workshop reference manuals or study guides for the master tailor exam and as such were created for an audience with specific technical understanding.[3] This observation helps to explain the general omission of labels on the diagrams for the pattern pieces and the occasional omission of entire pieces that were surely a part of a garment. Additionally, patterns for some kinds of clothes were not included in these texts. For example, garments such as doublets could be created from elements of other patterns. These kinds of omissions indicate that a high level of competence was required to work with the manuals. Barich and McNealy note, "These patterns were flexible tools in the hands of the tailors; constantly changing to meet the needs of their customers and adjust to the ever-changing whims of fashion and personal taste."[4] Additionally, sometimes a garment pattern was drawn in a manner that indicated individual pieces would exceed the width of the requisite fabric and it was therefore expected that a tailor would understand how to effectively execute the piecework.[5] Although the diagrams illustrated in these texts lack information that many a modern garment maker would likely require, a meticulous sixteenth century tailor, who scaled the diagrams carefully would have found that the diagrams were accurate, with elements like sleeve caps fitting properly into the armholes. Additionally, clients would have found that garments were crafted with the anatomy of the wearer and the intended use of the garment in mind, a point demonstrated by the cut of a riding gown that was conceived so that fabric covering the hips and buttocks was full enough to facilitate ease of movement but tailored enough so as not to bunch and impede the rider.[6]

Another early tailoring manual is Juan de Alcega's *Libro de Geometrica Practica* (1589), which, like the *schnittbücher*, contains instructions and diagrams for cutting clothes.[7] An early critical examination of this publication, which was designed for a nascent tailoring trade is notable for its comments pertaining to the contents. Nineteenth century tailor Edward Giles, who undertook a review of a great many early patternmaking sources in his text *The History of the Art of Cutting in England* remarked, "The instructions it contains are of the most meager description . . . It furnishes no instructions for measuring much less any method for constructing garments of various kinds for different figures."[8] Giles' palpable amazement at the paucity of specific information is interesting as a point of consideration, as he was working at a time when the procedures for tailoring were becoming increasingly systematic and codified, a point that was a long time in coming. Boullay's *Le Tailleur Sincere* (1671), published almost a century after Alcega's work, contained diagrams but still no instructions to help distinguish the meaning or orientation of the pattern pieces. Giles noted of this later artifact, "How this book could effectively aid a tailor in his labors it is difficult to conceive."[9] While Giles' response seems to assert an assessment of ineptitude on the part of the writer, it is probably more appropriate to imagine that Boullay was a writer who conceived of a wealth of prior knowledge within his intended audience. Just as illiterate churchgoers of the Renaissance had skills for reading paintings containing continuous narration (an uncommon skill in the twenty-first century), so too did tailors of this period comprehend technical drawings that later professionals construed as virtually incomprehensible.

At least two works of the eighteenth century survive: the 1789 manual *Instructions for Cutting out Apparel for the Poor* and *The Taylor's Complete Guide or a Comprehensive Analysis of Beauty and Elegance in Dress* (1796) which was produced by the Society of Adepts.[10] These early guides were again written for practitioners of the trade and included line drawings that could be traced and scaled-up, directions for making effective measurements of the body, and careful directions for laying out the fabric and cutting so that cloth could be meticulously conserved. Taken as a whole, however, these early works provide little in the way of methodology. Measurements (which were done with strips of paper not with standardized tapes or rulers) varied from author to author, and texts presented the author's impressions of best practices rather than systematic procedures. Giles noted that much of the early information about cutting clothes was likely transmitted in pamphlets that have not been archived and that through experience, practice, and time, the art of cutting probably "grew by degrees."[11] Additionally, it is important to note that the published examples that exist are part of the record of an apprentice system in which hands-on training and long-term tutelage by a master would have provided the knowledge necessary to work effectively with the aforementioned texts.

Throughout the eighteenth and early nineteenth centuries *ad hoc* techniques known alternatively as the "rock of eye" or the "rule of thumb" were implemented, refined, and passed on through the apprentice system, developing and improving over time through trial and error.[12] Although records of the precise evolution of early tailors' practices are incomplete, it is generally understood that some utilized an extensive series of meticulous direct measurements, while others used only select measurements such as breast or chest, shoulders and waistline to draft a pattern based on proportions. These approaches in the trade are understood through the sparse records that remain. Eighteenth- and nineteenth-century home sewers, whose "apprentice system" thrived within the domain of women's work, undoubtedly also evolved practices through trial and error, although documentation of such discoveries has yet to be found and/or published.

In the first half of the nineteenth century, drafting systems that relied on direct measurement of the body, a system of body proportions, or a hybridization of the two came into use, largely replacing the more labor-intensive and less systematic practices of old. Drafting systems were designed for women's and children's apparel, as well as for men's tailored clothes. These systems, which included some combination of an instruction manual, notched paper strips, perforated tools, or wooden and metal curves and squares were designed both for home sewers and for the trade. Claudia Kidwell, in her exhaustive survey of this topic noted, "In the nineteenth century, dressmakers drafting systems were heralded as a solution to the plight of downtrodden working women" as they eliminated some of the trial and error, problem solving, and fit work related to pattern creation.[13] Writing about late nineteenth century direct measure systems, Kidwell noted that the systems used "repeatable, systematic procedures instead of intuitive individualistic procedures."[14] Thus, over time, a dedicated seamstress could hope to make the pattern drafting process more time efficient and her final product would hopefully require little or no fitting to correct pattern drafting errors. Although drafting systems utilized formulae and included directions for implementing the proprietary tools and procedures, it is important to note that the systems were not foolproof and required significant skill and education (especially regarding measurement, calculation, and reading comprehension) to be effectively employed, thus the promise of drastic labor reduction often went unfulfilled. Writing of direct measure systems of the late nineteenth century, Kidwell noted, "A good deal of understanding of the entire procedure was necessary before an individual could be successful." In fact, so complex were many of these pattern-drafting systems, that the selling process for them typically included demonstrations and even individualized lessons.[15]

A close reading of specific examples of drafting systems for women's and children's apparel illuminates two issues: the commoditization of patternmaking and its related industries and products, and the level of skill that would be needed to utilize these systems. Among the most common promises of the drafting systems that were retailed from the middle of the nineteenth century into the first decades of the twentieth century were speed, ease, and accuracy. In fact, the makers of some systems suggested that the garments would virtually cut themselves. For example, the Bleeks' New Self-Calculating Ladies' Tailoring and Dress Cutting System boasted in the "Key" that accompanied its single cardboard tool that it was, "the only system ever invented that will cut all styles of garments (past, present and future) without the necessity of any calculation on the part of the user." The tool, which bears the smiling image of Tolbert T. Bleeks himself, combines a thirty-six-inch rule, small and large hip curves and scales, scales for hands, elbows, neck, and shoulders, as well as a skirt scale (Figure 1.1). The "Key," which claimed a waist (bodice) could be drafted in three to five minutes and a sleeve in one minute flat, was clearly written with the assumption that the user of this system would be endowed with both excellent measuring skills as well as exquisite reading comprehension as the dozens of scales and punched holes labeled with tiny notations were accompanied by just a few illustrations and only limited directions. Notably, the makers of this system maintained schools that charged hundreds of dollars to attend, an indication of the complexity inherent in this streamlined process.

In addition to the development of a great many drafting systems in the nineteenth century, a boom in publishing also occurred, especially in the latter half of the century. During this period, books and journals for the trade became more common, while manuals for homemakers and schoolgirls also proliferated. Notably, the publishers of books and journals also sold equipment, and in some cases ran bricks-and-mortar or correspondence schools. Essentially, the number and variety of resources available for professional tailors and dressmakers, as well as home sewers, was expanding and diversifying. Nineteenth- and early twentieth-century women's magazines were also important conduits for conveying information to seamstresses. Articles about garment creation and decoration were important monthly features in serial publications. Advertisements for textiles, trim, notions, and sewing equipment were featured alongside advertisements for

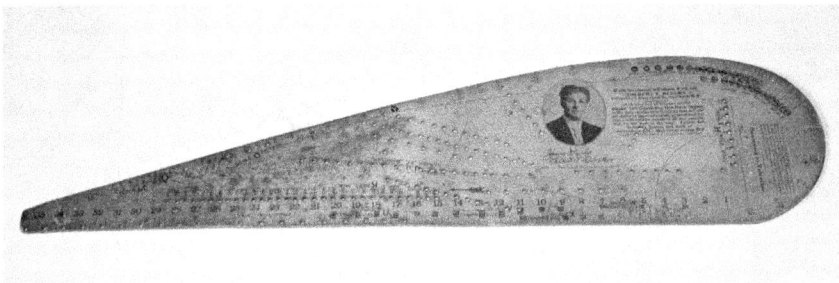

Figure 1.1 The "Bleeks' Self-Calculating One-Piece System," a cardboard tool (20¼" × 4⅞") containing at least twenty scales for calculating measurements including hip, neck, and sleeve. The book of instructions sold separately for $20 in 1914, the equivalent of almost $500 in 2018.

household cleaning products and health remedies. In addition, written directions for needlework, and patterns for garment creation were often featured within the pages of these serials, which were bound and kept by many women in the nineteenth century, a testament to the wealth of information they contained.

Rudimentary patterns that were typically printed on paper measuring 8½ by 11 inches or smaller were included in many ladies' magazines. These patterns

WORK DEPARTMENT. 169

DIAGRAM OF THE VICTORIA PARDESSUS.

(See engraving, page 106.)

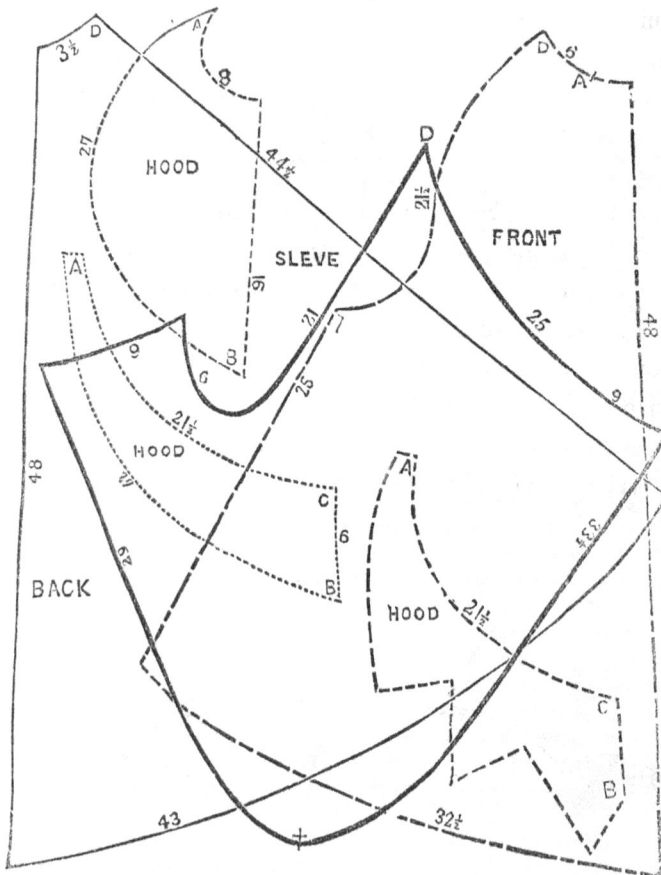

Figure 1.2 Diagram of the "Victoria Pardessus" (a hooded cloak) from *Godey's Lady's Book*, February 1859, p. 169. The diagram for all the pattern pieces of a long and voluminous cape was scaled to fit on a single page measuring 9⁵⁄₁₆ by 5¹³⁄₁₆ inches.

had to be carefully traced and scaled-up, typically using sheets of newsprint. Such patterns were available in popular publications like *Godey's Lady's Book*, *Peterson's Ladies' National Magazine*, and *Harper's Bazaar*. The garment and accessories patterns were presented as simple line drawings that included few if any measurements or labels of any kind. The outlines of each piece were printed on a single page with pattern pieces overlapping, thereby requiring keen discernment on the part of the person tracing the original to determine which piece was which (Figure 1.2). Patterns of this kind generally included no seam allowances, notches nor separate patterns for facings. Knowledge of garment shapes might lead the seamstress to understand that a particular piece needed to be cut on a fold or cut in multiples (perhaps with one piece cut in reverse), but this kind of direction was not typically labeled or otherwise indicated. Similarly, a home sewer of the day might have known that gathers would be required in an armhole or at a waist band but neither directions nor markings on the pattern pieces specified how to execute such fabric manipulations. Thus, the seamstress was left to figure out how to connect the pieces, was on her own to make decisions about where the apparel fabric should be included in the garment's interior, and was left to rely on her skill and instinct to determine how to draft the pattern pieces to the appropriate size and proportion. Patterns from ladies' magazines also generally omitted indications for the placement of closures and included only limited written directions. Directions were typically concerned with fabric type and yardage width as opposed to advice about basting, stitching, or fitting. The amount of prior knowledge required to effectively utilize these kinds of patterns and the skills that were necessary for both construction and fitting would have needed to be extensive and may lead us to consider the culture of sewing that was a part of nineteenth-century life. Just as the tailoring books of the sixteenth century would generally prove inadequate for twenty-first century pattern cutters, so too would these patterns produced in the nineteenth century prove insufficient to most modern craftspeople. However, the cultural necessity of sewing that was inherent in nineteenth-century life meant that many women would have had robust prior knowledge earned through a life of working with needle and thread and in all likelihood had a network of needlewomen in her family and community to advise her when problems arose.

In addition to the manuals, periodicals, and drafting systems, beginning in the nineteenth century, a garment maker could utilize commercially-produced tissue paper patterns. This aspect of the history of patternmaking has been well documented. Early paper patterns were often sold not as whole garments but as the components (such as bodice, sleeve, and skirt) that were required to make a garment. Early paper patterns were not sized and as a result seamstresses needed to be skilled in fitting by pinning either the cut-out tissue paper pieces or the cut and basted pieces of fabric to a dress form or to the body of the wearer.[16] Paper patterns for women's apparel were available as early as 1836 whereas full-sized paper patterns for men's garments were not widely available until 1849.[17] Commercially-made paper patterns were not sized until 1871. Additionally, it was only in this same year that written instructions and an illustration of the completed design were features accompanying the pattern.[18] The lack of image or text may be partially attributable to printing technologies and the fact that the patterns themselves were not printed; rather they were marked with punched holes and notches until 1921 when McCall's began to offer printed markings on the tissue.[19] Notably, the sizing of patterns changed over time with early patterns generally being sized based on bust or chest measurements for bodices and jackets. Additionally, until the 1870s patterns generally did not include a pattern piece for facings nor were notches a commonplace feature.[20]

By the 1880s there were six major paper pattern companies in the United States as well as numerous smaller companies that were forced out of business through competition before the close of the century. Market demand, as well as the development of papermaking technologies and postal systems (many patterns were purchased by mail order), meant that a paper pattern industry also flourished in Europe. In America, Demorest, Butterick, McCall's, Harper's Bazaar, Taylor, and Domestic filled the marketplace with patterns that could be selected from corresponding serial publications, some of which were also distributed in Europe. Notably, the product each company offered varied from brand to brand in any given period with regards to the markings that were provided and the information that was included (Figure 1.3). Furthermore, the markings and technologies used to make paper patterns changed substantially over time. Joy Emery, whose study of the paper pattern industry is meticulously detailed, notes that Butterick instructions of the 1920s "look very limited to today's consumers," but "were an immense improvement over anything that had been available previously."[21]

In addition to technical differences among paper pattern companies, there were also differences with regards to the origin of the designs themselves. In the nineteenth century, most companies touted their patterns as being of-the-moment designs, and (quite importantly) from Paris, but made no mention of who had created the design or executed the pattern in question. In some cases,

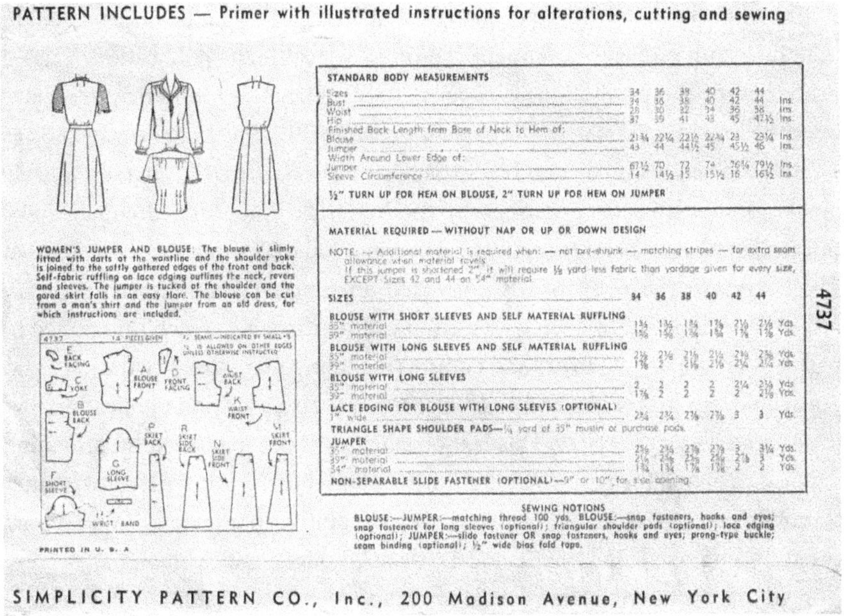

Figure 1.3 Verso of a Simplicity paper pattern envelope (Pattern no. 4737) from the 1940s showing a labeled thumbnail of each pattern piece and indicating that a "Primer with illustrated instructions for alterations, cutting and sewing" was included.

designs were attributed to specific French couture houses like Doucet and Worth, however there is no evidence of authorized line-for-line couture designs until McCall's began to offer authorized patterns in 1925.[22] Throughout the later part of the twentieth century and continuing in the twenty-first century, both American and European designers continued to license their designs to the makers of commercial patterns for home sewing. Popular musicians and television personalities also lend their names and signature styles to the creation of tissue patterns, thus the origins of many designs are featured in the marketing of some patterns. On an alternative note, in the twentieth and early twenty-first centuries, many publications like the national serial *Parade Magazine* or the New York newspaper *The Daily News* have offered patterns via mail order to their readership. In the case of these services, examination of the patterns and the packaging in which they came makes it clear that the patterns were coming from a company that licensed their designs to a great many brands or businesses. In such instances, the brand name (which sometimes evoked the name of a designer) was little more than a marking and the design origin of the pattern is not truly known.

The importance of the paper pattern industry should not be understated. In the nineteenth and early twentieth centuries, a great many publications existed primarily for the promotion of paper patterns. Ebeneezer Butterick may have been the first to do this when he began publishing *The Tailor's Review* in 1866 as a vehicle to sell his men's and boy's tissue patterns.[23] *The Delineator*, a monthly magazine that was also published by the Butterick Publishing Company—the title originated as *The Metropolitan Monthly* (1869–75) and then was retitled *The Delineator* (1875–1926)—is a detailed document of commercial patterns, fashionable dress styles, and sewing culture. The magazine, which functioned in part as a serial devoted to art and culture (including literature, illustrations, and household tips for recipes and child rearing) was also a fashion publication that documented current styles. This last objective was accomplished by providing detailed written information about color, recommended fabric type, construction features (such as darts and gores), and decorative treatments. In addition, carefully engraved and meticulously detailed black-and-white images were printed that captured the fine details of cut and trim. Importantly, placed in close proximity to both image and text were the critical pattern number or numbers to facilitate ordering. Pattern pricing, in both pence and cents, was necessarily included. *The Delineator* also provided extensive information about products that could aid both the professional apparel maker and the home sewer. Both advertisements and expository articles provided information about items like drafting systems, dress forms (some of which were made or marketed by Butterick), and reference books on skills such as lacemaking, crochet, smocking, and various forms of needlecraft (also published by Butterick). Notably, *The Delineator* also included advertisements for patternmaking products made by other companies. For example, a single issue of *The Delineator* (May 1900) included advertisements for a variety of drafting systems including the McDowell System, Buddington's Improved Dress Cutting Machine, and the Adjustable Skirt Drafting Machine.

Demorest's Monthly was also a vehicle for promoting the sale of paper patterns, which it advertised as being suitable for both ladies and the trade. Although the magazine included sheet music, literature, and decorative engravings, the lengthy descriptions of contemporary styles, which were accompanied by pattern numbers, were the main focus of the serial. Although patterns for garments and accessories were the primary focus of the publication, Madame Demorest also sold patterns for decorative treatments such as braid and embroidery. Like *The Delineator*, the publication also served as a vehicle for communicating a wide range of sewing products including tracing wheels, scissors, and notions in addition to Madame Demorest-branded items including the Madame Demorest Excelsior System of Dress Cutting and the Madame Demorest Children's Magic Dress Chart.

Among the many other publications that existed for the purpose of communicating styles, selling paper patterns and patternmaking accouterments, were *Modes*, published by the Modes Fashion and Pattern Company and *The Ladies' World*, published by S.H. Moore and Company, both of New York City. In Europe there were also numerous publications devoted to this kind of marketing including *Le Petit Echo de la Mode* published in Paris, and *Young Ladies' Journal* published in London. Interestingly, *Young Ladies' Journal* bluntly indicated in its masthead that the publisher, D. Nicolson and Company was able to "Supply all the Goods represented by these Illustrations." As vehicles for advertising and sales, publications of this kind provide very detailed information about paper patterns and the ways in which patternmaking and pattern use were supported with products and services. For example, patterns retailed through *The Ladies' World* included a flat pattern as well as a full size "Pinned Paper Model" of the garment. These patterns, which were sized based on bust measurement, seem to have been designed by a third party as language surrounding the directions for placing an order noted that the patterns were provided "by special arrangement with the manufacturers." *Young Ladies' Journal* was exceptional for the fact that it periodically provided large-scale diagrams for patterns in the form of their "Gigantic Supplements" (47¾ inches by 32¼ inches) in the late nineteenth century. A review of a sample of these supplements shows that significant prior knowledge would have been required to work with these patterns that were un-sized, did not include clearly marked grain or fold lines, and were illustrated with overlapping pieces that were usually all printed using the same kind of line. Further complicating the use of these patterns was the tendency to include pattern pieces that were larger than the paper on which they were printed. This matter forced the pattern drafter to show the ends of pattern pieces folded up (thereby overlapping even more lines) and to illustrate sleeves front and back as a single unit. Notches were almost never used and an indication of how many pieces to cut was always omitted. Thus, the full-sized pattern left almost as much to be interpreted and figured-out as the smaller line drawings provided in the sixteenth century *schnittbücher* or in *Godey's* in the middle of the nineteenth century. Through reference to engraved images printed verso and the yardage length and width requirements printed within one of the pattern pieces, an experienced seamstress would have had the basic information necessary to execute the garment, but would certainly have had to call on a robust arsenal of skills to create a pleasing, fashionable, and wearable piece of apparel.

It is important to note that high expectations about home sewer skills are evident in commercially-produced patterns and related products into the latter half of the twentieth century as well. The notion that home sewers had the ability to decode, calculate, and draft a pattern with only minimal support is evident in a wide variety of sources. An issue of *Le Petit Echo de la Mode* dated September 14, 1952 provided line drawings of two blouses and a skirt as well as photographs of the completed garments. Although the flat pattern pieces are depicted on a grid (a feature designed to facilitate scaling them up), many other aspects of the diagram are user-un-friendly. For example, the pattern pieces are drawn overlapped, the pieces lack alignment notches and seam allowances, and the pattern taken as a whole is incomplete, including facings for some parts, but not for others.

The techniques and technologies that have been discussed thus far all pertain to the practice of flat pattern drafting. It is this mode of pattern creation that has been most widely adopted in commercial ventures and distributed through forms of mass communication. However, a method of pattern creation that begins by working in three-dimensional space and is then usually translated into a flat pattern has also been used and has been documented since the nineteenth century. Draping, also known as *moulage*, is the process of pinning fabric (usually calico or muslin) onto a body or dress form. The fabric is pinned to the form to create the desired fit and effect, marked in pencil with lines and symbols indicating side seams, tucks, and darts, and then ultimately transferred to paper. Once transferred, the drape is brought into conformity with flat patternmaking techniques: seam allowances are added, notches are created, and grain lines are marked. The technique of working on the dress form or stand can also be utilized while working with the fabric that will be used for the finished garment. This approach is generally taken when a designer is making a one-of-a-kind garment. In such an instance the pattern and the garment are essentially one and the same.

The point of origin for the draping technique has not been documented. While it is understood that the practice of draping was used in the nineteenth century and it is documented that twentieth-century *couturières* like Madame Grès and Pauline Trigère used this method to create patterns, we are left to speculate as to the precise origin of the method. It seems logical to assume that the technique would have been applied by at least the sixteenth century when the skirts of women's gowns developed from basic gored constructions to more complex volumes. The size and quantity of paper required to draft a pattern would have been cost prohibitive if not unattainable. The need to connect numerous widths of fabric to create the necessary volume would also have made drafting on fabric difficult. Thus, it seems safe to assume that this technique began to be used in some form at the same time that apparel design began to move away from the straight lines and boxy shapes determined by fashioning apparel from loom widths.

In the twentieth and twenty-first centuries, patternmaking has been accomplished in a variety of ways, but perhaps the most remarkable is through the computer-aided drafting (CAD) software and hardware that facilitate the drafting and grading of patterns in both flat and three-dimensional forms. Beginning in the 1970s, patternmaking programs designed to generate and grade a pattern derived from a basic parametric set or block were employed in the fashion industry. Over time the software developed to include functions such as marker making (planning the layout for cutting) and cost sheet generation. CAD systems, which are often referred to by proprietary names like Gerber, Accumark, and Lectra, streamline some aspects of the patternmaking process. However, a widely levied critique of platforms of this kind is that the rules of grading do not always fully preserve the specified fit, thus the effective implementation of CAD systems that generate flat patterns necessitates knowledge and experience in traditional pattern drafting. CAD systems that create patterns using three-dimensional models are a more recent innovation. In some applications of this technology a virtual textile is draped and fitted on a virtual body form by plotting data points. The virtual textile is then removed from the form and a surface-flattening algorithm is applied to convert the "draped" garment into a flat pattern. In other instances, three-dimensional body scanners are employed to capture and model a real body, which is then used as the basis for simulating the drape. Three-dimensional CAD applications are utilized to insure a better fit and also to reduce the dependency on a master patternmaker.

Digital technologies have also impacted patternmaking by providing both a new way to publish patterns and a new way to distribute them. Fashion designers and patternmakers around the world are building websites to market patterns. Finished garments are shown on models in a way that reflects the retailing of ready-to-wear apparel. Patterns can then be ordered through the site in one or more ways. Independent pattern companies like Deer & Doe, Papercut, and Sew House Seven offer customers the option of ordering a traditional paper pattern or (for most designs) ordering a downloadable PDF of the pattern. The latter option, which is usually retailed for a few dollars less than the tissue pattern, is printed by the purchaser onto standard 8½ × 11-inch copy paper and then must be tiled together before the pattern pieces can be cut (Figure 1.4). This method of pattern distribution can also be found on a variety of personal websites and blogspots that are designed to share ideas about design and fabrication of apparel, accessories, and other crafted items. These patterns, which are often available free of charge, vary considerably in terms of the completeness of their markings and the clarity of the directions that accompany the pattern pieces. Both the commercial websites and the blogspots often offer tutorials and

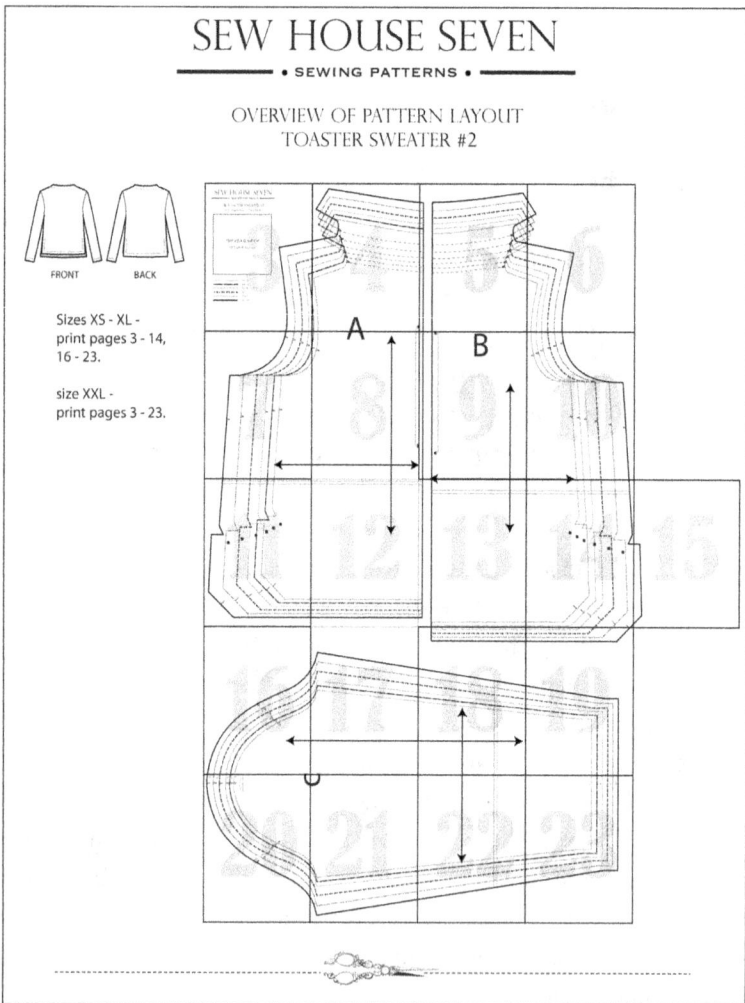

Figure 1.4 Overview of how to assemble the "Toaster Sweater" pattern from a downloadable PDF.

platforms to exchange information and ask questions, thereby demonstrating that the twin cultures of home sewing and patternmaking are very much alive in the twenty-first century.

One additional mode for creating a pattern remains to be discussed—the "rubbing-off" of a pattern from an existing garment. Comprehensive historical records of methodologies for lifting patterns from extant garments do not seem to exist, but this method of patternmaking has surely functioned as an important part of pattern creation since the advent of fitted apparel. Patterns may be copied from existing garments in several ways. Perhaps the most accurate method is to carefully unpick the seams of a garment (or a portion thereof), press the pieces of fabric, and then trace their outline onto drafting paper, whereupon markings for things such as the grain line, notches, and gathers can be added. This method is readily utilized by home sewers with garments that are badly worn or otherwise damaged. Notably there is evidence of this practice also being used for commercial means in the twentieth century. American designer Elizabeth Hawes whose journey in the fashion industry was documented in her memoir, *Fashion is Spinach* recalled working for a "good" French copy house in the 1920s. The moniker "good" was applied, she noted, because the house never made a copy of a dress unless they had actually had the original in hand.[24] Hawes recalled that original garments could be obtained through purchase, or by borrowing garments from private clients of couture houses, or could be surreptitiously scuttled away from the resident buying offices that temporarily housed fine apparel before exporting it from France. Christian Dior, writing in the 1950s, was also aware that patterns were being lifted from finished garments. He understood that one of his designs could be acquired by a manufacturer through a "model renter," who charged $350 to $500 for a three-day rental.[25] This practice is undoubtedly in wide use today as the demand for interpretations of on-trend designs proliferates throughout the fast-fashion marketplace; copying in this manner is both quick and easy.

Although the technique of copying a garment through lifting a pattern from an existing piece of apparel is used in both home sewing and in industrial applications, formal documentation of the practice is sparse. The Second World War-era text, *The Pictorial Guide to Home Needlecraft* provides a detailed example of tried and true practices for taking patterns from "made-up garments" which includes unpicking all seams, pressing the pieces of fabric and drafting around the edges; cutting a garment apart using the stitch line as a guide; and pinning calico or muslin to a finished piece of apparel and then tracing around the contours of the garment with a pencil (Figure 1.5).[26] Using this last process

TAKING PATTERNS FROM MADE-UP GARMENTS

It is sometimes wished to copy a favourite dress, but not having made the original nor having a pattern for it, it is difficult to know how to set about taking a pattern from the dress itself. Although a dress is mentioned in these directions the same processes can be carried out for any kind of garment.

It will be a very simple matter if the dress is too old to be worn again. In this case it can be unpicked, pressed, and the new pattern made by laying each part of the dress on calico or paper and cutting round it.

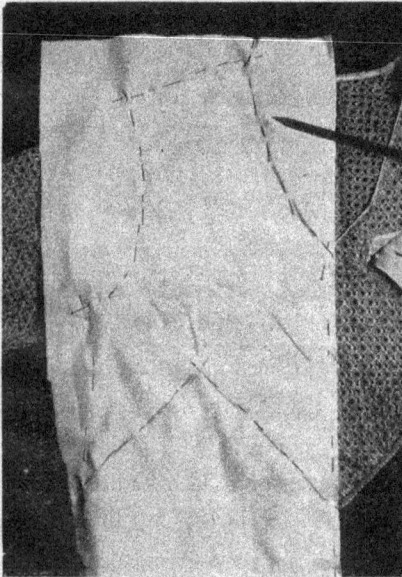

This will allow for turnings. If time is very limited, too short to spend unpicking the seams, take a pair of very sharp scissors and cut all seams on the stitching lines.

When the dress cannot be cut, the only other way to take a pattern is to lay each part of it as flat and smooth as possible, over an ironing-board, so that the skirt section can be moved round easily, place calico (not paper which will be too stiff) on it, and pin it on all seams and other edges. Mark the pin lines with coloured pencil, removing the calico and cut out with or without turnings.

1. Obtaining a pattern by undoing the garment.

2. Obtaining the pattern by pinning calico over the made-up garment.

207

Figure 1.5 Page from the Second World War-era *A Pictorial Guide to Modern Home Needlecraft* (p. 207) providing instructions for lifting a pattern from an existing garment.

the copy would necessarily need to have lines squared and contoured, seam allowances added, and notches determined. Notably, this practice was suggested by some authors of sewing guidebooks as the most effective way to create a pattern for a fitted garment,[27] while oral histories of women who lived and sewed during the Second World War document the practice of replacing parts of worn garments by drafting a pattern using the part that was cut away.[28]

The history of patternmaking for apparel and accessories is at least 600 years old. However, the early record is undoubtedly incomplete. The ephemerality of fashionable dress, coupled with the fact that apparel makers, until at least the middle of the nineteenth century, were generally regarded as working-class craftspeople whose tradecraft was not worthy of preserving in an archive, means that valuable evidence of the early part of this story has been lost. Innovations in patternmaking and commercial ventures to monetize this aspect of garment manufacture abounded in the nineteenth century and continue to develop to this day. In fact the wealth of resources is so great that the brevity of this review can only begin to capture the many interesting nuances of innovation that were developed over the course of the past several hundred years. Thus, the quest to locate additional records from the early history of patternmaking as well as efforts to locate, review, and document the vast wealth of content produced from the nineteenth century onward means that much more remains to be written about the history of patternmaking for apparel and accessories.

Part One

Approaches to Patterning Apparel: Formal Systems and Improvisation

An Education in Pattern Cutting *c.* 1950; the Work of E. Sheila MacEwan

Hannah Wroe

This chapter is centered on a close reading of a post-Second World War era patternmaking text. E. Sheila MacEwan's tutorial guide for direct-measure block pattern drafting was targeted at novice home sewers as a vehicle to help women assert taste and agency amidst the rise of ready-to-wear markets. Additionally, Wroe argues, the text was written to preserve a set of patternmaking skills that were in decline. Thus, this chapter serves as an historical counterpoint to the narrative of the introduction that emphasized the vast repository of sewing and patternmaking knowledge that was widely held by women in the nineteenth century. Throughout the close reading of MacEwan's tutorial guide, a keen consideration is given both to the tone and content of the text and how these would have been received by its user. The challenging nature of communicating patternmaking and pattern use are themes that are touched on throughout this book, especially in Chapter 4, "Making and Mending for Victory: Pattern Creation, Distribution, Use, and the Goal of Conservation for Home Sewers During the Second World War" and in Chapter 8, "Home Sewing Transformed: Changes in Sewing Pattern Formats and the Significance of Social Media and Web-Based Platforms in Participation."

Largely overlooked and unexplored as both historical and design education sources, there was a wide range of pattern cutting texts published in the early-to-mid twentieth century, many of which were authored by women. Through a close reading of one of these, E. Sheila MacEwan's publication, *Your Pattern Cutting* (1950), this chapter brings to light the multiple overlapping discourses which motivated MacEwan to publish and which shaped her text: the struggle to publish pattern cutting texts within post-war Britain, the promotion of hand-craft skills in a period of growing industrialization, an example of an educator's response to post-war austerity, and the positioning of made-to-measure pattern cutting methods as a domestic craft. This chapter will argue that, rather than this text offering revolutionary pattern cutting methods, it enabled MacEwan to preserve a set of pattern skills that were in decline and was a vehicle to help women assert taste and agency amidst the rise of ready-to-wear markets. *Your Pattern Cutting* offered the home dressmaker a comprehensive flat-pattern cutting system, which, through the adaptation of personalized foundation blocks, created individually-fitting patterns of a chosen style. MacEwan's pattern cutting methods utilized a direct measurement system that was created by taking body measurements to create accurate patterns.[1] MacEwan's papers and photographs at Hornsey College of Art Archive enable a deeper contextual understanding of how MacEwan's biography and experiences at Hornsey School of Art shaped her writing and design philosophies, and reveal an untold history of an early twentieth-century fashion educator. Through this text, MacEwan was able to extend her influence beyond her classroom, to generations of American and British seamstresses.

E. Sheila MacEwan as an educator

Euphemina Sheila MacEwan (1895–1982) was an author, educator, and craftswoman (Figure 2.1). For forty-three years, she both studied and worked at Hornsey School of Art, London (later Hornsey College of Arts and Crafts). Arriving as a young student in September 1913, she went on to set up and manage the Department of Women's Crafts until her retirement in 1956.[2] In 1950, while teaching at Hornsey, MacEwan published two books with the Sylvan Press under their *Your Home Crafts Series*: she wrote *Your Pattern Cutting* and edited *A Handbook of Your Children's Crafts.*

MacEwan was educated in a small private school in Bisham Gardens, London, which was run according to Frobel teaching philosophies. Fredrick Frobel (1782–1852), the originator of the *Kindergarten* system, introduced abstract toys, enabling children to explore ideas through play. Through using art materials and tools in the classroom, children were encouraged to explore aesthetic concepts.[3] This experience naturally prepared MacEwan to follow an art school education. When interviewed in 1981 for the *A Century of Art Education 1882–1982* exhibition,[4] MacEwan credited her understanding of visual measuring and proportion to her early education.[5] The understanding of shape and form, and two- and three-dimensional drawing, which Frobel's approach encouraged, are

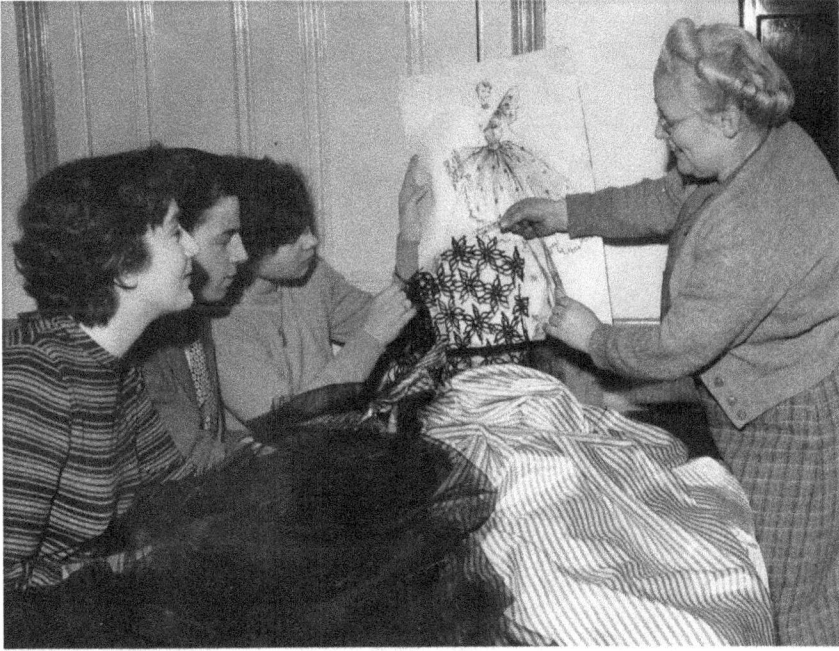

Figure 2.1 Portrait of E. Sheila MacEwan with Students *c.* 1950, International News Photos, London.

foundational skills used within pattern cutting and fashion design. MacEwan's own aptitude for drawing, and her understanding of the human form is demonstrated through her 263 hand-drawn diagrams in the text (Figure 2.2).

The Department of Women's Crafts was one of five in the school. In 1936, it offered eight courses, taught by six members of staff: Dress Design and Fashion Drawing, Ladies' and Children's Tailoring, Advanced Dressmaking, Elementary Dressmaking, Needlework and Lingerie, Millinery, Embroidery, and Hand-Loom Weaving. By 1956, the year she retired, MacEwan had expanded the department to offer sixteen courses, taught by twenty-seven members of staff. MacEwan was held in high esteem by colleagues and by those within the education sector, being credited as "a pioneer in the field of 'womens' craft' education."[6] Existing records show MacEwan teaching sixteen different subjects between 1936 and 1956, demonstrating her expertise in a broad range of interconnected creative skills around dressmaking, which were translated into her book. Hornsey graduates were well known for their applied approach to arts and crafts,[7] and MacEwan's practical instructions for pattern cutting aligned with this reputation.

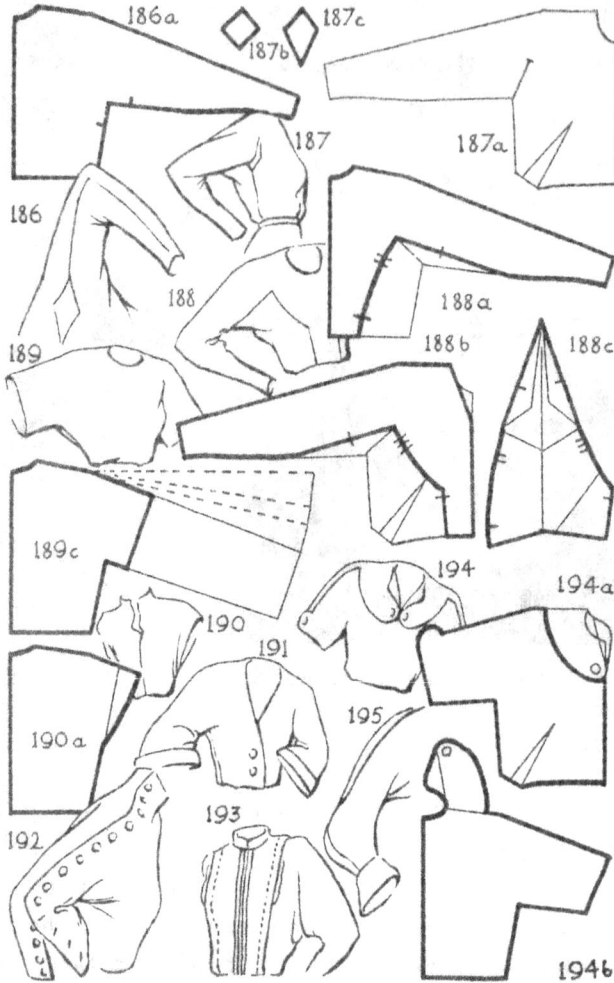

Figure 2.2 Integrated sleeve pattern diagrams, *Your Pattern Cutting* by E. Sheila MacEwan (1950), p. 89.

Publishing pattern cutting texts in post-war Britain

Books reflect the social, cultural, economic, and political context in which they are written and published.[8] Furthermore, technical educational texts, such as pattern cutting books, reflect the educational philosophies and practices at the time of publication. MacEwan's text was inevitably influenced by a variety of societal contexts. The impact of the Second World War on the British publishing trade was significant and long-lasting. Publishers struggled to provide an appealing range of books to meet consumer demand[9] and according to book scholar Claire Squires, the level of book production was low due to limited raw materials, the reduced availability of a skilled workforce due to conscription, bomb-damaged warehouses, alongside government legislation including wartime censorship and paper control, which was implemented from 1940 until 1949.[10] The result was fewer books published at an increased cost. Few pattern-cutting texts were published during the 1940s and 1950s in Britain, those that were commented on the impact of austerity. F.R. Morris, author of *Ladies' Garment Cutting and Making*, which was published in 1935, 1943, and again in 1950, commented that the "demand for this work has outstripped the publishers capacity to supply," and that the "dearth of technical knowledge on the ladies' tailoring trade," which he identified in 1935, was still applicable in 1950.[11] Furthermore, W.H. Hulme, author of two compact texts for clothing designers, teachers, and senior students: *The Theory of Garment-Pattern Making* (1945) and *The Practice of Garment-Pattern Making* (1946) writes of having to condense his work "within severe limits."[12] Publishers had to work within the government publishing priorities, and had access to limited resources, which impacted upon the size, layout, quality of paper, and number of pages that could be used. Despite this, there was evidently demand for educational pattern cutting publications.

These constraints of publication are supported by Kevin Seligman's reference guide, *Cutting for All*, which lists publications relating to the sartorial arts, related crafts, and commercial paper patterns. Seligman's comprehensive bibliography shows that between 1940 and 1948 (the years of paper rationing), of the seventy-two books listed, twenty-five were published in Britain (as opposed to forty-three in America), reflecting the impact of austerity on the British publishing trade. Of these twenty-five books, twelve were part of home-correspondence dress courses such as Bethjan, Meridian, Haslam, and Dreadnought. These offered flat-pattern drafting systems, similar to MacEwan's, based on the adaptation of foundation pattern blocks. These slim volumes included sparse written instruction, requiring the reader to have the skills to interpret the illustrations and the knowledge to adapt and fit the patterns once drafted. Additionally, this system only offered prescribed designs, and, though "on trend," they did not enable the dressmaker to create her own designs. Beyond what the home correspondence courses offered, however, *Your Pattern Cutting* included detailed technical instruction with clear written explanations of the theoretical underpinnings of flat-pattern cutting methods and training on how to alter these garments to fit the individual. The frequency with which these slim home correspondence volumes were being publishing suggests that a market for home pattern instruction existed. This was the audience for whom MacEwan's text was written.

Britain in the 1950s was a time of rebuilding, reskilling, and economic prosperity,[13] which was reflected in the expansion of dressmaking and pattern cutting publications. Seligman lists fifty-two texts published in Britain between 1949 and 1959, double the number in the preceding ten years. This expansion of newly printed material, including those produced by MacEwan's publishers, the Sylvan Press in their *Your Home Craft Series*, was both opportunistic, using newly available materials, and responsive to consumer expectations. Despite British publishing markets prospering both domestically[14] and globally,[15] the layout, format, and size of *Your Pattern Cutting* illustrates the significant concessions MacEwan still had to make in 1950 when publishing in Britain. She noted:

> My original scheme, on an altogether larger scale, was laid aside as a result of the late war, and now that books have become so costly, I have to decide whether it should be a well spaced, leisurely, and consequently expensive volume, or a small, very tightly packed text book within the range of every pocket.[16]

Consequently, MacEwan streamlined the essentials of her "craft" of pattern cutting into a compact 128 pages of a 19.5cm × 13cm book. The text boasts of having 263 diagrams, which were hand-drawn by MacEwan. These valuable illustrations were collated into thirty-six pages and are cross-referenced to pattern instructions, often many pages apart. Within heavily text-based descriptions, it is the quality of MacEwan's illustrations and her clear explanatory instructions, which enable the text to be useable.

The Sylvan Press and *Your Home Craft Series*

Out of a total 227 titles published by this small press, the *Your Home Craft Series* comprised eighteen technical instruction books, including: *Your Leatherwork; Your Handweaving; Your Embroidery; Your Rugmaking; Your Millinery; Your Linocraft; Your Textile Printing; Your Jewellery Making; Your Puppetry; Your Penmanship; Your Toymaking; Your Machine Embroidery; Your Light Furniture; Your Hand Spinning; Your Wood-Engraving* and *Your Yarn Dying* alongside MacEwan's two books on pattern cutting and children's crafts. All were published between 1947 and 1962, with thirteen of the series being published by 1951. Ten of the writers had taught or studied at Hornsey.[17] The caliber of the authors, with teaching experience in art schools, was noted as a mark of quality of the series.[18]

The *Your Home Craft Series* aimed to provide high-quality and clear technical instruction for the home craftsperson unable to attend classes. Learning a craft was promoted as an enriching artistic endeavor, offering potential economic enterprise, giving the opportunity to develop personal discipline and to experience the individual and communal social value of learning.[19] Across the series, the "call to action" against the contemporary acceleration of commercial mass production, was to master the skill to design and create something individual. Each edition followed the same format in size, layout, and typography with thematic dust jackets (Figure 2.3). They all contained hand-drawn

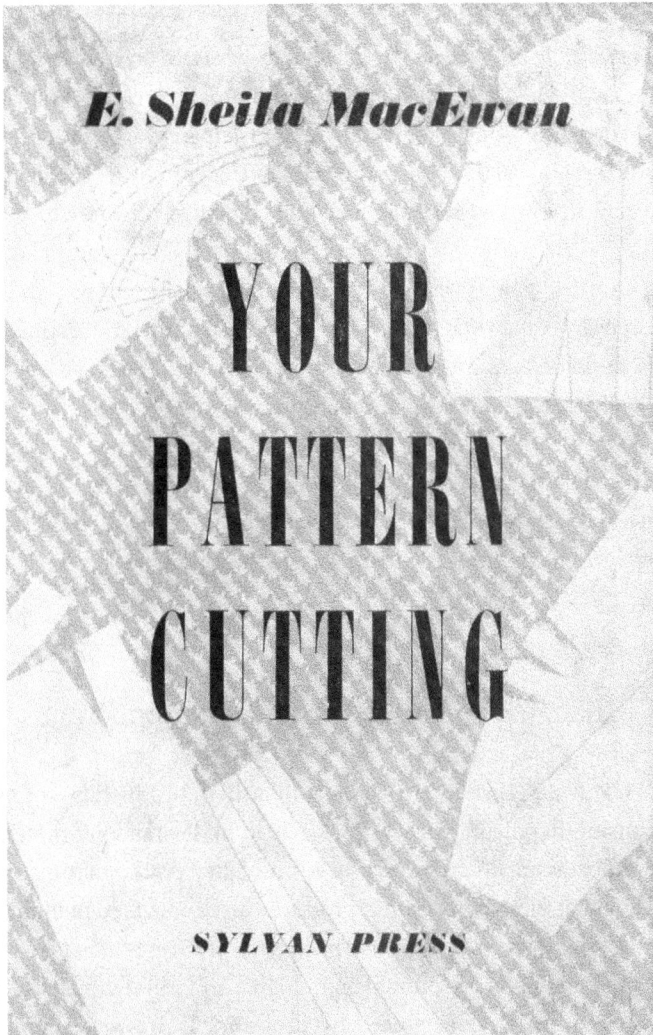

Figure 2.3 Dust Jacket of *Your Pattern Cutting* by E. Sheila MacEwan (1950), Sylvan Press, London.

illustrations condensed to single pages rather than being integrated within the text, this was a cost-saving measure. Later titles utilized multi-color pages and photographic plates, aesthetics that were not afforded to MacEwan, and although republished several times, no changes were made to the layout.

Situating pattern cutting within a "craft" series reflects its positioning as an attainable skill for the amateur home dressmaker, rather than just trained professionals. Similar home education craft series, such as Mills and Boon's *Craft Notebook* and *Pitman's Craft-For-All Series*, do not include pattern drafting or dressmaking. "Craft" has many fluid and changing meanings.[20] Within this context craft was normally associated with the decorative arts and home making,[21] and was not usually connected to dress (although the making of accessories such as gloves was). Dressmaking and related skills such as embroidery had traditionally been considered female domestic practices and viewed as lesser in value within the art/craft hierarchy.[22] The inclusion of patternmaking within this series reflects the challenge of where to place these skills within existing conventions. With commercial dress pattern companies producing affordable and fashionable patterns with instructions,[23] the complex skills required to cut patterns were now not essential to make one's own clothing. These texts could be used for reference, or as a home education course to enrich the reader's leisure time. An advertisement for a competitor, Oldham Press Ltd.'s *Practical Home Dressmaking Illustrated* (1948), noted, "books to-day are vital tools in the battle for increased production. They shape trained minds; lead to better efficiency in work; deeper and richer enjoyment of leisure." Beyond offering technical instruction, these books were being marketed as life-improving.

Changing landscapes in fashion production

MacEwan's text was shaped by the changes in fashion production in this period. Through considering these shifts, it is possible to understand her motivations to publish her book as an attempt to preserve individual pattern cutting methods.

In 1950s Britain, clothing was both produced and consumed in multiple ways: the growing ready-to-wear market produced mass-manufactured apparel, couture garments were made by ateliers in high-end fashion houses, and made-to-measure garments were produced by professional dressmakers.[24] London's post-war fashion trade was a changing landscape. The government Utility Scheme had expanded the mass-manufactured production of clothing, developing efficient uses of materials and higher standards of production.[25] Alongside this, court and society dressmakers were in decline due to changing class structures and economics.[26] Combined with growing consumerism and emerging boutique shops, this created multi-layered production and distribution models, which overlapped and co-existed.[27]

Against this backdrop of changes in the commercial production of clothing, the domestic home sewer was able to keep up with current fashion by using readily available commercial patterns.[28] As mass-produced clothing increased, professional dressmakers using bespoke pattern cutting methods, such as the ones demonstrated in MacEwan's text, gradually disappeared. MacEwan writes disdainfully about the compromised quality of fabric, and the lack of attention to detail and fit within the mass-production processes.[29] Marge Garland, the first fashion professor at the Royal College of Art, spoke in her inaugural lecture of the changing landscape of fashion:

> ...our clothes are the last item of daily use to be taken from our individual hands and put into the charge of industry. The change is very recent, and it is only during the last twenty years that the little dressmaker, on whose ingenuity in translating fashion plates to our own particular requirements we relied, and whose work was the basis of most wardrobes, has vanished from our midst.[30]

Garland's words resonate today, as the current *slow fashion* movement aims to create tighter production systems which reunite the relationships among designer, maker, materials, and traditional production methods, to develop more sustainable and meaningful models of clothing production.[31] Though MacEwan's motivations were rooted in the preservation of a declining industry rather than sustainability, her text promotes a "slow" approach to the values of dress design and production. For MacEwan, knowledge of materials, understanding of fit, quality of make, longevity, and creating a classic style that met the needs of the consumer, were imperative. This significant change in fashion production, which Garland and MacEwan had witnessed by 1950, moved the process of cutting individual patterns to fit (which was based on the designer/maker having a direct relationship with the customer) into the domestic sphere. MacEwan's text transmitted these skills to this alternative audience.

Whilst custom-made garments were still being made for select clients within couture houses,[32] cutting individually fitting patterns was only possible for the accomplished domestic dressmaker. Most relied on using and adapting commercial patterns. *Your Pattern Cutting* addressed this skills gap by offering the home dressmaker the opportunity to learn pattern drafting and fitting skills from the comfort of home. MacEwan identified her intended reader as those unable to access courses and addressed it "particularly to women of discriminating taste who wish to cut styles which appeal to them."[33] To learn this skill solely from a textbook, with no face-to-face tuition, however, would have been extremely challenging. There was an implied expectation that, due to the contemporary education curriculum and domestic necessity, the reader had an existing understanding of pattern shape and construction processes.

Your Pattern Cutting: approaches to cutting and design

Your Pattern Cutting was MacEwan's legacy as an educator. The first edition was published six years before MacEwan's retirement, and offered a comprehensive flat-pattern system through the creation of custom-made foundation blocks. These blocks were basic pattern templates made in card and, once fitted, could be

Figure 2.4 Hornsey fashion student (unknown) wearing her own design *c.* 1950.

manipulated and adapted into different styles. The publication enabled MacEwan to share her forty years teaching experience, and she used Hornsey staff and students to refine the system.[34] Indeed, alongside draping methods, this system of preparing block patterns and adapting them is listed within her class content for students training for the dress industry.[35] Photographs of Hornsey students wearing their own creations suggests that making garments to fit was common practice within fashion education. Although this text does not offer a complete

DEPARTMENT OF WOMEN'S CRAFTS

Miss E. S. MacEWAN, A.T.D., *Head of Department*

EVENING TIME TABLE

7 P.M. TO 9.30 P.M.

SUBJECT	DAY	INSTRUCTOR	STUDIO
Basketry	Wed.	Mackay, A.	T
	Fri.	A. Mackay	T
Dress Design	Mon.	Melliar-Smith, M.	5
	Tues.	Howard, D. W.	B
Dressmaking	Mon.	Gough, P.	3
	Tues.	Easton, M.	2
	Tues.	MacLeod, B.	3
	Wed.	Bullard, J.	3
	Thurs.	Bullard, J.	3
	Fri.	Bakkers, M.	3
Embroidery	Mon.	Short, E.	4
	Thurs.	Short, E.	4
Fashion Drawing	Mon.	Walton, S.	E
	Thurs.	Walton, S.	A
Fashion Illustration	Tues.	Mitchell, F. J.	E
	Wed.	Mitchell, F. J.	E
Flower Making	Tues.	Howard, D. W.	B
History of Costume	Mon.	Melliar-Smith, M.	5
Leather Dress Accessories	Wed.	Furst, G.	2
Leatherwork	Tues.	Piper, K.	X
	Mon.	Howard, M. D.	T
Lingerie and Needlework	Tues.	Bullard, J.	4
	Fri.	O'Hara, S.	4
Millinery	Mon.	Bickers, G.	2
	Fri.	Gregsten, R.	2
Pattern Cutting	Tues.	O'Hara, S.	A
	Thurs.	Kirwan, D.	E
Tailoring and Pattern Cutting for C. and G. Exam.	Fri.	Spratt, J.	A
Tailoring	Tues.	Wright, J.	5
	Wed.	Wright, J.	4
	Thurs.	Wright, J.	5
	Fri.	Wright, J.	4
Teaching Course, for M.C.C. Craft Teacher's Certificate	Wed.	MacLeod, B.	5
Theatrical Design	Thurs.	Agombar, E.	2
Weaving	Mon.	Barker, M.	I
	Tues.	Barker, M.	I
	Wed.	McCrae, J.	I
	Thurs.	Broadbent, A.	I
	Fri.	Broadbent, A.	I
Weaving, Dobby and Jacquard	Tues.	Barker, M.	I

For Classes from 4.30 p.m. to 6.30 p.m. see page 25.

28

Figure 2.5 Evening timetable of Women's Craft Department, Hornsey School of Art Prospectus 1955/56, p. 28.

education in fashion design, it does include condensed instruction on fashion illustration, dress design and making historical costume, all night classes MacEwan had taught at Hornsey.

MacEwan presents her system of pattern drafting from blocks as an up-to-date, reliable, and accurate system to cut clothing of any style, period, and fit.

> During the past twenty years, pattern drafting on paper, as opposed to modeling in material on a dress stand, has come into its own; far from being looked down upon as the Cinderella of the cheap dress trade, it can now be regarded as an almost exact science based on careful observation of the varying proportions of the figure in action and repose, coupled with the latest knowledge of garment fabrics in wear.[36]

MacEwan provides a standard sizing chart, which was to be used in conjunction with personal measurements to develop individually fitted blocks. Although she mainly focuses on flat patterns, she briefly discusses draping methods, as can be seen in her instructions for the sleeve block.[37]

Your Pattern Cutting has five sections, which develop in a logical sequence creating a linear approach to learning pattern-cutting skills. Readers with experience, however, would be able to use the text as a reference book. MacEwan views understanding the basics of fabric properties as essential to developing successful designs. In section one, to help understand the relationship between design and materials, she explores the weave and grain-lines of fabrics, offering a series of exercises to consider how fabrics drape. In section two, a series of step-by-step instructions guides the reader through taking personal measurements and plotting them onto a grid, to draft a foundation bodice block. Once the block pattern is drafted, the reader is shown how to transfer the pattern onto fabric to create a "mull" from cotton fabric, (also known as a *toile*), which is sewn together and fitted to the individual. This in itself can be a complex task, depending on the accuracy of measurements taken, the proportions and potential anomalies of the body being fitted, and the reader's ability to follow the written instructions exactly. These techniques require confidence in plotting patterns, understanding two-dimensional and three-dimensional shape, taking and recording accurate measurements, and knowledge in fitting and altering patterns to get a successful outcome. Although MacEwan does offer the reader additional fitting instructions and advice, the nature of bespoke flat-pattern cutting means that accurate and well-fitting blocks are essential to being able to progress to create fashionable styles. The completed bodice block was made in card and could be manipulated and adapted into different styles. The text is mapped out to create a set of personalized blocks including: bodices (with multiple variations—fitted, semi-fitted), skirts, sleeves and sleeve integrations, coats, lingerie, and maternity apparel.

MacEwan acknowledges "the apparently disproportionate amount of time which must be given to preparing and making foundation blocks."[38] The benefit of the process is that it enables subsequent patterns to fit with minimal adaptation. Offering this system to the home dressmaker potentially enables her to create well-fitting and individually designed clothing, which could be made within her budget. It is this personalized element which MacEwan values and promotes.

Once the initial bodice block was successfully made, MacEwan provides instruction on how to adapt the foundation blocks through adding and subtracting volume, changing seam lines and/or manipulating the position of the darts. This is a standard approach for made-to-measure flat-pattern cutting, though the choice of pattern adaptations does reflect the period in which MacEwan taught. There are 1950s duster coats[39] alongside bodices echoing day dresses from the 1930s with cascading ruffles.[40] Each section starts with the creation of the relevant block, and then offers design adaptations from this foundation pattern. For example, part three covers body and sleeve pattern integrations, such as raglan and kimono sleeves, and then leads into the creation of a one-piece dress block through using the bodice block from part one with the skirt block in part two. This linear approach builds the readers' skills and complexity in outcomes, if the text is followed as it is presented.

Part four introduces blocks for coats with a more complex two-piece fitted sleeve block. Lingerie blocks and designs for "nether garments," which include knickers, divided skirts, and "slacks" are also covered. This section also offers instruction for maternity and "adaptations for non-standard fitting" wherein MacEwan advises how patterns can be altered and specific designs chosen to flatter and accommodate fitting for different body shapes.

Overall, MacEwan believes that well-fitting and well-chosen designs make the wearer look and feel better, a very different experience from buying off-the-peg clothing. Her text offered the reader a broad overview of all the main traditional garment shapes and style adaptations, each illustrating a different pattern cutting principle. Her text is not about innovation or unique design, but offers practical, wearable components, which the reader would recognize within her wardrobe. In the final section, MacEwan moves beyond the nuts and bolts of practical pattern cutting methods and places these skills within a broader contextual understanding. Drawing on her teaching experience at Hornsey, she offers concise advice on "Interpreting Current Fashion," "How to Use Fashion

Drawings and Photographs," and how to pattern cut historical garments. This widens her audience beyond the home dressmaker to those making for amateur dramatics. MacEwan repeatedly presents the skills of pattern drafting as being outside the context of current fashion and as having a timeless relevance.[41] Her positioning of these skills establishes a sense of historical continuity.

MacEwan's design philosophy

MacEwan's design philosophy was to conceive and make garments with longevity through being well-fitted, well-made, with an understanding of materials, and which had good proportion and style. Ideals of good style—combining elegance, fit, and comfort—are embedded throughout the text. This was the opportunity to develop a relationship with clothing that is built around the needs of the individual, thus MacEwan is both preserving a method of producing clothing, and promoting its values and relevance: that of an individual relationship toward clothing. In this, MacEwan demonstrates the potential agency she believes these technical skills offer the reader to achieve a fashionable outcome.

Dress design is briefly considered within the text. MacEwan lists general design rules and ways to analyze both historic and contemporary design. The parameters within which she refers to design are limited, however, as she advocates the practice of interpreting current fashion rather than creating original designs.

> The ideal pattern cutter can extract what is best in current fashion and adapt it to the figure and personal characteristics of the ultimate wearer, and this quality, added perfect fit, should distinguish the work of the home dressmaker from ready-made clothes.[42]

MacEwan wanted the reader to be scrupulous in the quality of the designer studied. She advised studying only the "great designers" and recommended an annual subscription to a "high class" fashion journal, preferably French. MacEwan saw her readers not as designers, but as copyists, having the chance to interpret current fashionable images and recreate them to fit at home with guidance and practice. Just as dressmakers studied sketches from Paris,[43] MacEwan's home sewers could reinterpret the best of couture fashion by considering style, economy, and their own shape. This would include the process of creating a complete dress design (including the back), selecting appropriate fabrics, and adapting the pattern to flatter and fit the proportions of the individual, which are all design skills.

MacEwan's voice is authentic and encouraging, reflecting her experience as a teacher. Speaking directly to the reader, she addresses them as the "inexperienced worker" and the "inexperienced cutter," and refers to her text as a "companionable book." A practical and succinct text which offers the reader a technically comprehensive guide to becoming skilled at flat-pattern cutting, this is a textbook to learn with. The layout of the exercises builds incrementally on each pattern cutting principle, with clear instructions and an encouraging tone, often offering additional guidance. For example, when being measured, MacEwan advises:

> Stand quite naturally; you will want your dresses to hang well on you always, not only on the rare occasions when you remember your faults of posture! . . . Look straight ahead and remember that your part in the fitting is to stand patiently and to avoid making the fitter nervous by screaming if she sticks a pin in you inadvertently or by offering unwanted advice or criticism.[44]

MacEwan's ability to write clear, detailed, and humorous instructions (even to the point of how to hold a pencil) creates an approachable and accessible text.

Austerity and agency

Having taught through two world wars, MacEwan's response to experiencing austerity can be seen though her resourceful approach to materials and value of tools. For example, within the equipment list she offered, she included instruction in making your own yard stick from a "good straight lath,"[45] alongside encouraging the reader to protect her polished table with cardboard before starting work. Ways to economize reverberate throughout the text as she offered alternative pattern papers to use, and recommended buying a box of steel pins, which she noted was cheaper than buying them individually. Affordability was important to MacEwan, and in her preface she referred to the increase in the pricing of books. In 1951, the book cost seven shillings and nine pence, equivalent to £11.70 in 2018, making this an affordable book for the home dressmaker.[46] The aesthetic presentation of this text, with the illustrations compactly condensed onto single pages (sometimes up to thirty illustrations on a single page), and MacEwan's use of all the space available (she refers to providing an illustration template on the inside dust jacket), reflect her commitment to use materials to their fullest value.[47]

This system creates purposeful, lasting garments based on individual need, and in turn means that the garments would be worn, treasured, altered, and mended. Beyond an economizing response to austerity, MacEwan believes in meaningful design.

MacEwan advocated her system of pattern drafting as having lasting relevance and value, enabling the home sewer to make garments which nodded to fashion, but were made with the needs of the wearer at heart. This value of bespoke garments counteracted the loss of quality MacEwan identified as being a result of mass-production. By learning these skills, the 1950s home dressmaker would have been able to create garments that fit better and reflected her own style. This personalized process enabled the home sewer to be creative with her own wardrobe, moving her beyond passively consuming patterns, and offered an opportunity for self-expression. The potential for this method to facilitate the creation of true individual design was relative to the skill and knowledge of the pattern cutter: only the highly skilled cutter could create original designs beyond the cut and paste design elements covered in the examples. MacEwan referred to "moving beyond arithmetical instructions" and identified the understanding of materials and "good judgment" to be more valuable than the ability to carry out technical calculations correctly.[48] To be able to draft patterns well requires competency in multiple skills: material awareness, understanding of body shape, two- and three-dimensional shape and proportions, and a flair for fashion design. Through the development of all these skills women could play a more active role within fashion. This could be enjoyed as a hobby, developed for personal creative expression, or could become a home industry offering a way to supplement household income through making clothes for clients.[49] Being able to fit, alter, and adapt garments would have been important for all home dressmakers who used standard sized commercial patterns, or altered mass-manufactured clothing, whether building their own wardrobe or for paying clients. Offering flexibility and individuality, these were desirable skills within a culture of mass-produced clothing where standardized fitting was not always satisfactory.

Your Pattern Cutting was first published in 1950, and reprinted a further four times in 1951, 1956, 1960, and 1962, more than any other book in this series. No records exist identifying the number published; the multiple reprints, however, suggest continued demand for the text for over a decade. The text was also printed in 1951 by American publishers Chas. A. Bennett Company, which specialized in printing practical art instruction books.[50] MacEwan's text reached a global audience where it competed with titles such as E. Pivnick's (1948) *How to Design Beautiful Clothes*. Through writing this text MacEwan both extended her influence as an educator, reaching audiences for over a decade after she retired, alongside preserving and keeping the method of bespoke clothing production alive.

Conclusion

Multiple histories can be told through MacEwan's *Your Pattern Cutting*. Written at an interesting historical junction, this text demonstrates how MacEwan, as a fashion educator, promoted hand-craft pattern cutting skills beyond her classroom, in a period of growing industrialization. By positioning made-to-measure pattern cutting methods as a domestic craft, she offered women opportunities to define and express their own fashion taste.

MacEwan's motivation was to preserve a pattern cutting skill-set which she saw disappearing: making individual fitted blocks to develop personalized patterns, to make well-made, well-fitting, affordable, stylish clothing to meet individual needs and tastes. In this, she understood that although her work could not galvanize a dying profession, it ensured the essence of this profession (designing for the individual and value of hand-craft) was kept alive. This text offered the home dressmaker an alternative way to operate in a fashion system that was becoming depersonalized. Additionally, through this instruction, women could develop a practical understanding of the relationship of garments to their own bodies, enjoy the opportunity to explore their own individual tastes for their fashioned bodies, and become more active participants in shaping and creating their own wardrobes. These were complex skills, which would have required commitment to become proficient, and, although MacEwan did not view the home dressmaker as a designer, the process of drafting and fitting patterns placed the decision-making power—and by extension agency—in the hands of the home dressmaker.

Your Pattern Cutting revealed what is now referred to as a *slow fashion* approach to creating garments. It promoted the investment of time, resources, and skills to creating meaningfully-designed clothes, which focused on the individual. Echoing discourses today regarding the need to develop sustainable production methods which value materials, and build closer relationships between customer, maker, and designer, MacEwan's text is poignant and relevant, and offers the practical skills to help enable this change to happen.

This is a significant pattern cutting text from the period. Through documenting her methods and approach to pattern cutting in a technical instruction book before she retired, MacEwan ensured Hornsey's approach of promoting the practical application of crafts continued, and indeed reached a global audience. Her book was republished in 2010, amidst a wave of "print-on-demand" publishers reprinting out-of-copyright and orphaned works, thus seeing its reach extend beyond the author's own lifetime. This reinforces MacEwan's place in design education, enabling her to reach another generation of readers "of discriminating taste who wish to cut styles which appeal to them."[51]

"Knitting Instructions": An Analysis of Red Cross Clothing Patterns, 1917–65

Rebecca J. Keyel

This chapter explores the American Red Cross initiative to recruit civilians for a production program to create knit garments, hospital items, and surgical dressings between the years 1917 and 1965. This time frame notably includes the Second World War and thereby augments the story of civilian use of garment patterns that is explored in Chapter 4. Unlike all the other chapters in this book, which deal with patterns designed for cutting and constructing woven textiles, this chapter explores knitting patterns. A knitting pattern is a set of written directions that instructs the knitter with regards to stitch number, type and gauge as well as materials and tools. Only careful adherence to the text of a kitting pattern will produce the intended garment. This chapter explores how the Red Cross organized women volunteers to produce millions of items to aid servicemen, veterans, and civilians, and aimed to insure the uniformity that was necessary in a military context by writing patterns that accommodated a variety of skill levels. Interestingly, the author reveals internal Red Cross correspondence which shows an understanding that individuality may be intentionally or unintentionally expressed when executing even the most clearly written pattern and how patterns were written and revised with the end user of both the pattern and the garment in mind. Thus, this chapter is closely linked with a thematic consideration that runs throughout this text, namely the interconnectedness among patterns, users, and the broader socio-cultural context in which these blueprints for creation exist.

In August 1917, the Woman's Bureau of the American National Red Cross published its first nationally distributed instructional circular, an eight-page document titled "Instructions for Knitting." The small stapled pamphlet contained detailed instructions "prepared primarily for the use of hand knitters,"

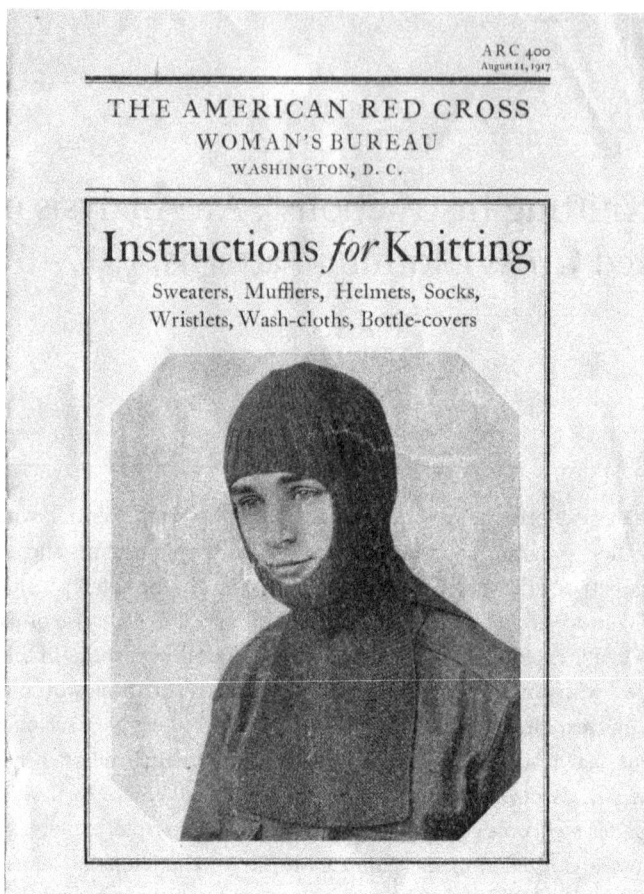

Figure 3.1 Instructions for knitting: sweaters, mufflers, helmets, socks, wristlets, wash-cloths, bottle-covers. ARC 400 August 11, 1917 printing.

and included directions for eight different items. "Instructions for Knitting" was only the first in a series of standard knitting patterns distributed by the Red Cross between 1917 and 1965, and it helped to set the standard for similar Red Cross-issued instructions that lasted for the next fifty years.

Using Red Cross knitting and sewing instructions like "Instructions for Knitting," American volunteers produced over twenty-three million articles for military relief during the First World War.[1] This was a frankly astonishing amount for the twentieth century, when industrial knitting mills could produce sweaters and socks in minutes and hours rather than days and weeks.[2] When the First World War ended with the armistice in November 1918, the Red Cross transitioned this wartime relief effort from a program that provided "comfort articles"—knit sweaters, helmets (balaclavas), and other warm knitted garments—to active servicemen into one that provided similar articles to veterans and civilians as part of Red Cross foreign aid. By the time the United States entered the Second World War, the Red Cross had a well-established Production program, with an extensive catalog of patterns for knit garments, hospital items, and surgical dressings. The Red Cross continued to reprint their standard knitting patterns as late as 1964,[3] only a year before the organization restructured their volunteer program.[4]

Red Cross volunteers used these patterns to produce millions of sweaters and other "comfort articles" to supply emergency needs. The patterns themselves were designed to produce simple, easy to complete garments that were distributed to wounded and active servicemen as a part of the Red Cross's charter-defined mission to provide aid to the armed forces. Each garment, from sleeveless sweaters to socks, was designed to reflect a "simplicity of design, reasonable uniformity of product, and as economical as possible a use of raw material."[5] The garments made from these patterns were simple to construct, utilizing few seams, basic knitting techniques, and little to no garment shaping. The simple construction and clear instructions given in each knitting pattern allowed the Red Cross to carefully control a program that was entirely reliant on volunteer labor and helped ensure that the men who received the donated goods had a serviceable garment to remind them what they were fighting for.

Over the five decades of the Red Cross's Production program, the physical patterns printed and distributed by the organization reflected the changing needs and values of the Red Cross's volunteer program. Over the fifty years of the program, Production officials revised each pattern based on fluctuations in the wool market, feedback from their volunteers, and even to match new military uniforms. But even when the patterns were revised, they continued to be written to accommodate knitters of varied skill levels and abilities, to produce a uniform garment, and to streamline the finishing process, ensuring that volunteers could make garments efficiently and well.

"Knitting now monopolizing women's attention"

The Red Cross's Production program lasted for five decades, but it was most popular during the two World Wars when it provided comfort articles to active service men and women. Three major factors influenced the success of this program.

First, the general popularity of knitting both at home and abroad in the years leading up to US entry into the First World War meant that "knitting for the boys" was already in the public consciousness. In August 1914, British women began knitting almost as soon as their armies marched, and American women soon followed suit. By December 1917, nine months after the United States entered the war, knitting was so popular that an article describing the work of "the College Women of the Nation" wrote, "Knitting—why speak of it? It is everywhere. [...] This work is omnipresent. In most cases it seems to be subconscious, and will, I presume, steadily increase without affecting any other product."[6] Knitting women appeared on the covers of magazines, knitting bags appeared in both fashion plates and as good gift items, and retail trade publications told department stores to "Push This Fad! Knitting Now Monopolizing Women's Attention."[7] Popular songs like "I Wonder Who's Knitting For Me?" and "The Knitting Song" were recorded and arranged for piano and voice.[8]

The second factor that influenced the success of the Red Cross's knitting program was directly related to the organization's status as a quasi-government organization. The Red Cross's 1905 federal charter placed a number of cabinet secretaries on its Executive Council, a connection that strengthened the Red Cross's relationship with the federal government. In addition, the close relationship between top officials and two presidents—William Taft and Woodrow Wilson—solidified it as the federal government's main avenue for both military and civilian relief.[9] This relationship was especially close during both World Wars, when the Red Cross worked directly with the military to provide knitted comforts and other relief items directly to servicemen.

Third, the leaders of the Red Cross during the First World War were part of the larger progressive era reform movement, and they created an organized system to direct the Red Cross's disseminated system of chapters that set a precedent for the duration of the Production program. Marian Moser Jones has argued that the Red Cross was emblematic of a particular strand of progressivism that attempted to create a more organized society that was aligned with a corporate style system of bureaucracy.[10] This system of progressive reform deeply impacted the knitting program and its systematic approach to organizing volunteers.

The Woman's Bureau: 1917

Individual Red Cross chapters began organizing knitting efforts to make knitted comforts for soldiers in their local communities as early as May 1917.[11] These localized efforts were almost certainly influenced by the knitting programs being run by organizations like the Boston-based Special Aid Society and the Washington, DC-based Comforts Committee of the Navy League.[12] Red Cross leadership soon realized that they would need to step in to organize the efforts of the local chapters. There was such an "intense desire on the part of women workers in the chapters to make useful relief supplies," that Red Cross officials at National Headquarters felt they needed to step in to "guide and systematize the work."[13]

The Red Cross established a Woman's Bureau to organize those women workers "in useful Red Cross activity,"[14] and created the Woman's Advisory Committee, a nine-member advisory board, to advise it.[15] One of the Advisory Committee's first tasks was to decide "what knitting work should be done by the Red Cross, and how the wool should be secured."[16] A major concern for the Committee was whether the Red Cross should adopt "<u>one</u> standard pattern to be used exclusively for each garment."[17] Adopting one standard pattern had several advantages for the Red Cross, and for garment production at large. A knitting pattern is a set of directions that provide written instructions for creating a garment. Knitting patterns typically include instructions for what materials to use as well as directions that tell the knitter how to construct the actual garment. The women on the Woman's Advisory Committee knew that adopting standardized knitting directions would help ensure that the thousands of volunteers knitting for the troops made consistent and uniform garments. In addition to providing guidelines on the actual construction of the garment, patterns provided directions on obtaining the right fabric texture by using the right materials and setting standards for gauge, the number of stitches per inch in knit fabric. Too few stitches and the fabric would be too loose and not protect the soldier on cold nights. Too many and the resulting garment would be dense and stiff and uncomfortable to wear.

The Committee assigned the task of deciding how to organize the knitting work to the newly appointed Director of the Woman's Bureau, a woman named Florence Marshall. At the first Woman's Advisory Committee meeting, held in June 1917, the Committee asked her to "investigate" the knitting and sewing already being undertaken by the chapters and report back. Marshall worked quickly. She consulted with "authorities from the British, Canadian and French Red Cross," and "with knitting experts from the commercial mills and the women's magazines" to develop and adapt eight patterns that would be useful for men in service. Based on similar knitting patterns that circulated at the time, it is almost certain that she adapted at least some of the existing patterns designed for comfort articles for servicemen.[18] She also worked with the Red Cross Bureau of Standards and Bureau of Supply to choose wool with a "four-ply No. 10's construction."[19] By the July meeting of the Woman's Advisory Committee, she had a knitting circular of the "eight patterns that are needed" ready for the printer, and was working with her staff writers on circulars for "various types of comfort bags," "hospital supplies and garments," and "surgical dressings."[20] She was tasked with communicating these instructions to the Red Cross's local chapters, who worked with their volunteers in Red Cross workrooms to produce the comfort bags, knit sweaters, and surgical dressings throughout the war.

Marshall's first knitting pattern circular, "Instructions for Knitting," was ready just in time. In early August 1917, Major Greyson Murphy, the Red Cross Commissioner to France, wired Red Cross National Headquarters in Washington, DC asking for "one million five hundred thousand each of warm woolen garments" for "our soldiers and those of our Allies who will suffer in their frozen trenches."[21] "Instructions for Knitting" provided clear, simple, standardized instructions to make the four different garments that Murphy requested, sweaters, socks, mufflers, and wristlets, as well as four other items Marshall and her team believed would be useful overseas. Volunteers were asked to knit the "comfort articles" using the specified yarn with a "4-ply 10's construction," in "either gray or khaki." These colors had "been carefully considered with the authorities of the War Department and with the American Red Cross Commissioner for Europe, in Paris."[22] No other colors were accepted for distribution to the troops. The circular even included scaled drawings of three sizes of "standardized Red Cross needles" so volunteers knew exactly what size knitting needles to use.

The patterns in "Instructions for Knitting" were simple and easy to knit. The design for each garment only required the knitter to know the most basic elements of knitting: knit and purl stitches and casting on and off to start and finish. The pattern for the sleeveless sweater, for example, was designed to be knit in one piece, folded over at the neck, and then sewn up the sides to create a rectangular boxy garment. There was no shaping in the fabric or any other design element that might require more advanced knitting techniques, which in consequence would make it more complicated for beginners. Other garments either followed a similar method of construction and were made by knitting a flat piece of fabric sewn together or were relatively simple shapes that only required the knitter to have one or two additional skills. The knitted helmet, the balaclava seen in Figure 3.1, and the pair of socks, for example, required the knitter to know a technique called "knitting-in-the-round," that created a circular seamless garment. However, despite this additional skill, the patterns were the simple straightforward versions that knitters with an intermediate skill level could produce relatively quickly.

Simple designs ensured that knitting wool was used efficiently and that the completed garments were as uniform as possible. Since knitting needle sizes were not standardized among manufacturers, establishing three "standardized Red Cross needles" ensured that volunteer knitters had the right tools in the right sizes to produce a uniform garment. Several of the garment patterns, including the sleeveless sweater, even included photographs so that the knitter could see what the finished garment should look like. Volunteers could work at home or in a Red Cross workroom and the carefully written instructions guided the knitter to create a uniform garment. The back cover of the circular even provided general shipping guidelines, advising knitters that finished garments should be sent to the volunteer's local Red Cross chapter, and to the Red Cross supply depot if there was no local chapter.

A half million circulars were printed and distributed to individual chapters in August 1917, and the patterns themselves were reprinted in the November 1917 issues of four of the most popular women's magazines, *The Ladies' Home Journal*, *The Modern Priscilla*, *The Delineator*, and *Good Housekeeping*. The eight initial knitting patterns were also reprinted in widely ranging publications including, *The Mary Frances Knitting Book* (a children's instructional guide), *The Touchstone* (a home and architecture magazine), *The Alaska Railroad Record* and even in the *"Win the War" Cookbook*.[23] The wide spectrum of publications represents the ubiquity of knitting for the armed forces during the First World War, when knitting was a constant preoccupation, which pervaded magazines, newspapers, and even music. The proliferation of patterns also represents the wide reach of the Red Cross as an organization, and the longevity of the Woman's Bureau's "Instructions for Knitting," long after the Red Cross published revisions to several of its most important patterns.

The Department of Development: 1918–21

The longevity of Red Cross patterns is even more interesting because the place of "Instructions for Knitting" as the official Red Cross pattern circular was short-lived. In December 1917, the Red Cross's managing council notified the members of the Woman's Advisory Committee that the board's responsibilities had been expanded to include "all Red Cross matters" rather than only those directly related to women's work. Two things happened as a result of the Woman's Advisory Committee's expanded responsibilities. First, Florence Marshall resigned as director. Second, the Woman's Bureau was discontinued as a separate bureau, its production work was absorbed by the Department of Development, and it quickly started building on the work Marshall had begun in July.[24] Marshall's resignation came after only six months of work. In that time, the Woman's Bureau developed not only an influential knitting circular, but also established guidelines for producing a number of other circulars that included patterns for infants' layettes, children's clothing, and surgical dressings, as well as guides for preparing comfort kits and Christmas packets for the armed forces.[25] Her work, and the work of the Woman's Bureau laid a foundation for the entire program that continued to develop over the next fifty years.

The Department of Development took over responsibility for organizing and systematizing relief work in December 1917. By May 1918, Development had introduced three new instructional circulars that completely superseded the original "Instructions for Knitting" circular. The three new circulars included revisions of five of the most sought-after garments originally included in "Instructions for Knitting," and reflected both the Red Cross's commitment to better fitting garments and simple directions, and a significant change of leadership. They also marked the second of what would be five major printing styles of Red Cross knitting patterns. This style is characterized by a single typeset half-sheet of high-quality glossy paper. Each included a new designation within the Red Cross's extensive record keeping system in the upper right-hand corner, along with the revision date. The three new circulars received the designation ARC 400A, B, and C, which distinguished them from both the original "Instructions for Knitting" booklet—which was designated ARC 400—and from other Department of Development circulars developed for relief.

Each pattern included an "Important Suggestions" section that provided basic information to the knitter while they knit, something that ensured they had proper instructions whether or not they were working under the guidance of a trained Red Cross volunteer. These patterns also included information about the yarn required to knit the pattern and used a manufacturer's designation rather than a retail yarn brand to ensure that chapters could always obtain the correct yarn weight. But in contrast to "Instructions for Knitting," the patterns of the second style did not specify a yarn color. This was almost certainly because by this point in the Red Cross's knitting program, individual chapters were asked to source their yarn through the Red Cross supply service, which purchased wholesale materials and distributed them to chapters. This helped ensure that the yarn was relatively uniform, and that the scarce wool supply was better controlled at the national level. The patterns also included two diagrams of the appropriate needle sizes, a side-view that the knitter could measure her own needle against to check the width, and a cross section of the needle with its diameter in inches, as seen in Figure 3.2.

The five garments the Department of Development included in the three circulars issued in May 1918 were a substantially revised sleeveless sweater (ARC 400B, shown in Figure 3.2), a pair of medium size socks (ARC 400A), and a sheet that included patterns for a helmet, muffler, and pair of wristlets (ARC 400C). The revisions to the socks, muffler, helmet and wristlet patterns included in ARC 400A and ARC 400B were slight and did little to change the overall look or construction of the finished garments. The sleeveless sweater pattern, ARC 400B, however, was a substantial rewrite that changed both the construction and finished product. The original sweater featured a ribbed hem, but the rest of the garment was constructed entirely in garter stitch with a rectangular opening for the wearer's head. Based on a contemporary reproduction knit by the author, the finished garment was uncomfortable and constricting, and knitters were warned that, "the necks of sweaters should be made sufficiently large to go over the heads of men, as otherwise the men cut the necks and the sweaters were ruined."[26]

ARC 400B included two patterns, a sweater in light-weight wool and a sweater in heavy-weight wool (Figure 3.2). Both were complete redesigns of the original sweater pattern. Both included a new, more flexible collar, with the addition of ribbing at the collar and shoulders that allowed the wearer to move more easily. This pattern was also successful. The overall design with minor modifications continued to be the standard Red Cross sleeveless sweaters for military personnel for decades. This revised version was slightly more complicated for the volunteers to make because the flexible collar included ribbing—alternating knit and purl stitches to create a stretchy fabric—but the overall construction of the garment remained the same. Just like the original sweater, the 1919 revision was knit as a single long piece of fabric that was finished by sewing up each side.

The Red Cross's production efforts during the First World War included items for both military personnel and civilians, but military relief was the main focus of the Red Cross and of chapter production work. The work for servicemen ended in December 1918, when the Red Cross determined that the current stocks of garments were sufficient to supply the men during de-escalation.[27]

ARC 400 B
Revised May 9, 1918

THE AMERICAN RED CROSS
DEPARTMENT OF DEVELOPMENT
WASHINGTON, D. C.

Knitting Instructions
Sweaters
Important Suggestions

Casting on and binding off MUST *be loose.*
When knitting with two needles, always slip first stitch.
To measure a garment, lay it on a level surface and measure with a dependable measure (wood, metal, or celluloid, not a tape line).
Terms used (applying to plain knitting with two needles):

    a "row" = once across;
    a "ridge" or "rib" = once across and back.

Sweater of Light-weight Wool

Quantity of Wool required:—about three-quarter pound of 4/10 yarn,
1 pair Red Cross needles No. 3:—(See diagram below).

RED CROSS NEEDLE NO. 3, SIDE-VIEW AND CROSS SECTION; NATURAL SIZE

Diameter = 1/5 inch

Cast on 78 stitches.
Knit 2, Purl 2, for 4 inches.
Knit plain 17 inches.
(A) Knit 28 stitches; Knit 2, Purl 2, for 22 stitches; then Knit 28.
(B) Knit 28 stitches; Purl 2, Knit 2, for 22 stitches; then Knit 28.
Repeat (A) and (B) for 12 rows (2 inches).
Knit 28 stitches; bind off 22 stitches (opening for neck); Knit 28.

First Shoulder: Knit 2, Purl 2, for 28 stitches; then
    Knit 2, Purl 2, back over the 28 stitches.
    Continue to knit and purl back and forth in this way 15
      times, which leaves the wool at *inner* edge.
    Break off wool and tie it on at neck-opening for

Second Shoulder: Purl 2, Knit 2, for 28 stitches; then
    Purl 2, Knit 2, back over the 28 stitches.
    Continue to knit and purl back and forth in this way 15
      times, which leaves the wool at *outer* edge.

    Knit plain 28 stitches; cast on 22 stitches; and Knit plain across the 28
    stitches of first shoulder.
(C) Knit 28 stitches; Purl 2, Knit 2, for 22 stitches; then Knit 28.

(OVER)

Figure 3.2 Knitting instructions: ARC 400B, sweaters, July 1918 revision. Front and back.

) Knit 28 stitches; Knit 2, Purl 2, for 22 stitches; then Knit 28.
Repeat (C) and (D) for 12 rows (2 inches).
Knit plain 17 inches.
Knit 2, Purl 2, for 4 inches.
Bind off loosely. Sew up sides, leaving 9 inches for armholes.
Single-crochet 1 row around neck and armholes.

easurements: { Neck (when stretched), 11½—12½ inches.
{ Across chest (*not stretched*), 17—20 inches.

Sweater of Heavy-weight Wool

Quantity of Wool required:—about one pound, or 4 hanks of 4/5 yarn.
1 pair Red Cross needles No. 3

Cast on 72 stitches.
Knit 2, Purl 2, for 3 inches.
Knit across and Purl back for 10 inches.
Knit 1 row.
) Knit 6, Purl across; and Knit last 6 stitches.
) Knit all the way across.
Repeat (A) and (B) for 8 inches.
Knit across and back 8 times; (making 4 ridges).
Knit 6; then Purl 1, Knit 1, for 11 stitches; Knit 6.
Bind off 26 stitches for neck.

rst Shoulder: Knit 6; then Purl 1, Knit 1, for 11 stitches; Knit 6.
Knit 7; then Purl 1, Knit 1, for 10 stitches; Knit 6.
Continue to knit and purl back and forth in this way 14
times, which leaves the wool at *inner* edge.
Break off wool and tie it on at neck-opening for

cond Shoulder: Knit 7; then Purl 1, Knit 1, for 10 stitches; Knit 6.
Knit 6; then Purl 1, Knit 1, for 11 stitches; Knit 6.
Continue to knit and purl back and forth in this way 14
times, which leaves the wool at *inner* edge.
Cast on 26 stitches; Knit 6; then Purl 1, Knit 1, for 11 stitches; Knit 6.
Knit across and back 8 times (making 4 ridges).
) Knit all the way across.
)) Knit 6; Purl across; and Knit last 6 stitches.
Repeat (C) and (D) for 8 inches.
Knit across and Purl back for 10 inches.
Purl 2, Knit 2, for 3 inches.
Bind off loosely. Sew up sides, leaving 9 inches for armholes.
Single-crochet 1 row around neck and armholes.

easurements: { Neck (when stretched), 11½—12½ inches.
{ Across chest (*not stretched*), 17—20 inches.

———————

CKS   For knitting instructions, see A R C leaflet 400 A.

RISTLETS
UFFLER } For knitting instructions, see A R C leaflet 400 C.
ELMET

Between the wars: 1922–39

Knitting for servicemen continued after the armistice, but there was a "natural relaxation of effort in some sections because of the lessening of the war tension."[28] This natural relaxation continued as the Red Cross pivoted toward a peacetime program. The Red Cross restructured several departments created specifically for the wartime emergency, including the Department of Development, in the first few years after the war.[29] In its place, the Red Cross created a new division, Production, to take up the relief supply program initially started during the war.

Over the next four decades, Production was responsible for developing and producing Red Cross relief supplies.[30] But compared to the Woman's Bureau and Department of Development, Production's reach during the 1920s and 1930s was limited. Facing the post-war reality of fewer resources and fewer members, Red Cross leadership made a deliberate choice to step back from program development and let local chapters develop and run their own activities.[31] This meant that although Volunteer Services and the Production Corps were in charge of relief production, individual local chapters bore the responsibility for organizing any local activities.

In addition, there was reluctance on the chapter level to continue Production work. The Minneapolis Chapter of the Red Cross reported that "interest in knitting had so completely gone" that they had serious difficulty interesting any of their auxiliary units in the effort.[32] The Red Cross ran one national knitting campaign for servicemen in the 1920s—a fall 1925 campaign to ask chapters to knit 30,000 sweaters for disabled and hospitalized veterans. National Headquarters released a new sweater pattern for volunteers that included instructions to knit a sleeveless version, along with additional directions to add sleeves. They asked volunteers to knit the sleeved version to supplement the sleeveless sweaters the Red Cross already had in their stores.[33] This sleeved sweater pattern marked the first pattern of the third style (1922–39) of the Red Cross's patterns and reflected the organization's reduced national presence and decreased resources.

Two types of knitting instructions were issued during the third style of Red Cross patterns: bound booklets that included knitting and sewing patterns and single sheet printed patterns. The bound booklets were a kind of expanded version of "Instructions for Knitting," known as *Garment Manual* (ARC 400). The earliest booklets included instructions and patterns for sewing various hospital supplies and clothing for domestic and foreign relief, as well as knitting patterns for civilians and hospitalized veterans. Starting in 1928, Production also released an abridged version (ARC 400-D) that only included basic guidelines for Production activities and Red Cross knitting patterns, rather than the relatively extensive guidelines for sewn garments issued earlier in the decade.

The knitting patterns included in *Garment Manual Abridged* (ARC 400-D) were also issued as individual patterns that could be more widely distributed (Figure 3.3). These patterns were lower quality than both their immediate First

See arc 400-1
and arc 400-3

ARC 400-B
Formerly NH 113

SUGGESTIONS TO KNITTERS

It is quite impossible to write directions or give suggestions for knitting that will always overcome the handicap of poor wool. Equally impossible is it to give directions that will always overcome the handicap of inexpert knitting. But correct needles for certain articles may always be obtained by using the correct gauge. Red Cross quotes to Chapters in these days are small, consequently the knitting given out to workers should be given only to competent knitters, — knitters who know how to use directions. Wool at present varies in the market, both in weight and quality, and quantities that Chapters can afford to buy are small. Therefore knitting should not be given to beginners for experiments. It is important that the director in charge of knitting know not only how to knit but to interpret directions. Some people never can learn to knit an "elastic stitch," — they are tight knitters, and they must of necessity use a needle a trifle larger than size mentioned in directions. If after knitting a given number of stitches the work does not measure the number of inches specified, one with "knitting sense" will know they must either use a larger needle or more stitches.

The directions for the heavy-weight sweater are based on a 4/5 yarn; all other articles call for 4/10 yarn. If yarn or needles used differ in size from those specified, the number of stitches should be proportionately decreased or increased.

A Red Cross needle gauge may now be obtained by Chapters from Headquarters. Chapters are earnestly requested to use this gauge.

Casting on and binding off MUST be loose.

Terms used: a "row" — once across; a "ridge" — once across and back. Abbreviations: K---knit; P---purl; St.---Stitch or stitches. When knitting with two needles, always slip first stitch.

To measure a garment, lay it on a level surface and measure with a dependable measure (wood, metal, or celluloid, not a tape line).

Always join wool by splicing or by running threads through each other with worsted needle.

SLIP-ON SLEEVELESS SWEATER

1 pair Red Cross Needles No. 3
Wool: About 3/4 lb. 4/10 yarn

Cast on 78 stitches; K 2, P 2 across; P 2, K 2 back for 4 inches.
K plain 17 inches.
(A) K 28 stitches; K 2, P 2, for 22 stitches; K 28.
(B) K 28 stitches; P 2, K 2, for 22 stitches; K 28.
Repeat (A) and (B) for 12 rows (2 inches).
K 28 stitches; bind off 22 stitches (neck); K 28.

51490

Figure 3.3 Slip-on sleeveless sweater, ARC 400-B, Formerly NH 113. C. 1930s.

World War antecedents and the professionally printed ARC 400 and 400-D. Instead, individual patterns were typed and stencil copied, a process that was likely done in house. Compared to having the patterns printed, in-house production would have allowed them to be produced quickly and cheaply. There was still demand for these patterns, as "sweaters and other knitted articles" for "disabled ex-servicemen government hospitals" were "not officially issued" by government hospitals during the 1920s but were in high enough demand that the Red Cross filled in the gaps. This demand kept "volunteer knitters busy" and encouraged the Red Cross to continue to reissue the sleeveless sweater patterns.[34]

Despite the differences in the print quality, patterns from this third style contained most of the same information as their immediate antecedents. They continued to include general suggestions and simple, easy-to-follow patterns that created basic garments. They also continued to include the manufacturer's name for the required yarn to ensure that chapters could source the necessary yarn locally. Additionally, they continued to specify one of the three standard Red Cross needle sizes. Both ARC 400-D and the single sheet patterns in this style also included a "Suggestions to Knitters" section, but instead of the brief instructions of iteration two, by 1928 they also include advice like:

> Wool at present varies in the market [...] and quantities that chapters can afford to buy are small. Therefore knitting should not be given to beginners for experiments. It is important that the director in charge of knitting know not only how to knit but to interpret directions.[35]

These extended guidelines reveal two things. First, the lack of control National Headquarters had over the Production program in the late 1920s and early 1930s. The directions indicate that local chapters had a significant amount of autonomy when it came to purchasing materials and appointing volunteers, and that National Headquarters was interested in cautioning them against potential waste where necessary. Second, they reveal a response to variations in the wool market and an awareness that knitting was an "art" and that "very few people knit alike."[36] Internal correspondence included statements like, "Of course the art of knitting is so individual a thing that no directions would be absolutely perfect for every knitter ... we strive very hard to overcome this difficulty."[37] Production worked hard to create patterns that produced uniform garments, despite variations in wool or knitter.

Despite lower interest, Production continued to release updates to knitting patterns regularly throughout the 1920s and 1930s. Production issued the last of the third style in September 1939, when a revision to ARC 400 was released and a number of individual patterns were reprinted. This release was almost certainly in response to Hitler's invasion of Poland on September 1, 1939. The updated packet included a limited number of sewing and knitting patterns intended for clothing and hospital supplies for foreign relief. This version of ARC 400 was a simple stapled packet of papers, but the individual patterns were printed on higher quality paper and included directions for packing and shipping abroad. The higher quality of these final patterns reflected Production's increased importance within the Red Cross as the Second World War began.

The Second World War: 1939–45

As the Second World War continued in Europe, public interest in volunteering for the Red Cross increased significantly. Between 1939 and 1941, membership in the Production Corps doubled, and it remained the most popular volunteer division throughout the rest of the war.[38] From September 1939 to September 1941, nearly all of the knitting efforts were focused toward civilian foreign war relief and hospital goods. Yet chapters began writing to National Headquarters as early as March 1941 to ask whether there would be a national knitting program to provide sweaters and other comforts to the servicemen in military training camps.[39]

Initially, the Red Cross was reluctant to begin a program for active, "able-bodied" servicemen because both the Army and Navy felt they could adequately supply their men.[40] Local chapters kept stocks of "supplemental supplies for the comfort of the men," but these were only distributed if a commanding officer directly requested the garments. However, despite the military's assurances, individual commanding officers wrote to both the Red Cross and other civilian relief groups to ask if knit comforts were available.[41]

At the end of September 1941, Red Cross Chairman, Norman Davis, moved to start a nationwide knitting program for the military. He gave two major reasons for the program. First, Red Cross officials felt strongly that knitting was one of the "traditional" duties of their organization and wanted to maintain their position as the main line of relief for the military. Second, there was some concern that the enthusiasm of Red Cross volunteers needed to be contained. When Davis announced the program to the Secretaries of War and the Navy, he wrote that women had been writing their chapters to ask whether the Red Cross would organize another knitting program.[42]

The Red Cross again took on the role of organizer and expanded the military production program to include able-bodied soldiers and sailors. Initially, the organization announced that two sleeveless sweaters would be available, a navy-blue sleeveless sweater with a round neck for men in the Navy (ARC 400-3), a maroon sleeveless sweater (ARC 400-3) for men in hospitals, and an olive drab sleeveless sweater with a V-neck (ARC 400-3c), for the Army, Air Force, and Marines. The "round necked" sweater was a familiar garment. Although it was labeled ARC 400-3, the pattern itself was a slightly revised version of the heavy-weight sweater included first introduced in May 1918 as ARC 400B.

These sweater patterns, along with a number of other patterns updated for the war, were part of the fourth style (1939–44) of Red Cross patterns. Between 1939 and 1943, Production expanded their in-house portfolio of knitting patterns for civilian and military relief significantly and again began having their patterns printed for distribution. Both stencil-copied and printed patterns exist in the Red Cross archives for this period, but it is likely that once printed versions were available only those were distributed to the chapters. The number of new patterns and the higher print quality reflected the fact that Production was a high priority for the Red Cross. The knitting program's popularity had grown enough during the early years of the war that it was worthwhile to have the patterns printed on durable glossy paper.

In addition to expanding their portfolio of knitting patterns, Production also updated the patterns themselves. A number of features remained the same, including the ARC designation in the top right corner, along with the print or revision date and a shipping code that determined whether the garment was intended for military or civilian relief. Each continued to include a simple, easy-to-follow pattern that produced an easy-to-finish garment. Each pattern also included the manufacture's term for the yarn required for the pattern and information about the appropriate needles, however both of these elements had slight but significant changes. A new "Equipment" section was added to the patterns that included the yarn and needles needed to make the pattern. Beginning in 1941, patterns issued for military garments also included the appropriate yarn color, olive drab for the Army, Air Force, and Marines, maroon for hospital use, and navy blue for the Navy. The needles the patterns specified also changed. Instead of recommending Red Cross needles in specific sizes, Production began issuing knitting gauges—a tool used to determine needle size—to chapters. Knitters were asked to compare needles they already owned with a needle gauge to determine whether the size was appropriate, a change meant to further simplify knitting for the volunteers and ensure a more uniform product.

Volunteers knitting for the Red Cross able-bodied knitting program made two different sets of garments, one set for the Army, Air Force, and Marines, and one set for the Navy. The actual garments made by volunteers for the Army shifted depending on what the military needed, but generally included sleeveless sweaters, socks, wristlets and gloves, helmets, and mufflers and cap mufflers, all knit in olive drab.[43] Like all the patterns the Red Cross designed, these were simple to make and finish. The socks, wristlets, and helmet patterns were similar to those initially issued during the First World War, with only slight revisions to accommodate different sizes or minor design changes.

The sleeveless sweater, ARC 400-3c (Figure 3.4), was a revised version of the original ARC 400B heavy-weight sweater pattern released over twenty years before. It included an updated V-neck, a design element introduced to "match the new V-necked Army uniforms."[44] This pattern was the first major pattern revision since the First World War, but it was still only a variation of the original heavy-weight pattern. The simplicity of the original designs was the key to the longevity of all the Red Cross patterns.

Despite the new V-neck, ARC 400-3c was still knit all in one piece and sewn together at the sides, a design feature that made it simple to make and finish. The new design also included a garter stitch border, the addition of two knit stitches on every row that made a firm border that made sewing the garment's sides easier. The updated pattern had ribbing along the hem, with a stockinette—a knit stitch that creates a smooth fabric—for the body of the garment. With the exception of the slightly more complicated neckline, the pattern itself was as easy to make as its square necked counterpart. In 1944, a slightly revised pattern was released for members of the Women's Army Corps (ARC 400-13). It was almost identical to the men's version but was adapted for a woman's frame.

While the Army's garment needs changed over the five years of the war, the Navy had a relatively stable list that included five garments knit in navy blue yarn, turtle neck sweaters, watch caps, helmets, gloves, and scarves. Initially, volunteers were asked to knit a slightly revised version of the heavy-weight sleeveless sweater released in 1918 as ARC 400B, a navy-blue counterpart to the olive drab V-neck sweater issued to the Army, Air Force and Marines. However, Navy regulations stated that sailors were allowed to wear hand knit garments on duty as part of the uniform, only if the garments conformed to their own specifications.[45] Consequently, ARC 400-3 was quickly dropped for active duty sailors and was relegated to use for hospital garments throughout the war.

ARC 400-3C
Rev. Aug. 1942
Code AF-57

MAN'S "V" NECK SWEATER
SLEEVELESS
U. S. Army, Air Corps, and Marine Corps

Equipment Needed:

Yarn: 10-12 ozs. 4/8 sweater yarn, olive drab.

Needles: 2 single-pointed needles to fit the Red Cross needle gauge for heavy sweaters. Gauges available from your area office. Needles slightly smaller may be used for the ribbing.

Scale:

5 stitches to the inch, 6 rows to the inch. Make a sample to find out how many stitches are required for you to knit an inch. If your scale is not that given here, try a smaller or larger needle until you obtain this scale. If you have to use a different sized needle from that called for above, it will not in any way alter the garment provided you knit 5 stitches to the inch and 6 rows to the inch.

Measurements:

Small: Chest 32-34. Length shoulder to bottom—23½ inches.
Medium: Chest 35-37. " " " " 24½ "
Large: Chest 38-40. " " " " 25½ "

This garment is worked up the back and down the front with no shoulder shaping.

INSTRUCTIONS FOR MAKING

Body Back:	Small	Medium	Large
Cast on	80	88	96 stitches
Work in ribbing of knit 2, purl 2 for	4	4	4 inches
Work in stockinette stitch (knit and purl alternate rows) for	10	11	12 inches

with the exception of the first and last 2 stitches which should be knit (garter stitch) to make a neat underarm seam. End with a knit row.

To Shape Armholes:

Bind off 3 stitches at the beginning of next two rows.
Next:

    1st row: K 5, P to last 5 stitches, K 5.
    2nd row: Knit entire row.
    3rd row: Same as 1st row.
    4th row: K 5, K 2 together, K to last 7 stitches, K 2 together, K 5.

	Small	Medium	Large
Repeat these 4 rows twice. There should now be on needle.	68	76	84 stitches
Keeping garter stitch border at armhole edges (by knitting first and last 5 stitches in each row), work in stockinette stitch until armhole measures	8	8	8 inches

from first shaping: End with a knit row.
Next:

	Small	Medium	Large
A. Knit 5, purl	12	15	18 stitches
Knit	34	36	38 stitches
Purl	12	15	18 stitches
Knit 5.			

B. Knit entire row.
Repeat A and B for 1 inch, ending with A row.

	Small	Medium	Large
Knit	22	25	28 stitches
and put on stitch holder. Bind off	24	26	28 stitches
for back of neck. Knit.	22	25	28 stitches

Next row, knit 5, purl to last 5 stitches, knit 5.

Figure 3.4 Man's V-neck sweater, sleeveless, ARC 400-3c. Revision August 1942.

The last twenty years: 1945–65

Production continued to release pattern revisions throughout the war, but these revisions were typically only changes to the typeface or layout, not revisions to the patterns themselves. The last revision of ARC 400-3 was issued in 1942 as a

ARC 400-3C
Rev. April 1944
Feb. 1959 Printing
Stock number 061641
(Olive drab)

MAN'S "V" NECK SWEATER (SLEEVELESS)
(U.S. Army, Air Corps, and Marine Corps)

Equipment Needed
Yarn--10-12 ozs. 4/8 sweater yarn, olive drab.
Needles--2 single-pointed needles to fit Red Cross needle gauge for heavy sweaters. Gauges available from your area office. Needles slightly smaller may be used for the ribbing.

Scale
5 stitches to the inch, 6 rows to the inch. Make a sample to find out how many stitches are required for you to knit an inch. If your scale is not that given here, try a smaller or larger needle until you obtain this scale. If you have to use a different sized needle from that called for above, it will not in any way alter the garment, provided you knit 5 stitches to the inch and 6 rows to the inch.

Measurements
Small --Chest 32-34.   Length, shoulder to bottom--23½ inches
Medium--Chest 35-37.   "   "   "   "   24½   "
Large --Chest 38-40.   "   "   "   "   25½   "
This garment is worked up the back and down the front with no shoulder shaping.

Instructions for Making

Body Back	Small	Medium	Large
Cast on	80	88	96 stitches
Work in ribbing of knit 2, purl 2 for.	4	4	4 inches
Work in stockinette stitch (knit and purl alternate rows) for	10	11	12 inches
with the exception of the first and last 2 stitches which should be knit (garter stitch) to make a neat underarm seam. End with a knit row.			
Back should now measure	14	15	16 inches

To Shape Armholes
Bind off 3 stitches at the beginning of next 2 rows.
Proceed as follows:
  1st row: K 5, P to last 5 stitches, K 5.
  2nd row: Knit entire row.
  3rd row: Same as 1st row.
  4th row: K 5, K 2 together, K to last 7 stitches,
            K 2 together, K 5.
Repeat these 4 rows twice more (12 rows in all), which means decrease on every other knit row 3 times.

	Small	Medium	Large
There should now be on needle	68	76	84 stitches
Keeping garter stitch border at armhole edges (by knitting first and last 5 stitches in each row), work in stockinette stitch until armhole measures	8	8	8 inches
from first shaping. End with a knit row.			
Next:			
A. Knit 5, purl	12	15	18 stitches
Knit	34	36	38 stitches
Purl	12	15	18 stitches
Knit 5.			
B. Knit entire row.			
Repeat A and B for 1", end with A row. Knit and put on stitch holder. Bind off	24	26	28 stitches
for back of neck. Knit	22	25	28 stitches
Next row knit 5, purl to last 5 stitches, knit 5.			

Figure 3.5 Man's V-neck sweater (sleeveless), ARC 400-3c. February 1949 printing.

garment for Navy hospitals, and was last reprinted in September 1964. Although almost fifty years had passed since its first release, the garment itself was remarkably unchanged. Two additional sizes had been added in 1942, but otherwise men who received this garment from the Red Cross in 1964 received the same garment as their fathers or grandfathers.

Sometime between 1944 and 1959, the Red Cross updated the print style for knitting patterns for the fifth and final time. These patterns (Figure 3.5) were a larger format with an updated typeface, but included the same information as those patterns issued during the previous print style. They reflect the place of the Red Cross's continued production program. After the end of the Second World War, production activities transitioned away from supplying active military personnel on a wide-scale and refocused on comforts for federal hospitals and civilian relief at home and abroad.[46]

Conclusion

The knitting program for able-bodied men continued on a very limited basis after the end of the Second World War. Volunteers continued to knit garments on a limited basis for emergency use in federal hospitals and military institutions, but the need for garments was largely superseded by military-issue protective clothing. Production in local chapters continued to meet emergency military needs as needed until 1965 when the Volunteer Services themselves were merged under one unified service and active production for the military seems to have stopped completely. Instructions about knitting do not even appear in the last Production brochure printed before the services were unified in 1965, a shift that likely reflected both knitting's decline in popularity and shift in focus for the Red Cross's relief efforts.

Over the nearly fifty years the Red Cross ran a Production program, volunteers produced millions of knitted sweaters and other comforts for active and wounded military personnel, veterans, and civilians. The patterns designed at National Headquarters provided clear and simple guidelines for volunteers to make easy to wear, comfortable clothing to protect servicemen from the elements and remind them that someone back home was thinking about them. The garments made from the patterns themselves changed very little, but the changing physicality of the patterns themselves is a reminder that clothing patterns have as much to reveal as the clothing made from them.

Making and Mending for Victory: Pattern Creation, Distribution, Use, and the Goal of Conservation for Home Sewers During the Second World War

Jennifer Grayer Moore

This chapter explores the ways in which civilians in both the United States and Great Britain accessed ideas and directions for accomplishing the related tasks of recycling and remodeling apparel and accessories, and points to the many challenges home sewers would have faced in their efforts to create and work with patterns, pamphlets, and instructional manuals. Many of the options for acquiring or creating a pattern that were discussed in "A Brief History of Patternmaking," including commercially-prepared paper patterns, block pattern drafting, transforming thumbnails and written directions into patterns, and drafting systems, are explored in this chapter and considered in light of the sewing culture of the middle of the twentieth century. This chapter also complements Rebecca Keyel's chapter pertaining to war-era knitting instructions while focusing exclusively on patterns that were used to work with woven textiles. Special attention is given to the challenges that the many methodologies presented within a socio-cultural context wherein sewing was a necessity and prior knowledge and development of the skills required to create apparel were highly varied. Finally, this chapter considers differences in resources and approaches in the United States and the United Kingdom and thereby explores themes that are considered in detail in section three of this volume.

The intertwined goals of conserving, recycling and "making do" with what one had were important, nearly omnipresent aspects of daily life in nations that militarized for the Second World War (1939–45). Governments in countries on both sides of the conflict including Great Britain, the United States, France, Italy,

Germany, and Australia sought to address the issue of consumption of valuable goods through official mandates such as the implementation of rationing books (that limited the purchasing of certain kinds of valuable products by civilians) or through official regulations governing mass production, including the L-85 regulations that directed American manufacturers of apparel to curtail the use of various kinds of textiles. Despite such efforts at conservation, shortages of crucial products were widespread and these shortfalls were shouldered first by civilian populations who were reminded regularly that it was their patriotic and civil duties to fuel, feed, and clothe combatants ahead of themselves. Recycling everything from animal fat and scraps of metal to fragments of fabric and yarn unraveled from old apparel; reworking curtains into coveralls and sheets into underclothes; and making-over household items and pieces of apparel were necessary tactics for survival and the quest for victory given the shortcomings of other conservation methods and the militaries' enormous demands for raw materials as well as finished products.

This chapter explores the ways in which civilians in both the United States and Great Britain accessed ideas and directions for accomplishing the related tasks of recycling and remodeling apparel and accessories. Specifically, focus is given to how sewing patterns were communicated, made, or acquired. The design features, the marketing and availability, and the use of commercial patterns (along with the challenges they presented for home-sewers) will be explored first. Next, the communication of pattern ideas through written text and diagrams that could be scaled-up will be considered in light of the benefits and challenges this approach presented. Finally, the teaching of pattern drafting techniques in classes, through pamphlets and books, with the use of specific tools, and in guidebooks for home sewers will be considered as a means for navigating a context of shortages, austerity, and deprivation. Exploring practices in both the United States and Great Britain provides the opportunity to understand how similar some approaches were across distance, cultures, and circumstances, but also demonstrates how coping strategies varied depending upon the direness of shortages and proximity to armed conflict.

Making, mending, and the culture of sewing

The many efforts that were made by civilian men and women to conserve, renovate, and generally make-do with less have been celebrated by later generations as patriotic acts and marvels of war time ingenuity. Certainly, all credits and accolades are due to those who labored at their small tasks to aid the war effort; however, it is important to note that the make-do mentality was not entirely new. Garment renovation, repurposing of cast-off textiles, mending, and darning were all established aspects of dress culture that existed to varying degrees across socio-economic demographics both in the United Kingdom and in the United States. It is also important to note these concepts were even embraced by *fashion* publications from the nineteenth century onwards; an important point to reckon with given the attitudes towards disposability that are inherent in mass fashion in the twenty-first century.

The contexts in which the make-do-and-mend attitude flourished are traceable. In America, "making over garments [had been] a time-honored tradition since pioneer days."[1] Instructions on topics such as "Making and Mending Men's Clothing" had been printed in publications like *New England Farmer* since the 1860s and became part of the curriculum of sewing classes during the Great Depression.[2] The privations of the Great Depression had definitively necessitated skillful salvaging of all manner of materials including saleable scraps (especially of metal) and preservation of oddments to facilitate the renovation of all kinds of items including equipment, furniture, and apparel. Patching, mending, darning, and myriad techniques to extend the life of a garment (and thereby save money) were standards of housekeeping. Similarly, in Great Britain, a culture of renovating and recycling was also in place prior to the

Figure 4.1 *Le Petit Echo de la Mode*. Directions for turning the usable parts of a smock dress into an apron. August 15, 1926 (p. 5).

Second World War, at least in some social milieus. Curators of the Warwickshire Museum in England gathered oral histories of women who had lived through the Second World War and derived, "most women can remember patching, darning, renovating and repairing, and fashioning new garments out of the most unlikely fabric and materials.... This concept was hardly a novelty for many women; those struggling to raise families on low incomes had been making do and mending for years."[3] It is notable that facility with needle and thread seem to have been closely tied to economic station and historical context. While the culture of making and mending clothes was present, it was not omnipresent.

Although there is evidence that a culture of sewing was thriving in both the United Kingdom and the United States prior to the Second World War, there is ample evidence of educational outreach to augment the existing skill sets of each populace and to provide necessary instruction to individuals lacking in foundational skills once the war was underway. This reality speaks to the point that the requisite skill set was neither held by all who needed it, nor honed to the level of sophistication that war-time demands required. In the United States, department stores including Macy's sponsored sewing classes, while Bloomingdales sponsored a radio broadcast that was accompanied by a McCall's booklet.[4] As early as 1942, classes that taught women how to remodel old clothes were taught in locations including the Pratt Institute in New York City and various locations of the Y.W.C.A.[5] "Salvage sewing rooms" were set up throughout the United States. Dedicated to "salvaging and reconstructing discarded clothing," these sewing rooms taught both sewing and patternmaking skills and made clothing both for personal use and for the project of sending bundles of garments to Britons and (after the bombing of Pearl Harbor in 1941) to American servicemen and their families.[6] Companies that had a vested interest in encouraging home sewing, including Singer, the sewing machine company, made education a pivotal part of their marketing mix. Outreach as advertising included publication of the *Singer Make-Over Guide*, a small paperback that promoted techniques for combining and reworking old clothes while also showcasing products like the Singer Skirt Marker, Singer Iron with Cord Control, and Singer Sewing Center classes. Non-commercial entities, including American welfare agencies also taught sewing and garment renovation to populations who lacked sewing and patternmaking skills.[7]

In the United Kingdom, needlework, including garment making, mending, and renovating, had been a part of the curricula in publicly funded schools since the nineteenth century, however, during the Second World War, thousands of sewing classes for adults were run through the Board of Trade,[8] a fact that may be construed as a need for refresher courses, development of skills, or the expansion of home sewing into echelons of society that had previously been less reliant on home sewing because of factors such as class, economic status, and education. During the War, the need to repair, repurpose, and renovate made sewing and patternmaking true necessities across socio-economic groups. Commercial connections to this reinvigorated culture of sewing were also evident. Oral histories as well as textual evidence show that producers of products for home apparel manufacture also promoted make-and-mend culture along with "coupon-free" craftsmanship (a reference to being able to make something without using rationing coupons), and women who lived through this era have recalled sensing that this was an effort on the part of companies to ensure "that their brand name remained in the public eye."[9]

Although mending and repurposing were heralded as important personal contributions to the war effort on both sides of the Atlantic Ocean, there is evidence that suggests these austerity measures were perceived differently in the United States and in Great Britain. A *New York Times* article written roughly two years into the war noted of the British citizenry, "The people here are worried because they see for themselves that after making all the sacrifices their leaders called for, the best they could do was not quite good enough." The reporter went on to note that Churchill's government needed to do more to "help people train themselves for the even harder tasks ahead."[10] In America, the revival of home sewing was heralded as a patriotic act[11] as well as an important boon for the economy.[12] Apparel made from salvaged textiles was celebrated in high style in competitive fashion shows (that attracted tens of thousands of entrants), which were held at swanky landmark hotels like the Astor, the Pierre, and the Waldorf Astoria.[13] Similarly, banks and businesses of all kinds made displays of war-era efforts to repurpose, fix, and refashion, indicating that amidst austerity a celebration of ingenuity and resourcefulness was also underway.[14]

The availability of materials was substantially different in the United States and Great Britain—a factor that may have impacted attitudes toward the apparel renovation process. Materials in Great Britain were notably harder to come by than they were in America. Blackout material, draughtsman's plans (which were printed on cambric), food and flour bags, muslin for butter making, discarded or irregular parachutes made of both silk and nylon, and retired service uniforms were all found to produce serviceable textiles for the making of apparel and home furnishings given the paucity of new materials that was available at retail textile counters.[15] In some instances, the acquisition and use of atypical materials was the subject of comment in educational texts. For example, the British manual

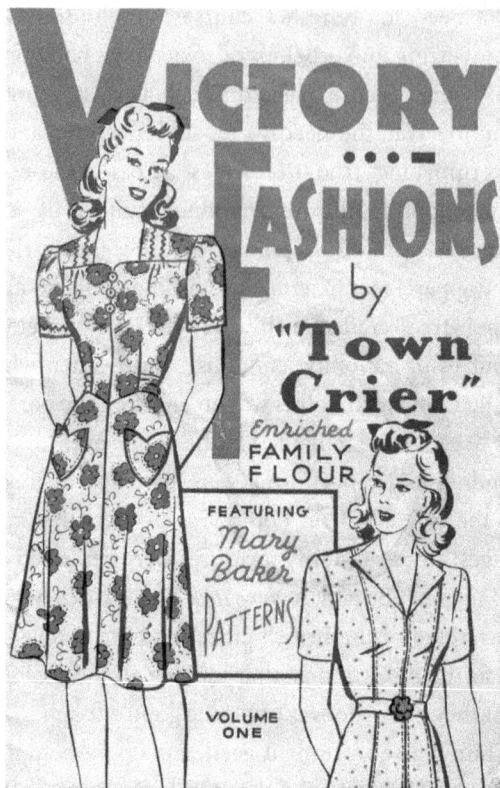

Figure 4.2 Cover of Town Crier Flour pamphlet promoting the use of flour sacks and Mary Baker patterns for the creation of women's and children's apparel. Undated.

Sew and Save encouraged women to purchase textiles from the "linens counter" or to acquire furnishing fabrics, which were deemed to be both cheaper and more durable, but most importantly more readily available.[16] Although textiles were more plentiful in the United States than they were in Great Britain, there is clear evidence that American home sewers were dedicated to the careful management of resources. This fact is demonstrated in part by a precipitous drop in donations to charities like the Salvation Army. Early in the war, American women devoted substantial efforts to bundling clothes and sending them abroad to clothe European civilians and refugees, however the shortages that were experienced in second-hand stores can also be attributed to the impulse to hoard textiles for future use—especially valuable, insulating woolen textiles.[17] Utilizing cambric food sacks (especially flour and sugar) was a concept promoted both in Great Britain and in the United States It was estimated in one American source that, "If all cotton fabric used in bagging were to be re-used in home sewing, the

1,000,000,000 yards so consumed would be sufficient to provide five dresses for every woman and girl in the United States."[18]

Paper patterns: design, availability, and challenges of use

Acquiring new yardage or salvaging fabric from an existing garment was just the first step in the quest to augment meager and worn-out wardrobes. In most cases, apparel and accessory manufacture or repair by home sewers would have required a pattern. Commercially-prepared paper patterns represented one of a range of possibilities for directing a home sewing project. Commercial patterns of the 1940s came with an illustration of the finished garment, a written description of its design features, a diagram for laying out the pattern on the fabric (the marker), clear markings of notches, seam allowance, and grain lines, notes on the pattern to guide alterations, as well as written directions. Although commercial patternmakers in the period made substantial efforts to make their products user-friendly, it is fair to assert that a novice seamstress would have faced challenges while attempting to use a commercial paper pattern. Specialized terminology such as revers, interfacings, darts, and bias were not defined within patterns. In some instances, a term would be used but would not be quantified in any way: for example, "gathering fabric" or "easing" a sleeve into an armhole. The seamstress was left to make a judgment and hope for a reasonable fit. Despite the many modern conveniences of commercially-prepared patterns, and because of the challenges of reading, translating text into action, measuring, and modifying, classes that were specifically designed to assist sewers with the use of these tools proliferated in both Great Britain and the United States. Notably, classes were sometimes sponsored by paper pattern and sewing equipment manufacturers and retailers. Supporting the requisite skills of cutting, basting, pressing, and fitting benefitted the novice seamstress in her efforts and her consequent success (hopefully) helped to ensure future purchases of commercial patterns.[19]

Many sources promoted the purchase of paper patterns. The British publication *Vogue's Book of Smart Dressmaking*, the cover of which proclaimed the text to be "the professional method that saves you coupons," promoted the use of commercially-prepared paper patterns. The introductory comments proclaimed, "Remodeling, renovating, making do with what you have is a vital part of war-time dressing. . . . There are many Vogue Patterns in our range which will help make these problems easier."[20] Commercially-prepared patterns designed to transform old clothes such as men's shirts and suits into women's and children's apparel were prepared in the United Kingdom and were generally designed to aid fabric conservation. The back of a war-era British Vogue Pattern envelope (5035) noted, "Every Vogue Pattern is carefully planned to comply with the spirit of the regulations for saving materials. As a result all are economical in the use of fabrics. In many cases you actually *save* coupons by buying Vogue

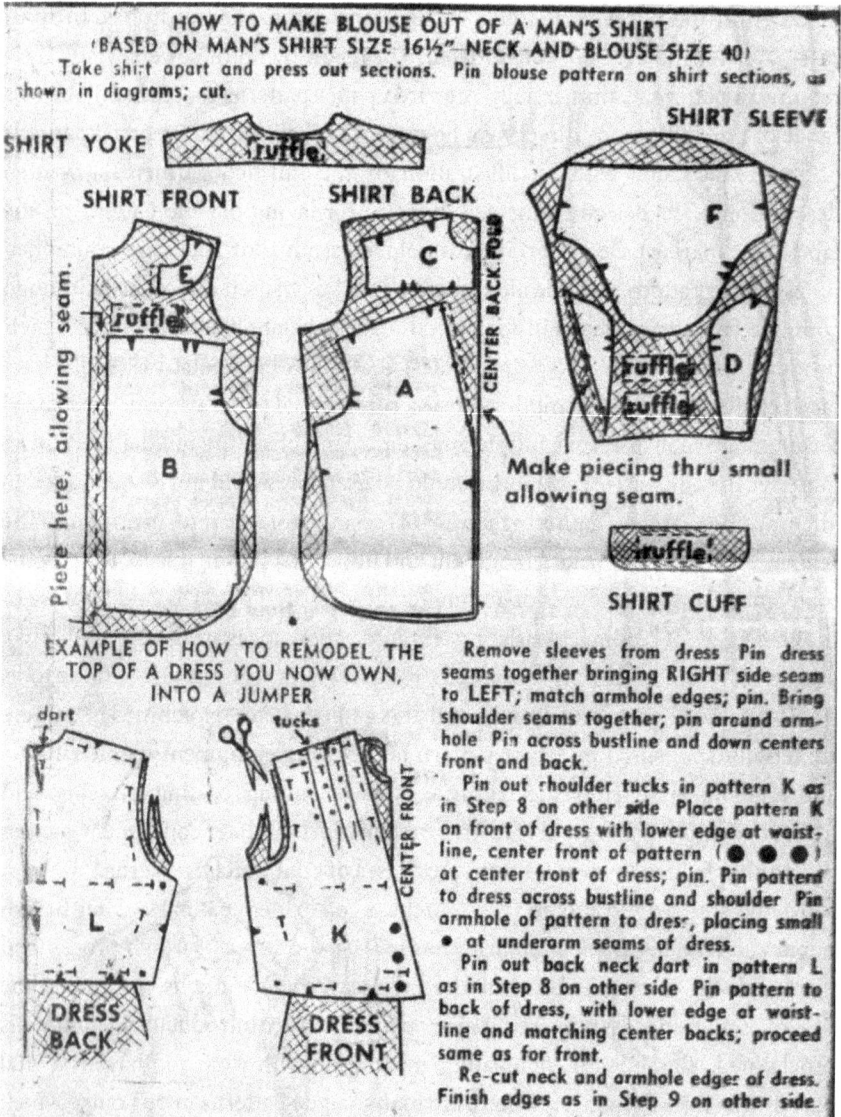

HOW TO MAKE BLOUSE OUT OF A MAN'S SHIRT
(BASED ON MAN'S SHIRT SIZE 16½" NECK AND BLOUSE SIZE 40)
Take shirt apart and press out sections. Pin blouse pattern on shirt sections, as shown in diagrams; cut.

SHIRT YOKE — ruffle.
SHIRT SLEEVE
SHIRT FRONT — SHIRT BACK
Piece here, allowing seam.
Make piecing thru small allowing seam.
ruffle.
SHIRT CUFF

EXAMPLE OF HOW TO REMODEL THE TOP OF A DRESS YOU NOW OWN, INTO A JUMPER
dart   tucks
DRESS BACK   DRESS FRONT

Remove sleeves from dress Pin dress seams together bringing RIGHT side seam to LEFT; match armhole edges; pin. Bring shoulder seams together; pin around armhole Pin across bustline and down centers front and back.

Pin out shoulder tucks in pattern K as in Step 8 on other side Place pattern K on front of dress with lower edge at waistline, center front of pattern (● ● ●) at center front of dress; pin. Pin pattern to dress across bustline and shoulder Pin armhole of pattern to dress, placing small ● at underarm seams of dress.

Pin out back neck dart in pattern L as in Step 8 on other side Pin pattern to back of dress, with lower edge at waistline and matching center backs; proceed same as for front.

Re-cut neck and armhole edges of dress. Finish edges as in Step 9 on other side

Figure 4.3 Marker showing how to lay out Simplicity pattern no. 4737 on the fabric from a deconstructed man's shirt.

Patterns." British war-era sewing guides including *Sew and Save, The Pictorial Guide to Modern Home Needlecraft,* and *The Pictorial Guide to Modern Home Dressmaking* all made suggestions pertaining to selecting, altering, and using commercially-prepared patterns. Advertising of the period makes it clear that paper patterns were available for purchase in Great Britain, however the emphasis on drafting patterns oneself is more pronounced in British publications than those made in America. Notably, the British Board of Trade pamphlet *Make Do and Mend* did not promote the purchase of specific patterns, although it was noted that "many good renovation patterns [exist] on the market."[21] However, the availability of such patterns across geographic regions and over time was undoubtedly uneven. Joanna Chase, author of the *Daily Mail* "Woman's Page" cautioned readers, "owing to the paper shortages, it will become increasingly difficult as the war goes on to obtain paper patterns."[22]

The promotion of commercially-prepared patterns was prevalent in the United States. The 1942 booklet *Make and Mend—For Victory,* which was produced by the Spool Cotton Company, offered advice for renovating men's clothes, presented layouts and illustrations to show how old garments could be repurposed, and promoted specific patterns (by number) from Advance, Vogue, Butterick, Hollywood, and McCall's. In fact the guide advised that all "major alterations" should be done using a commercial pattern.[23] Similar booklets like *A Bag of Tricks for Home Sewing* (1945) from the National Cotton Council and *Victory Fashions by Town Crier* (n.d.), a pamphlet sponsored by a flour brand, promoted ideas for renovating clothes while also promoting the purchase of specific patterns, which could be ordered from the back of each booklet. In the case of Town Crier, it was also suggested that the fabric used in the construction of garments be acquired from Town Crier flour sacks.

Commercial patterns for mass-production by the American trade were subject to fabric restrictions before commercial patterns for home sewers, a fact that may have contributed to home sewing with commercial patterns early in the War. In April 1942, the War Production Board (WPB) issued orders that directed patterns for commercial manufacturing to be cut in order to save cloth and predicted that 100,000,000 yards of cotton, rayon, wool, and "mixture cloths" would be conserved as a result.[24] This regulation impacted the appearance of mass-produced clothes. Austere, trim, and utilitarian are appropriate descriptors of much of the apparel cut under WPB orders. The arguably lackluster aesthetics of the garments in the shops undoubtedly encouraged some women to seek apparel elsewhere. A 1942 article in the *New York Times* noted, "A recent survey of leading pattern concerns" has revealed an "unprecedented" increase in sales, occasioned, it is felt, by the

WPB regulation L-85, which limits yardage and lengths in women's clothes.[25] Although patterns for home sewing were not initially subject to fabric limitations, pattern companies offered patterns that directed sewers to refurbish old cloth and clothes. Ultimately, patterns for home dressmakers were put to the same

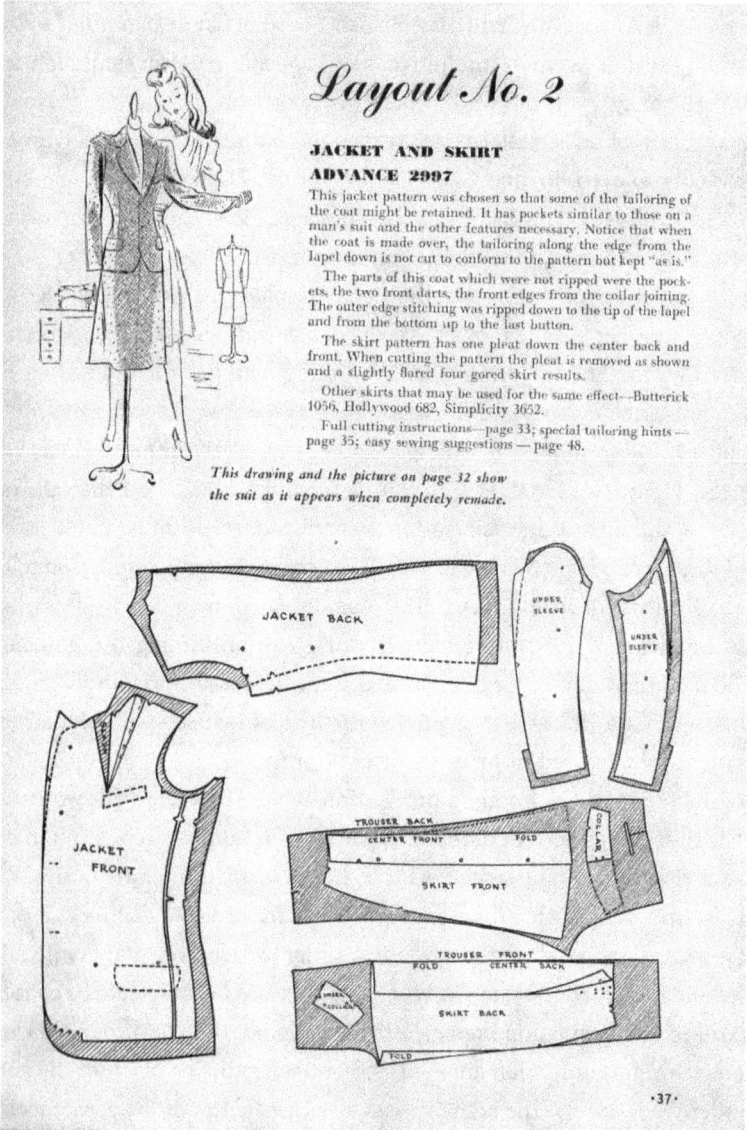

Figure 4.4 Diagram from the 1942 American pamphlet *Make and Mend* showing how to arrange pattern pieces from an Advance pattern (no. 2997) on a deconstructed man's suit.

standards as the trade about a year later; patterns cut after May 27, 1943 were required to align with all fabric saving measures.[26] Despite such restrictions there is ample evidence that pattern sales remained robust as the cost of apparel rose overall; a factor that continued to stimulate home sewing and the purchase of commercial patterns after the war.[27] American pattern companies also addressed fabric shortages by preparing patterns that encouraged home sewers to salvage materials from existing garments and to make apparel using old or outmoded apparel, especially menswear.

Although a commercially-prepared pattern has the ability to relieve the home sewer of a great many stressors related to the creation of apparel, it is important to note that commercial patterns were not without drawbacks and the potential for error was especially pronounced when using a pattern to repurpose an old garment. There is written evidence to suggest that the repurposing of apparel and other textiles presented problems for home sewers which pattern instructions did not adequately address. For example, the Bureau of Home Economics of the Department of Agriculture published a leaflet in 1942 that addressed some of the issues inherent in remaking a suit and cautioned that the sewer "needed to be resourceful" and that she should "think of ways of adapting a style to what you have." With regards to placing the pattern on the deconstructed suit, sewers were cautioned, "This takes great care, for there are no salvages [sic] to guide you in finding the straight of the goods."[28] Undoubtedly, a great many home sewers struggled to successfully apply a commercial pattern to used textiles that were unevenly worn and stretched.

Communication of pattern concepts in pictures, through diagrams, and in text

During the Second World War, patterns were also created by requiring the home sewer to render pictures into patterns, scaling-up thumbnail diagrams, and by translating written directions into pattern pieces. For example, the British Board of Trade publication *Make Do and Mend* included many general written directions for renovating apparel. In many cases, the adequate conversion of the written directions into a usable pattern would have required fairly sophisticated patternmaking and sewing skills. Among the written directions included in this Board of Trade booklet was the suggestion that one should "make a paper pattern" from the sleeves or neckline of a garment that one particularly liked.[29] The assumption that the reader would understand crucial issues like seam allowance and notches was taken as a given. This assumption of prior knowledge was echoed in a brief description for renovating a blouse that had become ill-fitting: "Open the front of the blouse which has become too tight and put in a contrasting button band, complete with collar."[30] A tiny diagram illustrated the finished product in this case, however the booklet provided no information about designing, cutting, or affixing the front placket nor directions for creating and binding buttonholes. British *Make and Mend* leaflets and directions published in newspapers and other serials routinely instructed home sewers to cut panels "to the right size" and to use existing garments to make a pattern. American publications also made suggestions for renovating a garment without any pattern whatsoever. For example, the *Singer Make-Over Guide*, provided written directions for making a man's suit into one for a woman. A brief excerpt demonstrates the kind of skill that would have been required to tackle the project: "The shoulders may be narrowed with a center dart tapered to the bustline in front and extending to about 3" in the back. Narrow the neckline at the center seams of the coat and collar."[31] A photograph of a charming model in the finished product and a line drawing of a woman fitting the man's jacket to her Singer Dress Form were the only snippets of guidance provided beyond the few brief paragraphs of text. Notably the written directions stipulated that the use of the dress form was an essential tool to facilitate this garment renovation. In both the United States and the United Kingdom an additional technique for communicating a pattern idea was to present a thumbnail diagram of a pattern piece (sometimes on a grid, but often not) along with a key to the scale. The home sewer was then left with the task of carefully replicating the contours of the diagram while scaling up and sizing the pattern pieces. Patterns of this kind typically did not include features such as notches or seam allowance, nor did they typically specify yardage requirements or textile type. Finally, textual advice pertaining to the creation of apparel, accessories, and home décor concepts also took the form of describing an idea and then asserting that no pattern was needed. For example, the American pamphlet "A Bag of Tricks for Home Sewing" asserted that some projects (like dickies, cuffs, and collars) were "so simple that no pattern is needed."[32]

In all of the scenarios described in this subsection of the chapter it is worth considering the many challenges that a home sewer would have faced as she tried to create a pattern (or in the last example to cut freehand). Creating accurate and aesthetically pleasing contours, judging proportions of pieces and their relationship to the body, and figuring ways to accurately align various pattern pieces to one another would have surely figured in the challenging quest to complete projects that were helpfully and happily suggested in war-era texts. The smiling models posing with their perfectly coiffed hair and their meticulously sewn apparel must have encouraged many home sewers to undertake such projects and may have irked (may have even seemed to mock) many a craftswoman as she struggled to correct bungled proportions, puckered seams, and misaligned pattern pieces that undoubtedly were produced by novice seamstresses.

Pattern drafting: texts, tools, and classes

Information about drafting patterns for tailored apparel appeared in a wide variety of sources that were directed to home sewers during the Second World War. Direct measure patternmaking techniques were commonly presented in sewing texts designed to help women through wartime austerity in both the United Kingdom and the United States, however the specificity of these instructions varied significantly. For example, the directions in the British publication *Sew and Save,* a general text devoted to wardrobe planning, caring for clothes, and shopping, as well as matters pertaining to garment construction, instructed the seamstress to begin by taking careful measurements of essential points including waist, bust, arm length, hips, armpit-to-armpit, throat to waist, nape of neck to waist, armpit to waist, and the back of the shoulders. Upon the completion of these careful measurements, the reader was presented with six short paragraphs of directions to guide the reader to translate these measurements into a sloper or block. Notably, some directions were rather vague. For example, one direction indicated that the shape of the armhole should be determined by cutting "in a very slightly sloped curve."[33] Directions for drafting a sleeve pattern from scratch were provided in four short paragraphs and included no diagrams of any kind.[34] Chase's text suggested that as long as the reader had carefully "taped" her measurements, it would "not [be] difficult to make your own paper patterns."[35] This optimistic comment belies the challenges of following written directions that were provided without any visual point of reference and assumes that the block alone would be sufficient to make period-correct apparel.

The Pictorial Guide to Modern Home Dressmaking and *The Pictorial Guide to Modern Home Needlecraft,* both Second World War-era British books, were entirely devoted to the subjects of patternmaking, sewing, renovating, and repairing both apparel and household furnishings. This text included comprehensive directions for the fundamentals of sewing, making alterations, and both altering commercial patterns and creating patterns from scratch. Herein the directions for drafting pattern blocks was again based largely on direct measure but the text provided detailed directions, diagrams on grids, and step-by-step instructions for plotting points on the block. In addition, the text provided instructions and diagrams for slashing and spreading patterns as a way to lengthen or widen a pattern cut too small, as a means to modify a commercial pattern for a straight skirt or narrow sleeve to a fuller style, and as a way to manipulate the basic block pattern. The text also included directions for taking a pattern from existing garments by either unpicking the entire piece of apparel and tracing each piece or by pinning calico fabric to the in-tact garment and tracing around each part. The text assumed little in the form of prior knowledge or skill and was designed to help a novice navigate the craft of bespoke garment creation.

An American text, *The Complete Book of Sewing* (1943), by Constance Talbot similarly provided comprehensive information for the aspiring home sewer making clothes during the Second World War. The *New York Times* book review for Talbot's sewing guide noted, "The limitations on wearing apparel, recently imposed by the War Production Board under the revised schedule of L-85, have simplified clothes to such a degree that a woman need no longer be half a genius to turn out a good-looking dress, coat, or suit. The vital need for conserving material has done away with excessive style and now it is the fashion to wear simple, basic clothes."[36] Talbot's guide for an American audience included ample information on sustaining existing apparel through careful laundering, mending, patching, and darning. In addition, the text provided extensive information on remodeling old clothes and repairing worn garments by creating pattern pieces from portions of existing apparel. This aspect of her tutorial is the primary place in which she guides her reader to create a pattern piece. It is notable that Talbot did not include pattern drafting of a block as an aspect of her instruction. Rather, she devoted substantial attention to the modification of commercial patterns and the vast majority of her course of instruction presumes the use of a commercially-prepared paper pattern. This is a notable difference that exists in multiple points of comparison between circumstances in the United Kingdom and the United States and suggests that British women had less access to vital resources such as paper and new yardage during the Second World War.

In addition to texts that advised women in the craft of pattern creation, a wide variety of classes devoted to apparel creation were run by both public and private organizations in both Europe and America. For example, in the United States

COATS WORN SHABBY UNDER ARMS

When parcel carrying has caused threadbare patches to appear in the front of a coat, the insertion of side-front panels made from fresh material is the only effective remedy. Such panels are best given a little extra shaping at the waist, as in the model sketched on this page. A slightly used material—that is, another old garment cut up—often blends better than a brand new fabric in this type of renovation.

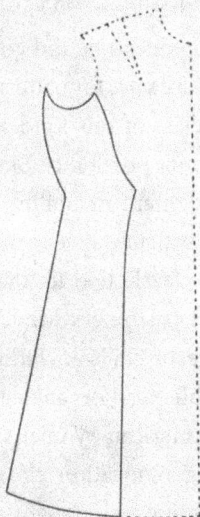

Contrasting fabric panel insertions for the coat renovation shown on the right must be designed wide enough to cover the worn parts on the original coat front. They should be drafted on a coat pattern which is itself based on the bodice and skirt blocks (see page 131). Care should be taken that one panel is cut for the left-hand side of the coat, and one for the right.

To insert the panels it is necessary to unpick the side seams of the coat and to take the lower part of the sleeves out of the armholes. Each panel should then be laid over its coat front and tacked satisfactorily in position, with edges turned in, before the old material beneath is cut away. Saddle-stitching, i.e. long running threads in embroidery silk or wool—makes a very attractive finish to the garment after the panels have been closely stitched or machined into position.

185

Figure 4.5 Diagram from the British publication *The Pictorial Guide to Modern Home Needlecraft* (p. 185) instructing the home sewer to pattern a new panel for a worn portion of a coat.

limitation orders impacted the manufacture of sewing machines and parts, making both scarce commodities for the general public. To alleviate demand, Singer offered rental machines, "giving priority to women who enrolled in Singer sewing classes."[37] These classes, which were largely devoted to clothing renovation, likely included instruction in pattern drafting of some kind. Sewing classes offered for free or at nominal prices were also held by department stores. In early 1943, 40,000 stores in the United States participated in "Sew and Save Week," an effort to teach women how to "remodel an out-of-date frock or refurbish old slip covers" and convert men's suits "hanging useless in the closet."[38] Ventures such as "Sew and Save Week" undoubtedly contributed to education and conservation efforts, but notably were also events that drove in-store sales for patterns, notions, textiles, and sewing equipment. It is unclear if a class of this kind would have taught pattern drafting skills, however it is a distinct possibility. Similarly, if a home sewer had "any doubts" regarding her "judgment or ability in making things over, personal advice and instruction [was] available at very small cost" at a Singer Sewing Center.[39] This example, which is clearly tied to a commercial interest to sell Singer products, also suggests that customers would have had access to skilled professionals with a wide range of skills including pattern drafting. Organizations to benefit the general public also organized classes to teach garment-making skills. For example, the American Women's Volunteer Services (AWVS) organized sewing and clothing renovation classes (which likely included some rudimentary patternmaking) that were taught specifically to welfare recipients.[40] In the United Kingdom, the Board of Trade increased the number of adult sewing classes being run during the Second World War as a part of Make Do and Mend.[41] While it is again unclear if pattern drafting was taught in those classes, it seems likely given the written suggestions and illustrations related to garment making and renovation published by the Board of Trade.

One additional pattern drafting option that would have been available to some women during the Second World War is the use of a garment drafting system. Pattern drafting systems, which had been commonplace in the latter part of the nineteenth and early twentieth centuries, would undoubtedly have been available in sewing cabinets and second-hand stores during the War. There is also some evidence that new versions were introduced during the Second World War. For example, a *New York Times* article from 1943 detailed a recently introduced "stencil-like" patternmaking tool that seems to have been a sort of adjustable block. The device was marketed with the promise that it could "lend a professional touch to amateur tailoring."[42] It is unclear how widespread the production of new drafting tools was during the Second World War, while it is also not certain how widely adopted specialized drafting tools were. It is also fair to argue that drafting systems are neither foolproof nor simple. While they solve some problems for the patternmaker, learning to use such tools effectively generally has a steep learning curve and requires strong reading comprehension and mathematics skills.

Conclusions

Women during the Second World War were faced with the daunting tasks of extending the life of their existing wardrobes throughout the duration of the War, while augmenting them with homemade apparel to offset the limited access to new ready-to-wear. Both of these approaches to dressing civilian bodies required sewing and pattern use, modification, and/or creation. While these are skill sets that some people in both Great Britain and the United States would have had (to some degree), the demands of the period would have pushed many home sewers to face new technical challenges. Whether using a commercially-prepared pattern, modifying a pattern that had already been drafted, or drafting a design from scratch, women of this period would have faced creative and technical challenges. The complexities of comprehending patterns and patternmaking, the skill required to adequately employ the pattern as a tool for creation, and both the creativity and the determination to see such projects through to completion deserve to be highlighted at the same time that we celebrate making and mending as patriotic acts.

Future research

This chapter has explored specific features of patternmaking and pattern use during the Second World War in both the United States and the United Kingdom, however there is evidence that this phenomenon existed elsewhere. The ways in which other countries and cultures directed their citizenry to make-do and make patterns is an area that deserves to be explored to both augment the historical evidence presented here and provide additional perspectives on the war efforts of other nations involved in the horrific conflict of the Second World War. For example, it is known that there were tremendous privations in Germany resulting from the mass mobilization of the Nazi military. Thus there were efforts in Germany to offset the need for raw materials. A version of make-and-mend known as "*Aus alt mach neu*" (from old make new) and "*Aus zwei mach eins*" (from two make one) were protocols to offset shortages in Germany.⁴³ In *Fashion Under the Occupation*, Dominique Veillon noted that information about garment renovation appeared in publications in France including *Le Petit Echo de la Mode, Marie-Claire, l'Oeuvre*, as well as a variety of daily newspapers.⁴⁴ Veillon also notes a 1942 text written by Hélène Pasquier entitled *Elegánte quand meme. Comment Tailler et Exécuter un Tailleur, un Manteau, une Jupe-culotte, Trasformations"* (*Elegant Against All Odds. How to Cut Out and Make Up a Suit, Coat, Divided-Skirt, Renovations*).⁴⁵ These textual references provide initial evidence of the need to make apparel patterns in Germany and France and suggest that similar initiatives may have existed elsewhere in nations that were mobilized for conflict during the Second World War.

The long-term legacy of making and mending and patterning homemade apparel is also fertile ground for exploration. It is clear that efforts to make-do-and-mend continued to be applied in the post-war years as shortages persisted and as austerity measures proved, in some instances, to be hard to give up. Gloria Mosesson, the author of *New Clothes From Old* (1977) noted in her introductory comments that the book was inspired by the salvage efforts her mother demonstrated from the Depression era onward and many of the projects and tips detailed in her book echoed principles propounded by make-do-and-mend. While Mosseson's book encouraged readers to use commercially-produced dressmaker patterns, a similar text, *Clothes for Children: Making New From Old* (1980) advocated pattern drafting in order to use salvaged material in the most economical manner. The Second World War-era impulses to make clothing as aesthetically appealing as possible also have emerged in very recent texts devoted to apparel transformation including *New From Old: How to Transform and Customize Your Clothes* (2006). Exploring the techniques presented in such texts and other sources, as well as the motivations for doing so has the potential to reveal interesting aspects of late twentieth-century and early twenty-first century ideas about self-sufficiency and conservation of personal wardrobes, an interesting counterpoint to the history of streamlined mass-production of fast fashion apparel.

Part Two

Perspectives on Technical Design and Technological Advancement in Apparel Pattern Drafting

The Tailor's Voice: Pattern Drafting Systems and the State of the Art

Catherine Roy

This chapter explores in keen detail the complexities of pattern drafting systems, a topic that is touched on briefly in both "A Brief History of Patternmaking" and "Making and Mending for Victory." In this chapter, Catherine Roy distils information gleaned from a study of 100 pattern drafting systems and shows how they reveal changes in ideology, technical practice, and the apprentice system in the realm of men's tailoring. As a growth in demand for tailored menswear led to growth of the tailoring industry, changes in means of production were necessitated. However, the importance of accurate pattern drafting that produced a good fit necessitated the communication of the many skills beyond careful measuring that are required to obtain the desired relationship between body and apparel. Roy begins by first walking the reader through the complexities of the tailor's craft from customer assessment, to cutting, to fitting, pressing and finally assembling a suit of clothes. Next, she explores how changes in pattern drafting systems progressed from conversational and suggestive that the user of the drafting system apply a wealth of prior knowledge to make corrections not specified by the system; to systems that included more scientific distillations of knowledge with step-by-step instructions, diagrams, and mathematical calculations to address abnormalities; to a final phase in which pattern drafting systems strove to quantify all aspects of making the draft. Roy is careful to point out that the latter two phases still required the cutter's *judgment* in order for a high level of artisanship to be attained. This is an important point that links with the overarching theme of the challenges of usership that are inherent in utilizing patterns.

Introduction

This chapter looks at nineteenth- and early twentieth-century menswear patternmaking as practiced in the rapidly changing world of custom tailoring. As the period progressed, economic and technological change impacted the trade. The craft relied on hand skills to mold woolens into sophisticated garments but it also required experienced judgment to create garment patterns to fit a wide variety of men. Larger tailor shops served the increased population and the patternmaker or cutter became an important player in the trade. Published pattern drafting systems began to replace apprenticeships as their authors struggled to convey their craft knowledge in a readable form that could be applied independently. I studied over 100 pattern drafting systems published between 1800 and 1920, applying my knowledge and skills as a practicing custom tailor to trace the development of written pattern systems.

The making of menswear in the nineteenth century

The process of having a suit of clothes custom-tailored has changed very little in the past 200 years. After greeting the client, the tailor offers or receives information about the fashion of the day to determine how fashionable an image his client wishes to present. The tailor discusses current men's fashion, perhaps offering some illustrations from a style periodical. Does the customer want a traditional morning coat for business or is he willing to try the new lounge or sack coat? How wide should the lapels be? Should the pockets have flaps? The occasions to which the garment will be worn also require careful consideration. From the tailor's stock, the client chooses an appropriate fabric. His body is assessed using direct measurements such as the chest and seat circumferences and the waist length. The tailor also observes the client's posture. A pattern for the desired garment can now be drafted. The tailor then cuts and assembles the garment pieces, molding them with steam heat and stitches, to conform to, or improve, the contours of the client's body.

   Garment patternmaking is *the* crucial step in tailoring. It combines knowledge of human anatomy, simple geometry, and garment styling with a nuanced understanding of how to create a perfect fit. Whether drafted directly onto cloth (using scant body measurements and a practiced eye), or first onto paper (using a complex system of body measurements, postural assessment, and applied proportions), the pattern largely determines a garment's success. That success is measured in many ways. Ideally the finished suit will be socially acceptable in the situations in which it is worn. It will be a technical masterpiece and will harmonize with the wearer's coloring and enhance his physique. Tailor-made dress, whether a small-town groom's wedding attire or that of a businessman in a major center, was created to bolster their public standing. Businessmen and the elite obeyed a strict etiquette of dress. Within the sober palette of menswear, superior quality was telegraphed by exquisite fit, providing the maximum comfort in these socially correct garments.

Challenges to the trade

During the nineteenth century, in the United States, the tailoring trade developed from an industry dominated by small-shop tailors into an industry that also included large custom tailoring manufactories. Fashionable ready-made frock coats, dress coats, sack coats, overcoats, trousers, vests, and shirts were produced in large centers such as New York City, Philadelphia, Chicago, and Baltimore, but many people saw made-to-order goods as preferable. Custom clothing manufacture was perceived as reliable and "low tech" in the face of innovation. Skilled tailors could fit anyone, regardless of bodily defects. By contrast, ready-to-wear was made for a range of imaginary, standard bodies, but it was increasingly accessible and ever more cheaply available to the growing population, many of whom now had waged employment. General improvements occurred in the business sector, such as rail transportation, warehousing, and gas lighting. These factors, combined with the development of an efficient sewing machine, benefitted the ready-to-wear industry. At the turn of the twentieth century, when a surplus of ready-to-wear garments became a problem for manufacturers, advertising encouraged sales.[1]

Tailors rose to the challenge of the increased competition. In the early nineteenth century, they established large workshops, run by a master or merchant tailor and staffed by journeymen sewing tailors. They produced custom menswear that was ready in a short time, for a fixed price rather than for credit. Historian Michael Zakim identified the role of the cash economy in transforming the trade and noted the "replacement of craft secrets with a burgeoning trade in new production technologies" including pattern drafting systems, the sewing machine, and the sectional system of garment assembly.[2] Of all innovations, the most important was the published pattern drafting system. Defined systems for making patterns replaced the drawing of pattern pieces onto the cloth when a garment was made, and led to the specialization of the patternmaker, or cutter, within the trade. Previously, master tailors had taught the art of patternmaking to favored senior apprentices or simply given them copies of their standard, or "block" patterns.

Published pattern drafting systems proliferated during the nineteenth century. As the century progressed, various patternmaking methods were set down in print, in increasingly detailed, precise, arithmetical form. The availability of drafting systems affected the trade at all levels because the reputations of all tailor shops were determined by the skill of their cutters. A large shop was able to hire a cutter who took the clients' measurements, made their patterns, and supervised the many sewing tailors he kept busy. The cutter in smaller shops was often the owner.

Eye, mind, hand—the work of the tailor

The tailor uses his (or her) senses and intellect to create sculptural garments. With the eye of a fashion aesthete, the tailor examines the client—his fashion sense, his posture and body characteristics. Does the client respect the tailor's opinions? The garments worn by the client—their harmonic proportions, fit, age, maintenance—are quickly registered by the tailor to determine the client's attitude towards dress. Nineteenth-century Glasgow tailor Joseph Couts asserted: "*Learn your customer's mind!* Fit that and all the rest is easy."[3] These observational skills continue to play a role during the drafting, the construction, and the fitting of the garments.

What particular fitting issues does the client present? Is his back straight or stooped? Is one shoulder lower than the other? Does he have a prominent belly or seat? These characteristics are recorded methodically at the measuring stage and assessed carefully, all without a mention to the client. Tailor Gunther Hertzer, writing in Tiffen, Ohio in 1892 suggested, "Better talk half an hour with your customer after he has been measured, in order to observe his build, rather than to spend half a day in altering afterwards."[4] At the 1911 convention of the International Custom Cutters of America Association, Charles Stone advised that a cutter must, "know how and inspire confidence with the customers and throw a sort of hypnotic influence over them."[5] Whether carrying out or supervising the craft, the tailor's eye continues to work throughout this sculptural process.

The tailor's mind, either schooled or through experience, has knowledge of anatomy. Where are the end points of shoulders and what is their relative proportion to the "norm"? Is a line across the client's shoulders parallel to the ground? How extreme is this deviation and does it have a strong effect on the pelvis? To what degree are his cervical and lumbar spine curved? How does the head sit on the spine? Is there any excess fat or muscular development on the body, and if so, where? Finally, is the client in a normal relaxed posture or is he holding himself in an unnatural pose while the tailor assesses and measures him? An article in *American Gentleman* in 1906 reported, "The Cutter's general skills include business tact and leadership—decision-making, planning, supervisory skills, attention to detail, and the ability to get work done on time."[6]

Before patternmaking begins, the tailor carefully considers his observations of the client's body and incorporates them into the measurements laid out in the notebook. He calculates any proportions necessary in laying out the grid of the draft. An article in *American Gentleman* from September 1909 advised, "Proportions should be cut close to average, even for the disproportionate, for it makes the client look normal."[7] The tailor may plan a slightly larger coat chest for the thin client, a slightly wider or narrower shoulder to achieve a proportionate look when needed, and use classical proportions based upon the client's height to determine the waistline and coat length.

Achieving a successful fit is more complicated than simply accommodating the body's circumference and height. The tailor understands, often subconsciously, the two-dimensional shapes required to dress a particular client's three-dimensional form. He recognizes which body points correspond to the pivotal points on the draft that ensure a perfect fit. The garment must hang from the shoulders, covering the front and back of the body in the manner that style dictates without creases, folds, or diagonal pulling. The tailor also understands the complex construction of the garments and where length or width may be needed to create the pleasing sculptural shapes dictated by style. He knows whether the extra fabric required should be built into the pattern (as for an expressive sleeve cap) or stretched with the iron (for the front shoulder point). Drafting system author John West prescribed stretching the side body at the waist, slightly, before attaching it to the front, drawing in the back armscye and the lower front armscye with thread, and easing the back shoulder onto the front shoulder. Chicago cutting school owner Charles Stone adds that the journeyman should check the waist length after stretching to ensure it has not been over-stretched.[8] I found this type of construction information articulated in many pattern drafting systems and other technical writings—only the vocabulary varied slightly from the twentieth century terms.

Figure 5.1 Drafting system author and owner of the Chicago College of Garment Cutting, Charles John Stone, *c.* 1892. Stone's dress coat and trousers illustrate the importance of understanding fit for the corpulent figure. Though obese, Mr. Stone looks sleek and distinguished in his custom-made attire. *Stone's Superlative Coat and Vest System.*

The finished pattern is laid upon the cloth and traced, and seam outlays are added to enable future alteration as the client's body changes. Providing extra seam allowance for increasing size enables a well-made garment to serve for many years. Once cut, the garment trimmings (pocketing, lining, the interfacing canvases, tapes, and threads) are assembled. In a large shop, this work was done by the "trimmer," often an apprentice to the cutter. Then the important reference points on the garment such as the center front, waistline, and pocket locations are marked with basting thread, and the garment pieces are press-shaped where desired (stretching in the upper front armscye and the front shoulder seam of coats or shrinking under the seat and stretching along the calf for trousers). The pockets are constructed. The interfacing (called the "hymo") is constructed of hair canvas to match the shape of the client and the coat front. The hymo is basted to the front, and the entire coat is basted together for a first fitting. The cutter supervises the fitting and notes how the garment fits the client, taking care to keep him relaxed and reassured that any discrepancies from an ideal fit are minor and easy to correct. Then, the garment seams are taken apart and the required changes are made to the garment pieces.

The coat fronts are then attached permanently to the hymo and the lapels are pad stitched. Pad stitching with short diagonal hand stitches rolls the lapel gracefully towards the body. The front edge is cut to its final contour and the edge and the lapel roll line are stay-taped for stability. Using the coat's front edge as a pattern, the facing and its attached front lining are cut and the two sewn together. Careful manipulation by the sewing tailor ensures that the coat curves in toward the body below the lapel roll line, and that the lapel edge (the underside of the front edge) curves in towards the coat front. The crucial front edge must not be puckered nor stretched. The other garment components are finished and lined, and the garment reassembled. The goal of all construction is for the garment and its components (pocket flaps, front edges, collar corners) to curve around the body, "building in" the sculptural aspect of the garment. Seated cross-legged, the tailor places one armhole over each knee to set the collar.[9] Shoulder pads are inserted and the sleeves hung. The armhole is "sealed" through the seam allowance, using big hand stitches of heavy thread through all layers of fabric, including the shoulder pad. Padding (a sleeve head) is inserted into the crown of the sleeve to maintain either an expressive or smooth effect. The linings are slipstitched closed and the top collar fabric is shaped and stitched onto the under-collar. Apprentices or tailoresses often performed this final stitching stage, called "felling." The coat is then "hard pressed" to set the edges and seams. Its front edges may be hand stitched for a topstitched effect or "bluff edged" by prick stitching (with fine back stitches) from the underside through the seam allowances, always pulling the coat towards the body to maintain its sculptural integrity. A specialist works the buttonholes. The buttons are sewn on, and then the coat gets its "soft press" or final pressing. Specially shaped pressing boards are used for each garment—jacket board, sleeve board, trouser board—to maintain their shape. The breadth of experience, skills, and knowledge required of the skillful tailor was garnered over years of refining eye, mind, and hand.

The development of printed pattern drafting systems

Garment patterns are the two-dimensional shapes that will result in a particular garment style. A pattern drafting system quantifies the method by which garment shapes are produced. Arithmetic formulae, based on body measurements and/or proportions of key measurements, are written in a systematic way, enabling the cutter to draw the pattern pieces for the style and size chosen. Throughout the nineteenth and twentieth centuries, quantified systems varied in their ability to articulate postural assessment, a crucial aspect of patternmaking achieved as a result of the tailor's experienced eye.

The pattern drafting system that I began to learn in 1976 was very sophisticated. Sabatino Roncucci (1922–2011) had been the cutter/fitter/owner of a tailor shop in Italy that made forty custom suits per week. This intensive work, completed over nearly two decades, led to a deep knowledge of fitting a wide variety of body types. When Roncucci began teaching at the Northern Alberta Institute of Technology in Edmonton, Canada during the early 1970s he had to develop a pattern drafting system that could be used successfully by beginning tailoring students. His system incorporated direct body measurements, aesthetic corrections based on proportions of the client's height, and a measurement system for determining posture and modifying his standard draft to fit postural issues. It worked for novice students to produce a well-fitting suit the first time used. My familiarity with this complex system gave me the confidence to examine and test a number of other pattern-drafting systems.

I found information about pattern drafting systems available for my study through the bibliographies of Patricia Trautman and Kevin Seligman. My training and experience as a tailor/cutter enabled me to interpret archaic instructions and to extract information from the systems. I considered a variety of content attributes including to whom the author directed his pattern drafting system (tailor, cutter, or the general public). I recorded whether fitting the corpulent man was considered by the author. I noted whether the system required an assessment of the client's posture and how this assessment was made—by observation, by measurement, or a hybrid method. I tracked the country and year of publication as well as the drafting medium (onto cloth or paper). Then I selected (by random number assignment) thirty-three of the systems to test by drafting in quarter scale. I recorded and interpreted the observations made during this practical work.

In total, I examined 102 pattern drafting systems published between 1800 and 1920. After my work was complete and the data was analyzed, the pattern drafting systems fell neatly into three time periods based upon the content

PATTERN DRAFTING SYSTEMS STUDY RESULTS

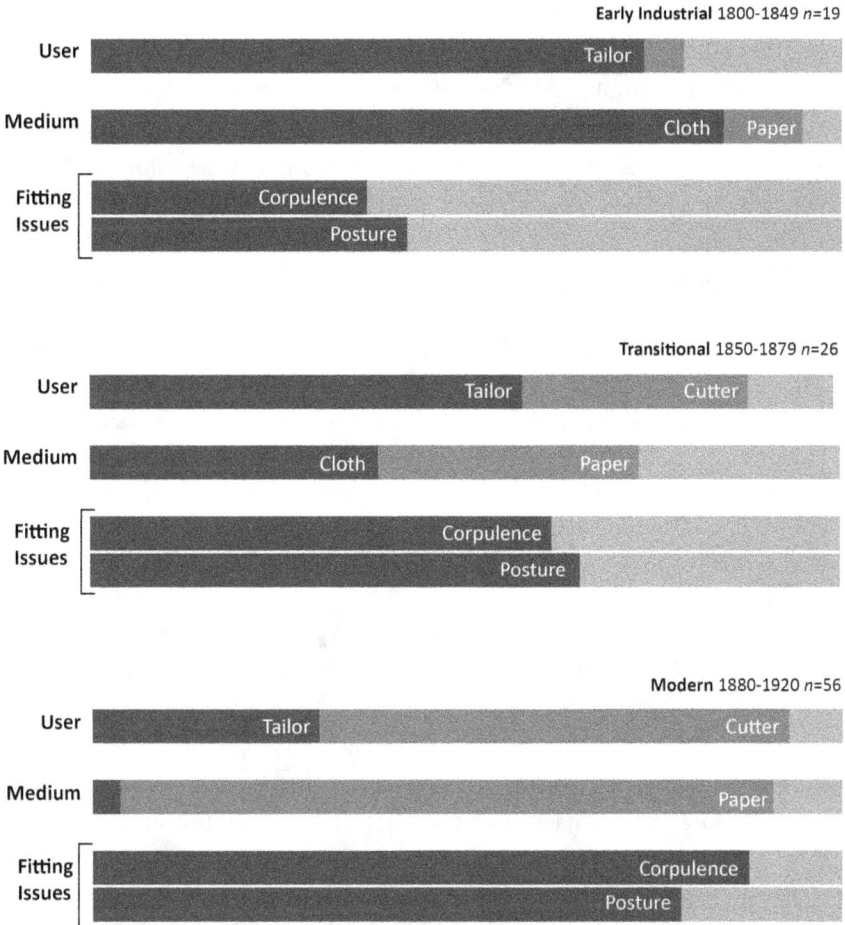

Early Industrial 1800-1849 $n=19$

User — Tailor

Medium — Cloth | Paper

Fitting Issues — Corpulence | Posture

Transitional 1850-1879 $n=26$

User — Tailor | Cutter

Medium — Cloth | Paper

Fitting Issues — Corpulence | Posture

Modern 1880-1920 $n=56$

User — Tailor | Cutter

Medium — Paper

Fitting Issues — Corpulence | Posture

Figure 5.2 Pattern drafting systems study by variables. The intended user of the systems and the drafting medium changed over time. Accommodations for complex issues of fit were always a concern to tailors.

and style of their presentation. I found that the authors of pattern drafting systems in the early industrial period (1800–49) tended to present their methods in a conversational way, rather than systematically. Instructions for drawing a pattern were brief, so successful use depended upon users' familiarity with pattern shapes. For example, John Killey of Liverpool advised that "On forming the back ... I shall not propose anything new of my own ... as any person at all acquainted with Cutting knows that the back is easily formed."[10] Most early systems drafted the back directly onto the cloth, then cut it out and used it to establish key points on the garment front, such as the neck point, the shoulder length and angle, the front neckline, and the side seam lines. Some authors relied upon the cutter's eye to determine the armscye shape, the neckline, shoulder line, and to position the front edge of the coat. Tailors had methods for accommodating postures and body shapes that deviated from the normal form and many early systems included advice to make such accommodations. Corrections of defects were made by a knowledgeable eye or by prescribed methods.

Tailor Gabriel Chabot of Baltimore commented in 1829, "The only guide to precision that has ever existed has generally been the tailor's judgement."[11] He went on to note:

> Those in this [corpulent] class who dress fashionable, should (for their comfort) wear their pantaloons above the round prominence of their stomach ... It follows ... that the difference in the depth of the crotch ... should be greater in the front than at the side seam, and diminish proportionately behind.[12] [viii] ... in the first place you have taken the length A ... paying proper regard (as you always have to do,) whether the person be straight made; ... inclined to stoop ...; stooping; or portly.[13]

Chabot, in addition to this discussion, offered tables of corrected measurements for drafting for different body types.

In 1845, master tailors Young and Rathvon gave the vague advice that, "where the first shoulder measure is the largest, it shows the person to be straight with the head more thrown back, and consequently requires the shoulder to be pitched further back."[14] Glasgow-based tailor Joseph Couts used "check measures" to determine differences in the left and right sides of the body. "If both sides of the person you are measuring be not alike—if one shoulder blade be fuller than another, as often occurs with lawyers and other professional men who stoop much to a desk, as well as to most mechanics—you ought to take the measurements of both sides in the manner described."[15]

The drafting systems began to evolve from the conversational format with roughly sketched images. During the transitional period (1850–79), a more scientific approach emerged. Point-by-point drafting instructions were laid out in paragraph form and improved printing technology facilitated better diagrams. More systems accounted for the client's posture and for corpulence and some addressed these subjects objectively, using body measurements to improve the standard draft. Some systems used a divisional scale—a ruler divided into fractions of, for example, the chest circumference—to simplify the arithmetic

Figure 5.3 John Moxley, 1823, *Every One His Own Tailor*. The draft "floats" on the page without any guidelines to anchor it.

required of the cutter. Other systems employed scales of the author's invention, perhaps intended as a tool to safeguard the author's secrets and as a moneymaker if his system was widely adopted. During the transitional period, more mention was made of drawing patterns onto paper. Paper patterns could be reused for returning clients, and by drafting onto card a tailor could create his own set of standard block patterns. The drafting systems were addressed primarily to custom tailors and cutters but it is not known whether the systems were used by small shop tailors or by master and merchant tailors in larger city custom tailoring shops. It is notable that many of the systems were directed to the new role of the cutter. The sewing machine came into use during this period, and paired with better pattern drafting systems, the new technology improved the efficiency of the large custom tailoring shops and ready-to-wear factories.

Pattern drafting instructions in point form and drawings based on a grid were consistent features during the modern period (1880–1920). These systems look

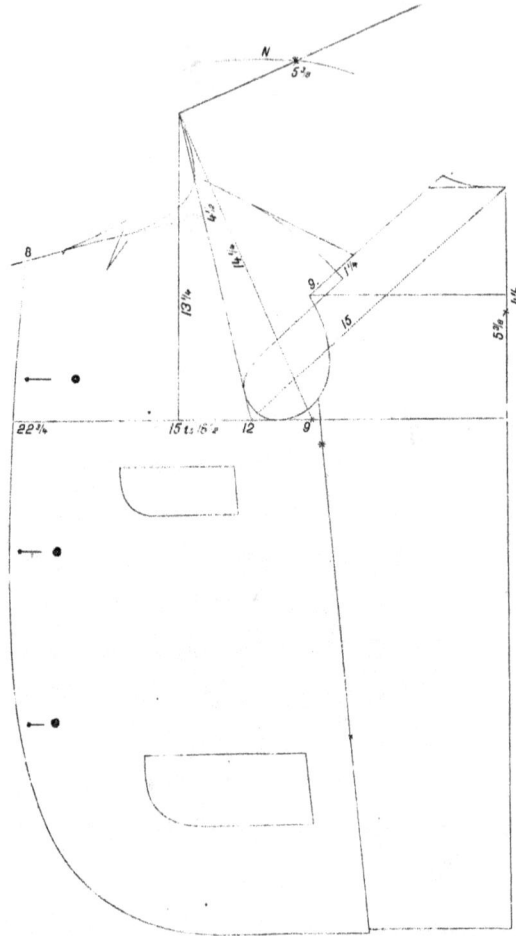

Figure 5.4 W.W. Brundage, *A Complete System of Cutting*, 1867, offers a clearer diagram, but few gridlines.

like the published pattern drafting systems in use in the late twentieth century. Nearly all authors of systems specified changes to the standard draft to accommodate posture and corpulence. Many systems quantified modifications to the draft but all relied on the cutter's judgment. Harry Simons, a prolific author of cutting systems, published a draft for "Stout Pants" with extra height at the center front and a very narrow back dart.[16] He also had solutions for fitting "Bow-legged and Knock-kneed" men.[17] *The Popular Gentleman System*, 1917 showed the use of a hand-held yardstick to measure the curvature of the client's spine. Its advice on "How to Take a Depression Measure" instructed:

The yard stick must be held straight up and down and not lean in or out at the top or bottom ... Measure in for the waist depression from the edge of the yard stick to the hollow part of the waist which is 2 inches for a normal man, but can be more or less.[18]

The author then directly applied the waist depression measure to the coat draft to assist in determining the center back curve. The system included instructions for measuring a large prominent seat, stooping back, and seat depression or flat seat.

Charles Hecklinger used a table of heights to determine the client's waist length. He then made use of this table in determining corrections for erect and stooping postures. However, his method still relies on the cutter's experienced judgment.

If we measure an erect figure, we satisfy ourselves whether it is one or two sizes more than [the] proportion [indicated on the table], and then select the numbers on the table accordingly. As an erect figure increases in the front at the expense of the back, which decreases, find on the table the numbers corresponding to one or two sizes larger for the front, and the same for the back, only so much less.... It requires but little judgment to decide how far and how much to deviate from the regular standard.[19]

It was during this period that drafting schools emerged, and the use of these systems in teaching may have led to the clarity of the directions. The tone of the systems' authors changed from information shared with other tailors to one of instruction. Prolific British tailoring author William D.F. Vincent said, "Our advice to the student is, thoroughly master one method for all styles and all shapes, make it the basis of your cutting room practice."[20]

The tailor's skill of observing the client's form, evidenced as early as the first pattern drafting systems, is the key to successful fit. Drafting front and back correctly depends on being able to identify "deficiencies" from the ideal normal body—deviations such as girth and posture. The curvature of the client's spine—forward (stooping), very straight (erect), or "normal"—as well as client corpulence determines the length of the front and back garment pieces from the balance point. Debate about the location of the balance point for tailored coats took place in trade journals and at cutters' conventions throughout the nineteenth century. Today it is agreed that garments hang from the point where the shoulder line intersects with the base of the neck—the "neck point." The methods for achieving garment balance vary from the use of practiced observation and applied "know how" to systems that attempt to apply a direct measurement of posture to the draft to guarantee success.

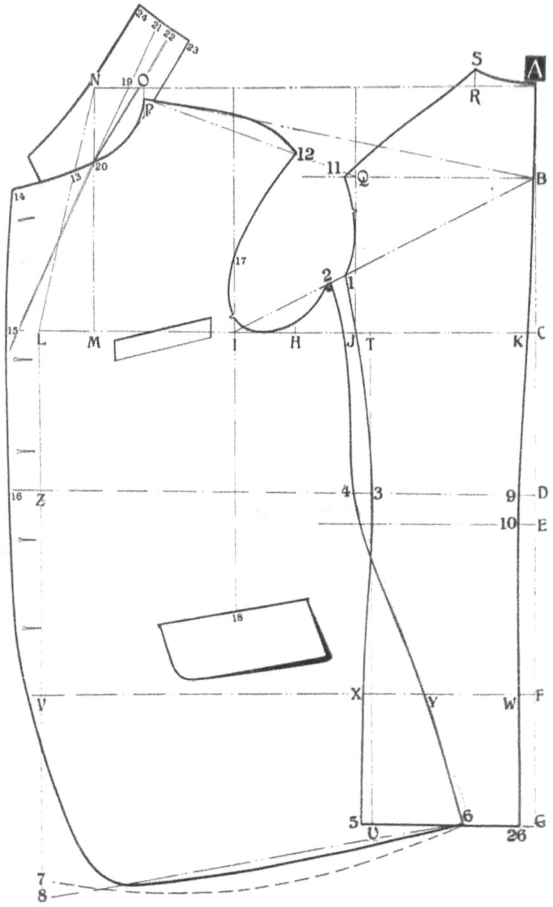

Figure 5.5 *Stone's Advanced Superlative Coat and Vest System,* 1910. The drafting grid varies little from the systems of the late twentieth century.

Each author had his own parameters but laying out horizontal and vertical lines upon which to style the garment made the process of drafting easier to replicate. Here is one example. In 1892, Frank Van Aarle published *The Key Line System,* setting out vertical lines to establish the armscye width, neck point, and waist suppression. He theorized that since the width of a proportionate figure equaled his height (cf. Leonardo's Vitruvian man) these eight parts could also be used to successfully establish proportionate garment widths. He also used the concept of eight "cubits" to set horizontal lines such as the proportionate armscye depth, waist and seat lines. Van Aarle experimented further and established proportions of the chest and waist measures that he found worked to determine neck, hip, calf, etc. circumferences.[21]

British vs. American differences

Of the systems in the study, 90 percent were published in the United States and 10 percent in Britain. This proportion remains true in each era examined and it is interesting to compare the American and British trade. In general, the British systems had an authoritative, instructional tone and seemed directed to improving the craft. British tailors' guilds had been in place for centuries. North American tailors came from diverse immigrant backgrounds and, as clothing producers, were important members of early communities and towns. The American pattern drafting systems had an entrepreneurial air about them. The authors were self-promoting authorities on their craft, selling their systems as the newest and best system to date. For example, the title page of H.J. Hansen's 1889 Goshen, Indiana system: *Hansen's Seamless and Artistic Frock Coat System: A Method which is Clear, Simple and Complete and Its Involving Ideas Have Never Been Heard or Thought of Before. A Work Which Has Been By Careful Study and Practice Successful. Elaborated.* One author used ever-inflating adjectives for the titles of his drafting systems. Charles J. Stone, tailor and cutting system author, published his first system in 1887, *Stone's Paramount-Cutter*, followed by *Stone's Superlative* (*c.*1892), *Stone's New Superlative* (1900), and *Stone's Advanced Superlative* (1910).

Technical differences existed among the pattern drafting systems of the two groups. The British relied more on "rock of eye," the practiced judgment of the tailor, to assess client posture. The Americans attempted to quantify anatomical characteristics, rather than to rely on the "mere" observation of an experienced craftsperson. As early as 1874, American William Crawford used a yardstick and ruler to measure the "incline of the neck," a measure that was then used to place "Scale A" in the correct position when drafting the coat. Crawford's drafts referenced a variety of his scales for use in drafting for stooping, erect and corpulent figures.[22] By contrast, London author J.P. Thornton urged the development of an eye for the "disproportion" of the figure as well as the conscious memorization of how well the correction to the draft worked in the finished garment. In this manner, the young cutter builds his skill in assessment. Thornton also prescribed an optional complex measurement system useful in drafting for the "over erect" (very straight) spine. He considered this measurement unnecessary for the stooping figure.[23]

All the British systems in my study mentioned and provided accommodations for the corpulent client. American author Chabot commented on corpulence in 1829, "Happily there are but very few men of this make."[24] Though the American cutters may have had fewer corpulent clients, they accommodated well-developed chest and shoulders. The British called this deviation from their norm "the American shoulder." In contrast, the British tailor's sophisticated client was more likely to appear well fed, with the distinguished profile seen in portraits of the titans of industry and commerce.

Block patterns for standard sized, standard styles of coats were available for purchase from the pattern cutting schools in major garment centers. The schools taught courses in the adjustment of the blocks for a range of client "deficiencies." Standard blocks could be purchased in sets by size and style or individually. There was disagreement within the custom tailoring industry about the use of blocks, which were in popular use by cutters of ready-to-wear. Custom cutters in the United States argued that the adoption of blocks was a threat to the profession and would lead to a reduction in the cutter's wage, which was, at the time, amongst the highest paid to United States trades. George W. DuNah, in *The Custom Cutter and Fashion Review* of September 1890 argued that, "Block patterns have been a curse to tailors, they have stunted his intellect, and have obstructed the development of any genius he might possess; making it possible for anyone who has no knowledge of tailoring to be its dictator."[25] The British, however, embraced their use and published instructional manuals on how to adjust blocks for fashion and for postural defects. Tailor T.H. Holding noted, "A block pattern is a base from which you can deviate into any style you like."[26] Holding's book included many adaptions for block patterns to accommodate postural changes (e.g. for very broad shoulders, moderate stoop, small chest and big waist, hump back, and excessive thinness).

Authors of tailors' pattern drafting systems during this period of rapid change in the trade expressed concern about preserving their knowledge and skills. Tailors used their applied observational skills combined with objective measurement of the client, and considered the properties of the cloth chosen, the dictates of fashion, and the client's personality, to produce sophisticated, high-status garments. Today "table drafting" is in limited practice, in small shop situations. Computer-aided design attempts to replace the experienced human eye, and the patternmaker's mind and hand.

Conclusion

Many nineteenth- and early twentieth-century resources dedicated to the cut and construction of menswear are available for study, but only recently has menswear gained the concentrated attention of dress scholars. Tailoring was among the fields publishing trade journals in the late nineteenth century. Menswear publishers were in the vanguard as early as 1840 with style serials.[27] Leading practitioners shared skills in print, on topics such as dealing with clients and staff to run successful businesses. Naturally, the trade published technical materials needed to cut and construct complex, well-fitting garments, but elements of humanity emerge in the technical writings as well. Journals and pattern drafting systems allow us into the working lives of tailors, where we can observe the fashion, workshop practices, technical issues, and their reactions to the business challenges of the day. Understanding the producers as well as their production methods is an essential part of material culture methodology. Today, the ethical production of fashion is a concern to many. Our studies of historical dress must include an examination of the lives and working conditions of the makers of garments. This information is there for the taking in the rich documents of the tailoring trade.

6

Computer-Aided Patternmaking:
A Brief History of Technology Acceptance
from 2D Pattern Drafting to 3D Modeling

Fatma Baytar *and* Eulanda Sanders

This chapter studies the introduction, dissemination and adoption of 2D and 3D CAD (computer-aided design) technologies in apparel patternmaking. The authors trace the introduction and dissemination of 2D and 3D CAD technologies, citing the technical and financial boundaries that the technology itself initially presented to widespread adoption in apparel patternmaking. The authors discuss 2D flat pattern design, 2D-to-3D pattern design, and 3D-to-2D pattern design. They then proceed to a discussion of the importance of using computer-aided technology to streamline the apparel production process in the global apparel marketplace. The authors discuss how CAD facilitates increased collaboration and communication among different departments within a company and how parties throughout the world who are involved in decision-making can view and evaluate computerized workflow. The authors demonstrate that use of CAD platforms increases productivity, and results in reduced costs, improved fit, and quick response time. While this chapter provides an important and necessary contribution to scholarship pertaining to patternmaking it also reinforces a narrative that courses throughout this text: the development of technologies to facilitate, expedite, and improve patternmaking. Viewed in contrast to Catherine Roy's discussion in Chapter 5, the reader may come to understand how many more aspects of the patternmaking process have been quantified and honed to greater precision given the advances in technology of the latter part of the twentieth and early twenty-first centuries.

Introduction

In competitive industries where time is money, drafting two-dimensional (2D) patterns for three-dimensional (3D) products requires specialized computer-aided design (CAD) software, which uses vector graphics. The earliest users of CAD software in the 1960s were large automotive and aerospace companies such as Lockheed, General Motors, and Citroën. Internal research groups within these industries were collaborating with university research teams at Massachusetts Institute of Technology (MIT) and Cambridge University to develop 2D (for drafting) and 3D (for solid and surface modeling) CAD software.[1] The 1970s saw the shift from research into commercial use of CAD software; which was supported by computer hardware's increasing processing power and decreasing prices, allowing smaller companies to afford such systems. Thanks to the increased industry support for innovation, by the mid-1980s CAD systems evolved significantly, for example AutoCAD (2D) and CATIA (3D) emerged, and technological advancements empowered design engineers to complete the work themselves, rather than working with trained CAD operators.[2]

In the apparel industry, 2D flat patternmaking methods progressed with the introduction of CAD software, such as ApparelCAD, in the 1980s. During the adoption of computer-aided patternmaking in the 1990s, working on flat table surfaces was replaced by a computer screen, and pattern drafting instruments evolved into digital tools activated with one click of a mouse. Patternmaking became more effective as CAD systems allowed a speedy and accurate process of pattern manipulation from existing databases, and ease of data transmission for decision-making and production.[3] During the infancy of CAD adoption, CAD systems were costly and a majority of patternmakers were not trained to use the technology. Most apparel companies still preferred manual patternmaking, but many used software for grading and marker making.[4] Gradually, as the diffusion of CAD innovation continued in the apparel industry and accessibility increased, companies started integrating computers into their patternmaking processes and hiring patternmakers with CAD skills.

In the twenty-first century, the gap in linking 3D designs to 2D patterns is closing fast due to powerful 3D visualization technologies, allowing patternmakers to visualize the drape and fabric appearance as they synchronously draft patterns in the 2D workspace of CAD software. The same 3D CAD technology also allows reverse engineering, as garments can be taken apart and analyzed digitally, removing instant haptic feedback and requiring new mindsets when working in a digital environment. This chapter examines the introduction and dissemination of 2D and 3D CAD technologies in apparel patternmaking, and their stages of adoption in three distinct markets. In that context, adoption of new 3D CAD patternmaking technologies, which have taken 2D patternmaking practices one step further, is also presented with a review of existing studies. The chapter also presents examples of widely used commercial CAD patternmaking software systems, and concludes with a discussion of how future patternmaking trends may facilitate an integrated approach to consumer needs and domestic production.

Emergence of CAD

Innovations cannot be separated from the political, social, and cultural environment of their time. This is exactly what happened during the Cold War era when technological advancements and computers were seen as key factors for becoming the world's supreme political and military power. The foundations of CAD technologies were laid in the 1950s, at MIT, to address the need to automate milling machines for manufacturing complex shapes for the aircraft industry.[5] In an attempt to design the first numerically controlled milling machine to allow operators with no programming skills to use machine tools, the MIT Computer-Aided-Design Project was funded by the United States Air Force between 1959 and 1970, and run by the team of engineers and designers led by Douglas Ross and Steven A. Coons. As Cardoso Llach (2015) explained, the phrase "computer-aided design," manifested the team's view of a computer's role in production as supportive of, not a replacement for, humans.[6] CAD evolved from the necessities of driving numerically-controlled machines, and significantly decreased the time and energy devoted to turning "someone's idea into a usable physical object."[7]

During the first phase of CAD evolution between the 1960s and 1970s, remarkable milestones were achieved. The introduction of interactive computer graphics by Ivan Sutherland's Sketchpad system, which allowed users to draw with a light pen on a monitor, demonstrated several characteristics of modern CAD software systems such as constraint-based modeling and "rubber banding." Additionally, Bézier's mathematical representation of a family of curves facilitated intense research towards CAD.[8] CAD technology was disseminated as alumni of the CAD Project continued their work at companies and other academic centers. The second phase of CAD evolution occurred between approximately 1971 and 1982 and CAD evolved from 2D into 3D simulations through the formulation of CAD functionalities such as wire-frame, solid, and boundary-modeling.[9] The third phase of CAD development and importance happened from 1982 until 1996 when industrial needs for CAD systems escalated, personal computing and digital networks appeared, and a product life-cycle oriented thinking became important in production. The fourth phase, highlighted by the terms "virtualization" and "collaboration," lasted roughly between 1996 and 2005, and 2D and 3D CAD tools became more sophisticated. The most recent phase of CAD evolution is from 2006 until today and so far the dominant trend is applying CAD to new domains.[10]

CAD terms and definitions

In their most commonly used form, CAD software programs are based on 2D vector graphics; which are composed of primitives as basic building blocks (i.e., lines, Bézier curves, circles, etc.) that connect key points at certain Cartesian (x, y, z) coordinates and form polygons or other shapes. Based on these coordinates, each CAD drawing can be easily edited and stored. Lines can be given some graphic qualities by changing their color, type (dashed, dotted, etc.) and weight (thin, wide).[11] Planar objects (i.e., 2D shapes) are created on the xy plane whereas 3D objects use the xyz dimensions. "Solids" refer to 3D models that represent objects in 3D space. Cubes, cylinders, cones, spheres, etc. can be given as examples to simple solid primitives. Vector objects can be drawn, edited and transformed in both 2D and 3D spaces by altering specific points that shape the object, and maintain clarity without being pixelated when transformed by scaling, reducing, rotation, or stretching.[12]

3D vector graphics have been heavily used in industries requiring drafting and modeling, such as architecture, mechanical engineering, and aerospace. Some of the CAD developers in these industries include Autodesk (AutoCAD®, Inventor®, Fusion 360®), Dassault Systèmes (CATIA®, SOLIDWORKS®), 3D Systems (Geomagic®), PTC (Creo), Adobe Systems Incorporated (Adobe Illustrator), and CorelDRAW (CorelCAD). The adoption rate of 3D vector graphics has been slow, as compared to 2D graphics, due to several factors including a steep learning curve, the price of full-feature software packages, and maintenance fees. However, solutions such as cloud-based CAD can be a cheaper and more flexible alternative to traditional CAD.[13]

In the apparel industry, vector-based CAD software programs are used for 2D (or flat) patternmaking accomplished on a computer. Some of the developers of such specialized patternmaking software include Gerber Technology (AccuMark) and Lectra (Modaris). In addition to these, generic vector graphics software platforms that were not specifically designed for pattern drafting can be used for drawing patterns (e.g. Adobe Illustrator). It should be noted that specialized CAD used in the apparel industry is different than the systems used in engineering and architecture. Especially from the 3D modeling perspective, CAD for apparel design and development needs to simulate the drape of soft materials on human body forms rather than modeling rigid objects.[14]

Importance of CAD in the apparel industry: big picture

The apparel industry is one of the most labor-intensive industries in the world, therefore its production economics are highly affected by labor costs. Global and regional trade agreements, differences in workers' wages between "high and low-wage" countries, varying consumer demands, and advances in computer technology have challenged the apparel industries in developed countries, such as the United States.[15] To decrease the overall price of garments, apparel companies moved their manufacturing activities offshore to lower-wage countries. During the first half of the twentieth century, Japan was the destination for production, then other countries such as Korea, Taiwan, and Hong Kong gained prominence. By the 1970s, jobs started to move to China, Vietnam, Cambodia, India, and Pakistan.[16] In 1960, less than four percent of the apparel purchased in the US was imported. By the late 1980s, imports continued to increase and became the major factor for the loss of domestic apparel production.[17] In 1995, for the first time, the majority of the apparel purchased in the US was imported.[18] Based on the Bureau of the Census data (1996), Bean (1997) reported that 281,000 jobs were eliminated from the apparel industry between 1983 and 1995.[19] The Bureau of Labor Statistics of the US Department of Labor reported that, employment in the apparel industry dropped from 938,600 in January 1990 to 116,500 in January 2018.[20]

Since the 1970s, the use of computer technology and automation has played an important role for the US textile industry and helped it stay competitive with foreign textile producers.[21] Following this example, technology can play an important role for the domestic apparel industry by automating skill-intensive design and production processes.[22] Although earlier technologies developed in the apparel area were not integrated to communicate with each other; the third phase of CAD development has placed the emphasis on coordinating and integrating the preproduction (e.g., patternmaking, marker making), production and postproduction (e.g. distribution) processes in apparel manufacturing. For this purpose, product data management (PDM), which manages the process of product development from start to end, and product lifecycle management (PLM), which grew out of aerospace and manufacturing industries, and built on PDM, software programs were developed. PLM software can store all the digital files about a garment style in one location, and make it possible to streamline and monitor each stage of preproduction, production, and postproduction.[23] Through increased collaboration and communication among different departments, parties involved in decision-making can view and evaluate computerized workflow. For instance, a virtual prototype of a garment can be developed from 2D patterns in CAD and draped on a digital body to be used in computer-supported remote fit evaluation sessions. Based on the decisions made, CAD pattern files can be altered and uploaded to the system. This way, an apparel company can also produce more items in a season by using the same resources.[24]

Off-shoring has gradually resulted in the development of complex and long global supply chains. Consequently, the phenomenon of fast fashion, which generates massive quantities of cheap garments that imitate high-fashion trends, has been growing.[25] Off-shoring causes a geographical split between "source and destination." As a result of this distance, lead times involving the preproduction processes increase, thus increasing the product costs.[26] Linking the once-separated, computerized apparel design and production into a synchronized whole while integrating people, processes, and business strategies increases productivity, and results in reduced cost, improved quality, and quick response time.[27] Quick response (QR) is an approach to flexible manufacturing that reduces the production time, and costs, to design, manufacture and deliver garments to the retailer.[28] Consumers want products "now," and with the help of technology, there is no reason why production times should take so long.

CAD patternmaking technologies can facilitate efficient production of goods in a short amount of time, and they can enable on-demand manufacturing by providing consumers with high quality and personalized apparel products. There are opportunities for domestic manufacturers to continue apparel manufacturing in novel ways and compete with the current practices of fast fashion. Progressive changes in enabling technologies (e.g., digital communication, retail, and production technologies) can decrease response times to changing trends, and contribute to innovative business models, thus re-shoring (i.e., reversing off-shoring and bringing production back to home country).[29]

CAD in technical apparel design and manufacturing

Overview of technical apparel design from patternmaking to marker making

When designers work, they generate fashion illustrations, but do not include all the technical information necessary for production. These sketches are meant to give clues for production, therefore it is a technical designer's job to realize the fashion designer's ideas for a garment and manufacture it effectively. Technical designers develop two-dimensional patterns; test fit of garments on fit models; create specifications for garment measurements in various size ranges, assess material properties, and develop sewing instructions to communicate production specifics to other parties involved in the decision-making process. Patternmaking is both a creative and an engineering process involving turning a fashion illustration into an actual garment, and creating a set of templates with a precise roadmap to manufacture the garment.[30] Enabling a quick and accurate translation from a designer's mind into a 3D object, makes patternmaking the most important activity in the fashion industry.[31] As Stott (2012) indicated, a pattern is more than a simple template to cut fabrics. It is a crucial document embedded with the information in an "international language" of grain lines, notches, seam allowances, etc., which needs to be spoken in detail very clearly and accurately as it sets the standard for entire production.[32]

Once production patterns are ready, fabrics are cut using these garment patterns, and sewn together to prepare a sample garment, which is a prototype of the fashion sketch, for verification of fit and style. During fit sessions, prototypes are repeatedly adjusted on fit models until the desired outcome is achieved. The process of assessing fit and adjusting prototypes is a long, iterative process that is heuristic in nature, and involves the team of decision-makers including fashion designers, technical designers, and merchandisers.[33] After this step, corrected and finalized patterns are graded. Grading is the process of increasing or decreasing sizes, and is a very important step for mass production as any mistake in the finalized pattern would be amplified in the smallest and largest sizes.[34] After this step, all the pattern pieces are arranged in a layout (marker). Based on the fabric direction, pattern pieces can be rotated, flipped, and moved around to achieve the maximum usage of fabric to minimize waste and decrease production costs. This process is called marking or marker making.[35]

Preparing "soft patterns": overview of 2D and 3D CAD in patternmaking

CAD plays an important role in apparel technical design and product development processes by reducing the time to prepare patterns, grade them and develop markers; thus, speeding up the manufacturing process to shorten lead times. Digital or "soft" patterns can be created by directly drafting in a CAD software, digitizing physical patterns into the software, or using the digital versions of the basic blocks in the software and further modifying them. Digitizing is the process of converting a tangible flat pattern that was developed by draping or drafting into a digital pattern. The most common input devices/peripherals needed for digitizing are a table (or a portable roll-up digitizing surface) that is a flat electronic board, and a cursor (i.e., a mouse-like input device with cross-hair and buttons to enter grade rules). By converting physical patterns into digital ones, a designer can generate a library of patterns. Digital patterns save storage space and can be sent to contractors via email, or uploaded to a PDM/PLM system for sharing information with multiple teams.[36]

When designing garment patterns in CAD, three different approaches can be executed: 2D flat pattern design, 2D-to-3D pattern design, and 3D-to-2D pattern design (i.e., flattening).[37] The following sections give a brief overview of these methods and research associated with them.

2D flat pattern design

A CAD patternmaking software allows designers to draft pattern pieces from scratch, import patterns draped from muslin or drafted on paper by digitizing them into the system, or use existing basic blocks in the system and modify them further by applying the flat patternmaking rules. 2D CAD systems allow faster, easier, and more accurate pattern alterations as compared to manual flat patternmaking. These alterations are executed with a combination of special functions (e.g., manipulating darts, adding fullness, etc.), as well as the generic ones (e.g., adding/deleting points, editing segments, etc.) that can be found in most of the vector-based software programs.[38] With traditional apparel CAD patternmaking systems without 3D functions, digital patterns need to be plotted to develop physical prototypes for fit testing, which is an iterative process and makes up 4–6 percent of total garment costs.[39]

2D-to-3D pattern design

Today's powerful computer graphic systems took CAD patternmaking one step further by incorporating 3D capabilities. Propelled by the developments in computer speed and performance, as well as the increased importance of online retailing for apparel retailers, some major advancements were made, such as in 3D human body modeling (static or animated avatars), and 3D garment simulation on digital human models.[40] The 2D-to-3D pattern design approach is an attempt to link 3D original design with 2D patternmaking. Garments can be visualized in the CAD software's separate 3D module after developing the patterns in 2D, stitching them digitally, applying fabric mechanical properties (weight, stiffness, etc.) and surface designs, placing the stitched patterns around a 3D fit model (either parametric, or a body-scan avatar), and draping them on the model. Garment simulations can allow designers to see the garments from various views (sometimes on animated models), evaluate the design, and alter it if necessary, without developing physical prototypes. These 3D virtual samples can be quickly sent to decision-makers for a fast approval process, and cut down time and material used to develop prototypes.[41]

3D visualization of garments was not an unfamiliar topic in the apparel industry in the 1980s and 1990s. However, its use as a design and a merchandising tool in fashion did not gain acceptance until the early 2000s. Before then, its use was limited to "a few adventurous manufacturers."[42] For example, in 1988, during the American Apparel Manufacturers' Association 15th Annual Apparel Research Conference, Roe Van Fossen, the president of Computer Design, Inc., demonstrated their 3D CAD software on "a powerful Silicon Graphics computer" to show "the drape, pleats and even wrinkles of a given fabric could be displayed in three-dimensions on a full-color, high-resolution video terminal." Six US apparel manufacturers, including the activewear company Russel Corp., were reported to be using the system. During the meeting, Mr. Fossen indicated that 3D design systems were the only way to accelerate the response to new styles, and the only way to re-shore some apparel manufacturing. He announced they would develop an animated version of the software so that designers could see "how fabrics drape when, for example, a model raises her arm or walks."[43] Collier and Collier (1990) reported that as of the 1990s 3D systems lacked the ability to realistically predict and represent garments.[44] As of the first decades of 2000s, garment simulation techniques have advanced greatly, but more studies are still needed to improve garment visualizations, such as by incorporating paddings and lining.[45]

3D-to-2D pattern design

In the 3D-to-2D process, 2D digital patterns are created by drawing lines on the shape of the 3D body and flattening the selected areas. Then, they can be altered, digitally stitched, and draped on the body to test the fit (2D-to-3D). With the advancements in 3D human body modeling, 3D laser scanning, and surface reconstruction technologies, more emphasis has been placed on the flattening technique.[46] The 3D-to-2D process is especially found to be very useful for tight-fitting apparel products such as bras[47] and protective gear.[48]

Numerous studies have been conducted to develop efficient reverse methods in CAD for use in apparel product development, especially for mass customization (i.e., a production method to provide consumers with high quality and personalized apparel products). For example, Wang, Smith, and Yuen (2002) proposed an innovative method of using a triangular mesh to represent a surface, and establish an energy-based model to flatten a 3D surface into a 2D pattern. They used an interpolation function to show the energy distribution on the developed surface and based on this distribution applied surface cutting to improve the flattened surface.[49] In another study conducted to define and quantify the ease allowances in 3D, Thomassey and Bruniaux (2013) scanned a body with and without a shirt, and then superimposed the shirt scan onto the body scan to calculate the ease amounts. Then they designed the same garment on the 3D body scan by using the 3D-to-2D method while incorporating the measured ease values, and compared the shirt patterns to the flattened patterns.[50] Although there is a vast amount of literature on the 3D-to-2D process, difficulties in determining the ease value on a 3D garment, and residual stretch and distortion in the flattened surfaces from the 3D model are some of the most pressing challenges to be solved.[51]

Commercial CAD patternmaking software suppliers

As shown in Figure 6.1, various commercial apparel CAD patternmaking software suppliers serve a diverse group of customers such as apparel companies, fashion designers, freelancers, professional patternmakers, fashion design educators and students, and home sewers. All of the major software platforms offer the same functions for basic flat patternmaking such as drafting patterns from scratch using measurements, using basic blocks to develop patterns, grading and marker making; but each software uses its own tools at different levels of efficiency.[52] These companies also provide 3D modules with their software to help designers check the fit and drape of the garments as they design 2D patterns. 3D modules allow users to wrap 2D patterns on a 3D body, adjust avatar size and shape and animate it. A few companies such as EFI Optitex offer a flattening module for the 3D-to-2D pattern development.[53]

Table 1.Examples of commercial CAD patternmaking software developers

Company	2D CAD software	3D module (2D-to-3D)	Flattening module (3D-to-2D)	Website
Gerber Technology	AccuMark	AccuMark VStitcher	N/A	www.gerbertechnology.com
Lectra	Modaris	Modaris 3D fit	DesignConcept (for furniture)	www.lectra.com
EFI Optitex	O/DEV Pattern Making Suite	3D Creator	3D Flattening	optitex.com
Human Solutions	Assyst	Vidya	N/A	www.human-solutions.com
Tukatech	TUKAcad	TUKA3D	N/A	www.tukatech.com
GRAFIS Software Dr. K. Friedrich	GRAFIS CAD	VSticher	N/A	www.grafis.com
Audaces	Vestuário	Audaces 360	N/A	www.audaces.com/en
CLO Virtual Fashion Inc.	CLO	CLO3D	N/A	www.clo3d.com/
PAD System	Pad Pattern	N/A	N/A	www.padsystem.com
Browzwear	VStitcher	VStitcher	Lotta	browzwear.com
StyleCAD	Pattern Xpert	N/A	N/A	www.stylecad.com
Polygon Sofware	PolyNest	N/A	N/A	polypm.com
eTelestia	Telestia Creator	N/A	N/A	www.etelestia.com/en
Wild Ginger	Cameo, PatternMaster	N/A	N/A	www.wildginger.com
Cochenille Design Studio	Garment Designer	N/A	N/A	www.cochenille.com

Figure 6.1 Table listing examples of commercial CAD patternmaking software developers.

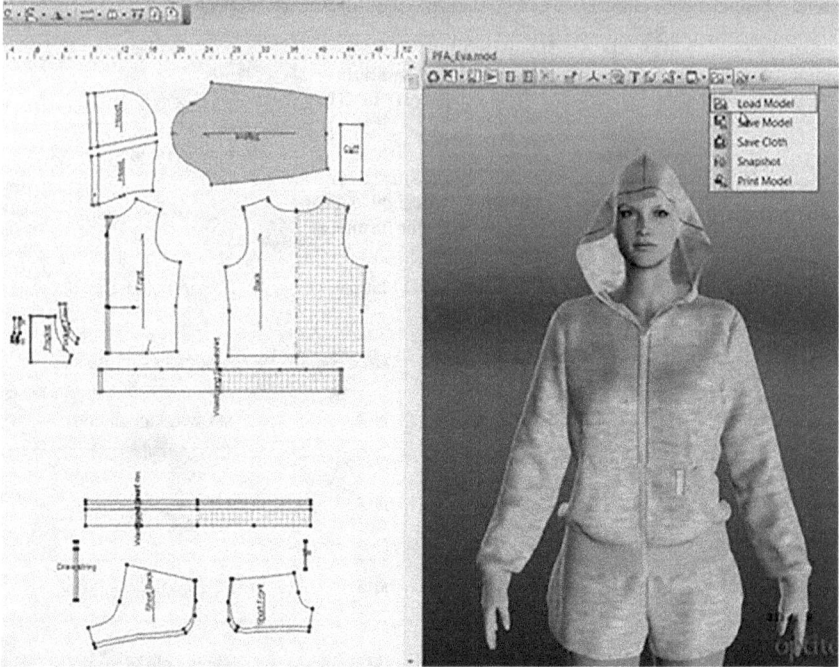

Figure 6.2 Image of Optitex 2D and 3D patterns on a model.

Software programs such as eTelestia, Wild Ginger, and Cochenille are affordable "scaled down" CAD options with some limited functions designed for the needs of small companies, individual designers, and home sewers.[54] For designers who do not have access to these commercial CAD patternmaking software, generic vector-based CAD programs such as Adobe Illustrator, CorelCAD, and AutoCAD can also be used to create digital patterns.[55]

Technology acceptance and diffusion of CAD patternmaking

CAD patternmaking software users must be competent in basic patternmaking, grading and marker making as software training does not cover such fundamentals. Required skills for each group is similar and include computer literacy; patternmaking, draping, and construction knowledge; familiarity with grading and marker making; basic math skills; attention to details; and enjoying using a computer for a long time, as CAD patternmaking takes time and patience.[56] There are three groups of people to adopt CAD patternmaking software programs: fashion/technical designers working freelance or at companies, home sewers, and design educators and students.

Adoption of CAD patternmaking in the apparel industry

Computer technology was first applied to the apparel industry in the form of grading in the late 1960s, in marker making in the early 1970s, and in patternmaking in the early 1980s. Initial technologies were bulky and slow as compared to today's systems. With the first CAD patternmaking software, designers were able to develop and modify patterns, as well as create a library for production patterns on a mini-computer, which was a much faster version of the 1970s mainframes.[57] When small, medium, large, and giant-sized apparel companies in the US were compared to understand their CAD adoption, no difference was found among their approaches. They were reacting slowly to adopt these technologies for patternmaking. However, grading and marker-marking were the two most frequently used functions executed in CAD as they were the most tedious operations that needed to be computerized to decrease labor costs.[58]

In the 1990s, the price of CAD systems drastically decreased (e.g. grading/marker-making systems costs dropped from $250,000 in 1980 to $50,000 in 1995) and computer-processing power significantly increased.[59] As a result, the adoption of CAD patternmaking gradually increased in 1990s, but it was still slow. Implementation of CAD technology in a company depends on complex relationships among organizational, technological and social factors.[60] Therefore, some of the main reasons for slow adoption were: (a) companies did not want to commit to expensive new equipment and technology but instead waited until they saw proof of these systems' usefulness as well as a decreased cost; (b) there was not a sufficient workforce possessing the technical skills to operate such systems; (c) companies were not sure if they could adequately manage constantly evolving new technologies; and (d) companies felt overwhelmed with the number of technological choices.[61]

Although computers became much more affordable in the early 2000s, specialized CAD patternmaking software remained an expensive investment, especially for new companies. Nonetheless, adopting CAD patternmaking software saved time and money by streamlining tasks such as naming pieces and adding seam allowances.[62] Additionally, CAD patternmaking was offering other advantages to manufacturers such as improved productivity and quality, flexible production, and process control. Applying grading to all pattern sizes after making alterations to them, creating markers for these updated patterns, and calculating the cost of garments based on the marker efficiencies became especially simple.[63] In their study of the determinants of the CAD/CAM technology adoption in the American textile and apparel industries, Yan and Fiorito (2002) found that manufacturer's attitudes toward CAD/CAM systems were positive and the major reason against adoption was the cost of the systems.[64]

Adoption of 3D CAD in the industry has been following a somewhat similar path to the adoption of 2D CAD in the 1980s and 1990s. Studies of 3D CAD in the 1990s predicted that the technology was not mature enough to realistically simulate fabric drape and human bodies, and therefore would not be immediately feasible to use.[65] Easters (2012) interviewed a group of apparel designers, and managers to understand the apparel CAD adoption and use in British companies. He found that, although 2D CAD tools were effectively used in most apparel firms, the industry was resisting full adoption of 3D CAD technology.[66] A recent article about Walmart's pilot testing of 3D CAD adoption reveals all the steps the company took to implement a 3D CAD system.[67] In an effort to increase speed and flexibility in the sample product development cycle, the company decided to work with Browzwear after comparing and evaluating the existing software companies. Because of the vast number of choices to be made, Walmart hired a consultant company for help. Building the right team was another key factor and the company looked for team members who were passionate about technology. The company also needed to build the team's trust in 3D (e.g., the accuracy of fabrication, drape, fit, etc.). Another consideration they had to make was to identify the product categories that would be most suitable for the 3D software (the company initially started with just two styles of girls' activewear), and who, internally (e.g. buyers, technical design teams, graphics, design teams, etc.) and externally (e.g. suppliers), would be impacted from this change.[68]

Adoption of CAD patternmaking in home sewing

The growing home sewing segment is another area on which commercial CAD patternmaking software companies have been focusing. The motives behind home sewing vary from doing it as a creative outlet; dissatisfaction with ready-to-wear garment fit, feeling in control of garment attributes including style, fabric, color, and fit; engagement with a more ethical clothing practice; and saving money.[69] Because fit is the key factor shaping decisions about purchasing a garment or sewing it, pattern companies such as Burda, Kwik Sew, and Vogue have offered home sewers a wide range of fashionable styles.[70] However, in their study to investigate consumers' use of and satisfaction with home sewing patterns, LaBat,

Salusso, and Rhee (2007) found that home sewers were dissatisfied with the patterns available to them and their dissatisfaction increased with larger sizes and pants.[71] Strategies such as using computer-aided patternmaking to customize patterns would be a solution to this issue while providing attractive and well-fitting apparel.[72]

Software programs offered by companies such as Wild Ginger and Cochenille Design Studio, allow users to select a style, enter their measurements to customize basic blocks (or, fit garments) and then modify 2D patterns to fit the style to their body by using the tools to transfer darts, slash/spread, slash/pivot, add seam allowances etc. By helping home sewers draft patterns to fit their measurements, these software eliminate fitting trial and error in the sewing room.[73] Tech-savvy home sewers usually form networks to communicate with each other. One of the discussion threads on PatternReview.com indicates that this group of home sewers exchange ideas on patternmaking software and operating systems. Most of them agree that using a computer to create patterns instead of altering commercial paper patterns is "more fun" and "time-saving" when they possess computer and patternmaking skills.[74]

One of the innovative attempts at software development was made in 2007 by introducing home sewers to 3D digital fitting of 2D patterns on parametric avatars. Launched in partnership with Siemens, Optitex, and Bernina, Bernina MyLabel offered home sewers the option to create parametric fit models by entering their measurements and altering the default avatar (Eva). The software also offered a set of patterns that users could alter by entering their own measurements. Styles were limited, but users were able to shorten, lengthen, widen and narrow existing patterns. They were also able to select from a large fabric library or scan their own fabric swatches. Users also had a wide selection of buttons, embroidery, and machine stitches.[75] Before being withdrawn from the market in 2012, Bernina MyLabel attracted many technology-savvy home sewers who are still using it as of 2018.

Adoption of CAD patternmaking in academia

In the apparel industry, there is a growing need for a workforce capable of using CAD patternmaking software programs. This need necessitates the development of CAD patternmaking courses at universities.[76] Upon seeing its transformative potential, CAD was first implemented in two apparel design programs in 1982.[77] Some programs started by using AutoCAD technologies for patternmaking, then Dr. Phyllis Bell Miller developed ApparelCAD, a program that used the AutoCAD platform. ApparelCAD provided additional tools for patternmakers that AutoCAD did not have.[78] Miller also presented workshops and presentations for academics to encourage the integration of CAD into curricula.[79] The answer to whether it should be offered as a standalone course or as a part of an existing course depends on who would teach it, the availability of funds to purchase CAD hardware and software, and redesign of the curriculum. High costs of industry-specific CAD software usually make the adoption of these technologies difficult. Moreover, instructional materials such as textbooks are limited, thus discouraging CAD adoption by instructors.[80]

In addition to training the future workforce and increasing their software competency, there are other benefits of using CAD for educating apparel designers. In the earlier days of CAD, it was believed to be a replacement of hand drafting and just another tool. However, this tool requires different knowledge and skills,

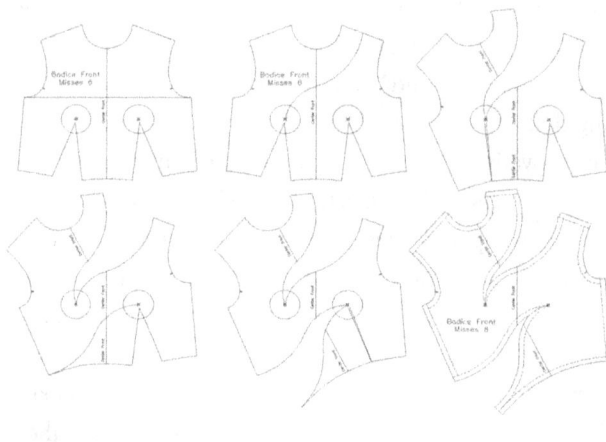

Figure 6.3 A screen shot from ApparelCAD patternmaking software and image of Dr. Phyllis Bell Miller with knit garments created from ApparelCAD patterns.

and complex interactions occur when working with digital technologies. CAD stimulates human creativity by taking care of routine operations, and reducing cognitive load.[81] In manual flat patternmaking, "darts are folded and seams are joined" to create a 3D shape. However, CAD patternmaking requires stronger mental manipulation and spatial visualization skills.[82] This is especially true when working simultaneously between 2D and 3D workspaces, and designing patterns in 2D while placing them around an avatar and draping them to evaluate fit in 3D. A recent study conducted by Baytar (2018) examined how students' interaction, imagination, and problem solving skills were impacted when using 3D simulations across three consecutive class projects in a standalone CAD patternmaking course. Student learning was continuously monitored by questionnaires completed after each project. The results showed that students' visualization skills, which helped with evaluating virtual prototypes, interactions with the 2D/3D CAD patternmaking software, and problem-solving skills gradually improved by the end of the semester.[83]

Future trends pertaining to CAD patternmaking and conclusions

This chapter has focused on the development of 2D and 3D CAD apparel patternmaking technologies, technology acceptance, and applications. Digital technologies and equipment that help generate digital data, such as 3D body scanners, are becoming more powerful, cheaper, and portable. As computer technologies and approaches to production methods continue to evolve, there will be more exciting developments with regards to CAD. For example, Liu and Yuen (2010) proposed two research directions for future garment CAD development as follows: (a) artificial intelligence and machine learning techniques in 3D garment design (e.g., automatically detecting sketches of fashion designer and determining sizing tables and material properties); and (b) real-time collaborative environment for 3D CAD data sharing and manipulation to support interaction among garment product development teams across the globe.[84]

Mass customization is a concept that still has not yet been perfected and matured for the apparel industry. However, advancements in 3D CAD design systems and body shape measurement systems can offer a new level of customization and on-demand manufacturing.[85] For example, in 2017, Amazon received a US patent for on-demand apparel manufacturing to domestically design, produce, and ship garments in hours instead of weeks or months.[86] Development of 3D CAD systems for garment simulation, improving the way a 3D human body and fabrics are modeled in 3D CAD, and creating a better environment for interacting with garment simulations can significantly change the practices in apparel product development.[87] Such new dynamics would also change the needs for skills in the workforce. For example, there would be an increased need for technical designers who can use these technologies to make garments by looking at the fashion drawings.[88] Moreover, these technologies would change how consumers shop for garments. Consumers may design their garments directly by using retailers' CAD systems and send their designs for production.[89] Using improved CAD technologies will shape the apparel industry in the future by providing more integrated and speedy manufacturing opportunities.[90] These strategies can help the industry develop attractive techniques to compete with imports and making re-shoring come true.

Patternmaking Methods for Creating Size-Adjustable Garments

Ellen McKinney *and* Bingyue Wei

In this chapter the authors explore the concept of making a pattern that produces a product that can be adapted by consumers to change the size and/or the style. The chapter commences by detailing the ways garments have been made adjustable and the patternmaking methods that have been used to create size-adjustable garments. The authors explore the types of garments and garment parts that have been made adjustable for both length and circumference, detail the methods that have been implemented for creating adjustability, and note whether each approach resulted in an adaptation that was permanent or reversible. This discussion reveals not only a specific kind of approach to patternmaking but also points to the ability of a patternmaker to address fit issues that exist among customers who have bodies of differing sizes and encourages the reader to consider the challenges of creating an exceptional fit in a different way. Finally, the authors note that exploring the possibilities of adjustable garments has the potential to advance the agenda of sustainability by prolonging the use of clothes that can be adjusted for size over the span of their use. This contribution to the volume introduces a concept that is not specifically dealt with elsewhere in this text, however it does speak to the idea that a given pattern (be it a commercial paper pattern or a pattern hand-drafted from a block or using CAD technology) can be modified by the designer or the user to accommodate specific stylistic or size requirements. This subset of patternmaking (pattern modification) can be explored for both creative intentions as well as to solve more workaday problems of necessity by both home sewers and professional patternmakers.

Introduction

Mechanical engineering professors, Gu, Hashemian, and Nee[1] introduced the concept of *adjustable design*, which is categorized into two types: *design adaptability* and *product adaptability*. "Design adaptability aims at reusing the same 'design' for the creation of different products."[2] For example, Chevrolet Sonic, Chevrolet Cruze, Chevrolet Malibu, and Chevrolet Impala share the same general design (chassis, silhouette, and accessories). "Product adaptability refers to the ability of a product to be adapted to various usages or capabilities."[3] For example, fold-out sofa beds can be reoriented to become a bed. The adjustable garment is one of the applications based on the concept of *product adaptability*. It provides an alternative option to consumers to change size or style without purchasing new products.

Some fashion designers and retailers have provided adjustable/transformable clothing in the market for consumers. Canadian fashion designer Rad Hourani[4] launched his transformation collection at the Fall 2010 New York Fashion Week. Zippers, used as transformational design details, were applied to most of the clothing. A Hourani jacket can be transformed to a T-shirt or a vest by zipping-off the sleeves. Lemuria, by Susanna Gioia,[5] designs and sells transformable clothes by applying soft fabric that is easy to wear in multiple contexts. For example, one dress can be transformed into five different looks including a one-shoulder empire style, a short-sleeved V-neck style, and racer-backed style. HipKnoTies, another adjustable/transformable fashion brand created by Sarash Levenson,[6] provides consumers with convertible garments that can be worn multiple ways for multiple events. For example, the same rayon jersey dress can be worn throughout an entire pregnancy. The tubular garment does not include neck or arm openings. Instead, a clear elastic band is used to hold together any two garment parts to create infinite styles. Garment size is also completely adjustable, depending on how it is fastened. For example, two points along the edge may be secured behind the neck to create a halter style. To adjust the size, the user simply secures excess fabric in the back with another elastic band. The soft rayon jersey fabric drapes around the body from these securing elastic bands.

The purpose of this chapter is to provide the reader an understanding of the ways garments have been made adjustable throughout the years. In particular, we describe patternmaking methods that have been used to create size-adjustable garments that may be changed in order to fit bodies of differing sizes. We also consider how these strategies can be applied in current fashion. Understanding garment adjustability concepts is useful to students, instructors, and designers, who may create size-adjustable garments in the future. There are potential benefits to retailers who may sell garments to a wider range of individuals. Size-adjustability may allow for increased garment lifespans and sustainability within the fashion industry. Means of adjusting garments may provide creative ideas for solving design problems with other types of garments or worn products.

Improving garment fit potential

Knowledge of patternmaking methods to make garments size-adjustable may be useful to apparel designers as they seek to design better-selling garments. The current Western mindset is that garments have a relatively close-to-the-body fit. Human bodies vary in their height and in their proportions, yet there is rarely a mechanism built into the garment to allow measurement change, and thereby, its fit on the body. Research indicates the areas of greatest fit dissatisfaction are overall lower-body as well as specific sites below the waist (hip and thigh).[7] If the garment incorporates the opportunity for the consumer to self-adjust the garment's size in certain "fit problem" areas, then more of that garment may be sold to a wider range of consumers.

Improving apparel sustainability

Knowledge of patternmaking methods to make garments size-adjustable may be useful as a reference for those that would like to design garments with a longer lifespan. Size-adjustable garments may have longer lives of use, increasing their sustainability.[8,9,10] Size-adjustable garments provide a solution for extending the lifespan and utility of garments and eliminating apparel waste due to garments being discarded when the body size changes.[11,12,13] Size-adjustable garments are considered a sustainable alternative in the fashion industry to reduce overall clothing consumption.[14]

Home sewers may also use this information to adapt sewing patterns for size-adjustability as well. Research has indicated that home sewers invest much thought, time, and money into creating garments for themselves.[15] If sewers could adapt their patterns to create garments that could continue to fit despite weight gain or loss, they could then enjoy their investment for a longer lifespan and increase the sustainability of their self-made garments.

Method

As the purpose of this chapter is to uncover ways of making garments adjustable and describing patternmaking methods that have been used to create size-adjustable garments, the following guiding questions were developed:

1. How have garments been made adjustable?
    a. What types of garments have been made adjustable?
    b. What garment parts have been made adjustable?
    c. What dimension is it adjustable?
        i   Circumference?
        ii   Length?
    d. Is the adjustment permanent or reversible?
    e. How were the garments made adjustable?
    f. What pattern changes were made to make the garment adjustable?
2. What are the current and future applications of this knowledge of patternmaking practices to make garments adjustable?

Information sources

The search to discover the ways that garments have been made adjustable began with a search of Google Scholar. Using the search engine, the following terms were searched: adjustable garments, adjustable clothing, changeable clothing, and garment adjustment. The primary source of historical data that appeared was garment patents. The data was sorted by relevance without time period limitation. Over 140 relevant patents were found, which were categorized into two types of patents: garment patents and garment-related patents. An example of the latter is the adjustable garment hanger. The researchers eliminated the garment-related patents, patents for garment adjustability in style only (not in size), and patents repeating an adjustability concept already represented in another patent. A total of twenty-two patents were investigated. Dates of included patents ranged from 1911 to 2014.

While patents are a source of historical information on size-adjustable designs, they do not indicate the actual use or effectiveness of the inventions. It is also possible that there may have been additional garment-adjustability designs in use, which were never patented. To uncover additional ways that garments have been made adjustable, we consulted the Textiles and Clothing

Museum at Iowa State University. This collection includes European couture and designer ready-to-wear, US designs that are innovative or manufactured with high quality, clothing owned or donated by prominent Iowans and those connected to Iowa State University, examples of traditional dress from global cultures, and student and faculty work.[16] As such, it represents a diverse gathering of backgrounds, experiences, and tastes for garments. A total of six adjustable garments were found in the collection and were investigated. We physically reviewed each garment. The collection's digital information record for each of the six garments was downloaded and saved as a PDF document. Dates of included garments ranged from *c.* 1919 to *c.* 1995.

Information exploration approaches

Each document was loaded into Max QDA qualitative data analysis software. To explore the first guiding question and its sub-parts, the following items were coded in each document: garment type, garment adjustment location, dimension adjusted, type of adjustment, and means of adjustment. *Type* of adjustment was whether the adjustment was permanent or reversible. *Means* of adjustment was the way in which the garment dimension was changed. Further, each document was read to understand what changes were made to the pattern and how the garment adjustability functioned. Most documents did not include the garment patterns. However, we were able to infer necessary pattern adjustments based on our collective thirty-plus years of experience with patternmaking. The outcomes of each of these categories are discussed in the findings. Discussion of the necessary patternmaking modifications is incorporated in each area.

To address the second guiding question: "What are the current and future applications of this knowledge of patternmaking practices to make garments adjustable?" the overall findings were considered. Usefulness of the uncovered patternmaking methods and opportunities for future improvements are discussed in the conclusion section.

How garment patterns have been changed to make garments size-adjustable

In this section, we discuss findings relative to the types of garments made size-adjustable and the garment areas that were adjusted. Further, we discuss what types of garments were adjusted for circumference and for length and the permanence of those adjustments. Much analysis and discussion was devoted to uncovering the ways that garments are made adjustable.

Type of garment

Patterns for outerwear, underwear, full-body garments, lower-body garments, upper-body garments, and sleepwear have been modified for size-adjustability. Outerwear patterns included coats and jackets. Undergarment patterns included slips, bras, and supporters. Full-body patterns included dresses and surgical gowns. Lower-body patterns included skirts and pants. Upper-body patterns included vests and shirts.

Part of pattern adjusted

The following parts of patterns have been modified for adjustability: side, shoulders, chest, sleeve, hem, waist, and neck. Methods used in each area are summarized here. Pattern adjustments are discussed in detail in the Means of Adjustment section.

Side. The inventor applied multiple parallel buttons on the side seam of the garment (woman's coat) to achieve a change in the size of the garment.

Shoulders. The adjustable slip straps or fasteners were applied on the shoulder of the garment (dress and bra), to achieve a change in the length of the garment.

Chest. The inventors created the adjustable breast positioning system for the bra, which was located directly on the underbust of the garment. By adjusting the breast positioning system, the volume of each breast cup can be changed.

Sleeve. Buttons were applied on the edge of the sleeves. The length of the sleeves can be extended or reduced by folding the extended length of fabric to the sleeve through the connection between the buttons and the buttonholes.

Hem. The inventors created the adjustable hem systems for pants or skirts. The length can be lengthened or shortened by folding up the extra length of fabric to the inside of the pant or removing one or more selvage-edged bands of the knitted skirt.

Waist. The adjustable waistbands were widely used by the inventors of skirts and pants to allow a change in the circumference.

Neck. The inventor added removable pleats at the neckline of the garment so that the circumference of the neck of the garment can be increased or decreased by loosening or tightening the pleats.

Dimension adjusted

Pattern changes have also been implemented to allow garments to be adjusted in circumference and in length. The following types of garment patterns have been modified for circumference adjustability: vest, maternity supporter, woman's wrap dress, laboratory coat, brassiere, skirt, and pants. The most prevalent adjustability strategy was to apply an adjustable waistband. Zippers and multiple buttons have commonly been added on adjustable waistbands to vary the circumference. The following types of garment patterns have been modified for length adjustability: dress, pant, sleeping garment, and skirt. The common adjustability strategy in changing the length of the garment was to add length along the entire hem that can be extended or reduced by folding or unfolding the extra length of fabric to the inside.

Type of adjustment

Garment adjustments were coded as either reversible or as permanent. Reversible means that the garment can be changed back and forth among multiple sizes or styles. Permanent means that once the garment is changed in size or style, it cannot be changed back. The majority of the adjustments we found were reversible.

Means of adjustment

Adjustable garments typically have some extra fabric incorporated in the design using an extension or tab, which will allow it to be expanded into a larger size. Sometimes a narrow portion of the garment, such as a strap, is extended. Other times, it may be a larger area, such as the entire hem or side seam. Most designs include one or more methods of reducing the excess fabric from the garment length or circumference and one or more methods of securing that reduction. If the garment needs to be made bigger or longer, the excess fabric may be released. Extra fabric can be reduced by using a belt, fold or pleat, gather, or by wrapping. Garment adjustments can be controlled by: loops, buckles, string, hook-and-loop tape, hooks-and-eyes, snaps, buttons, zippers, or other unspecified fasteners. In the case of unspecified fasteners, the inventor simply stated *fastener* in the patent. Sometimes, a specific type of fastener, such as hook-and-loop-tape or a snap could be seen in the illustrations. However, other times it was completely unstated.

A simple way to allow a change in garment dimensions is by creating an extension of a garment part, which is then controlled by some means. One common example is the extra length of a slip strap, exemplified by the Snip-It Slip that was introduced in 1950.[17] The extra length of the strap is folded under and controlled by a buckle, which slides up and down to adjust the length as needed. This feature is commonly used in bras. The necessary pattern design is to simply extend the length of the garment part (in this case the strap) to the maximum desired length. The pattern would also have to be modified to allow application and operation of the desired method of securing the excess fabric (a sliding buckle, in this case). Henderson[18] designed another way to adjust bra strap length. The design was intended for sports bras. The strap pattern was split at the shoulder and extended on each side (front and back). The extensions would overlap to create the desired strap length. The overlap would be held in place with a hook-and-loop tape.

Extensions of tabs may also be used to make garment circumference adjustable. This adjustability strategy has commonly been used in bras. A typical bra[19] has an extension at the center back of the band that encircles the body beneath the breasts. The extensions can be more or less overlapped to vary the circumference of the bra. The amount of overlap is controlled by a series of three single hook-and-eye closures on the extension. Again, the patternmaking for this type of garment adjustability is simple. The designer adds length to achieve the maximum desired circumference. Of course, there are limitations to the practicality of this strategy. As the back width is increased, the straps consequently become farther apart. Further, adjusting the back width does not allow for a change in the spacing or volume of the bra cups.

Michel[20] invented an adjustable bra closure system in which tabs extend out at the center front of the bra. The tabs wrapped over each other and were controlled at the desired location with hook-and-loop tape. In this system, adjusting the front width allows for a change in the spacing of the bra cups on the front of the body. Perhaps, the ideal bra would use a combination of adjustable front closures and adjustable back closure to allow users to customize fit to their own bodies. Such a system might also allow consumers to extend the wear-life of their bras despite weight gain or loss.

The length of a garment may be made adjustable by adding length along the entire hem of a garment. This could work on any type of hemmed garment, for example, pants, skirts, and shirts. A number of approaches have been used to make garment lengths adjustable. Most approaches add length to the hem. The extra length is then usually folded (or sometimes rolled) inside the garment and secured with a range of devices. Designs also vary in the range of adjustability. The number of length variations range from infinite to one or two up or down settings. The number of variations possible is often related to the type of closure used to secure the excess fabric. In other approaches, the extension is removed, either permanently or in a changeable manner such as using a zipper.

Sanchez[21] developed a method of garment hem adjustment in which it could be rolled inside the garment and held in place by one of a series of snap sets. LeTourneau[22] developed a system to adjust trouser length in which excess fabric length was folded up inside the garment and held in place with a series of hook-and-loop tapes inside the pant leg. Howard[23] further developed this hem adjustment design by utilizing hook-and-loop tape stitched to the garment. Howard[24] also provided tabs spaced at intervals adjacent to the interior strip of tape, which could be used to cover any used portions. Ryan[25] further developed this concept into adhesive hook-and-loop fasteners that could be attached without sewing.

A different approach may be used for garment length adjustability when the limbs are enclosed within the garment (e.g. children's pajamas). Extensions may be added to the end of the arm or leg on one side and then folded over the fingertips or toes to overlap the opposite side (Figure 7.1). The overlap is designed to provide the required length. A number of fasteners in increasing distances from the garment edge can be provided to secure the extension in place.[26]

Chung[27] proposed "separable clothing" in which extensions to garment length (including sleeves and skirt and pant hems) could be added and subtracted with zippers, hook-and-loop materials, or snaps. McKee[28] proposed a design in which the garment length could be changed by removing or attaching panels along the edge with a separating zipper. The design also included a lapped application of the zipper to camouflage the lengthening panel. To pattern this type of adjustment, it would be necessary to draft an extension of the hem as a separate piece and then add seam allowances appropriate for the lapped application of a separating zipper or other desired closure.

Biern[29] invented a way to permanently alter the length of a knit skirt (Figure 7.2). Three extra strips of the knit fabric would be attached to the skirt hem by a thread, which, when pulled, would release the fabric strip from the skirt. One, two, or all three extra fabric strips could be removed to easily modify a ready-to-wear knit skirt to the individual's desired length. While most length adjustments are for pants or skirts, Peyser[30] proposed a design for a jacket with adjustable sleeves. It can be worn with the sleeves at wrist length or with the sleeves rolled up to the shoulder to suit the wearer. To secure the sleeve in the

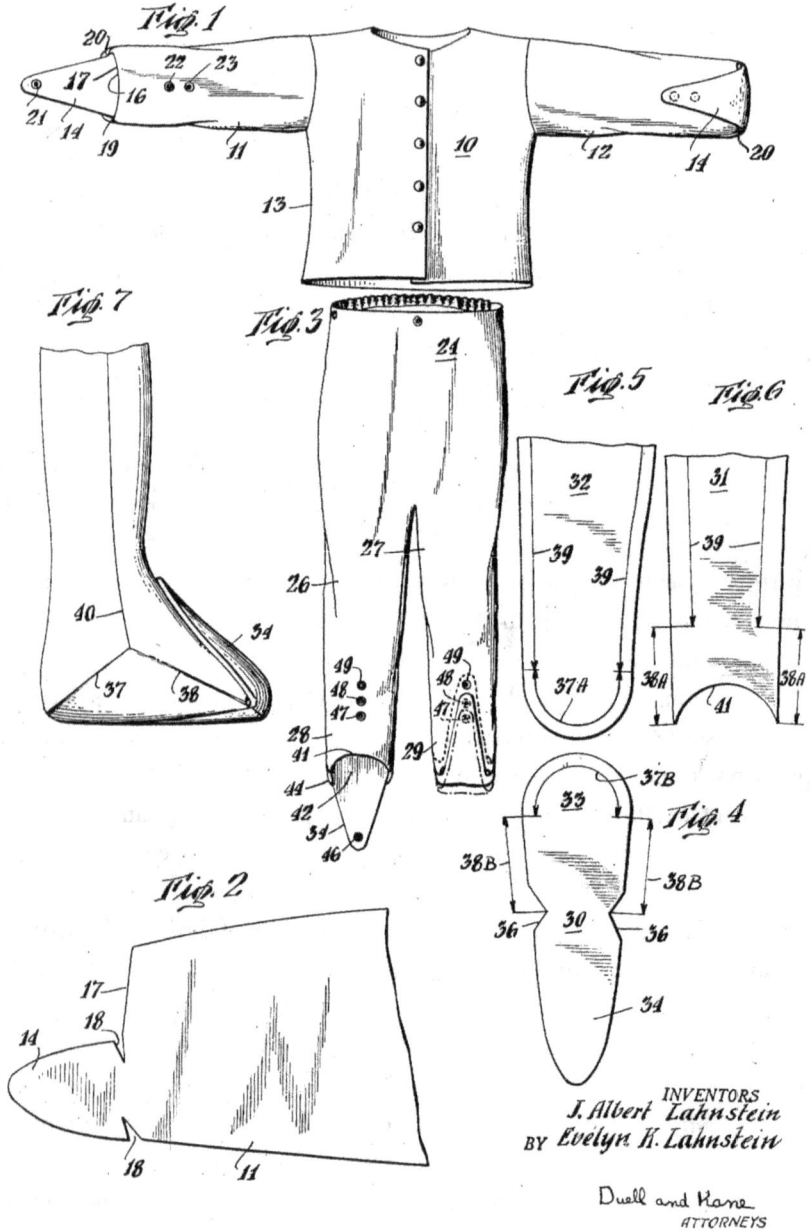

Figure 7.1 A method for lengthening sleeves and pant legs in children's pajamas. Patent 2,705,326. Adjustable Garment. 1955. Joseph A. Lahnstein and Evelyn K. Lahnstein, New York.

Nov. 22, 1955   N. BIERN   2,724,120

LENGTH-ADJUSTABLE READY-TO-WEAR SKIRTS

Filed Jan. 3, 1952   2 Sheets-Sheet 1

FIG. I.

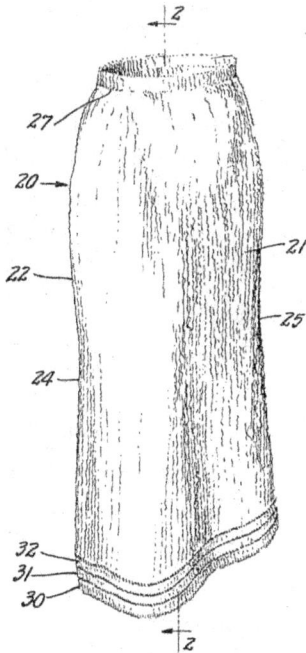

FIG. 2.

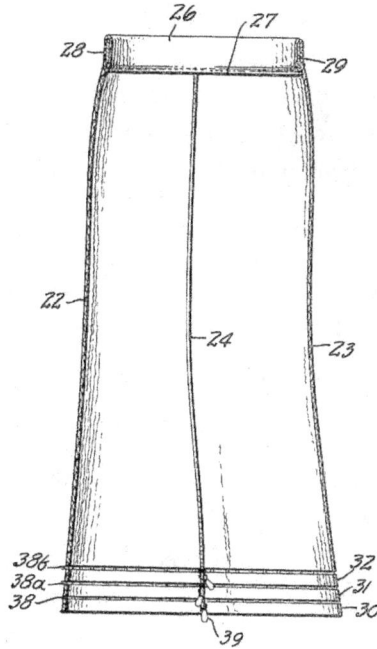

FIG. 3.

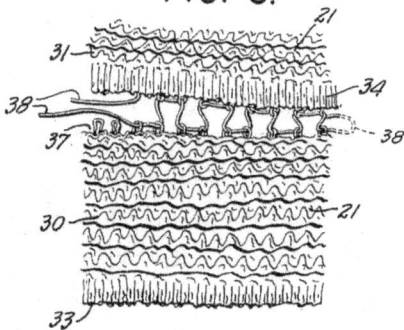

FIG. 4.

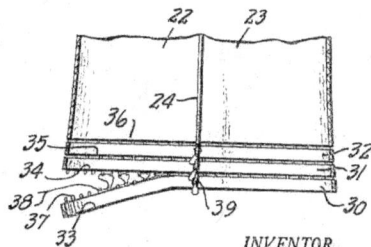

INVENTOR.

NATHANIEL BIERN

BY

Charles W. Morton

ATTORNEY

Figure 7.2 Method for shortening knit skirts. Patent 2,724,120. Length-Adjustable Ready-To-Wear Skirts. Nathaniel Biern, New York, NY. Credit: The United States Patent and Trademark Office.

rolled-up position, a loop on the inside of each sleeve is threaded with an adjustable epaulet on each shoulder of the jacket. The epaulets are fastened by snaps.

Extensions may also be added at a garment's waist to allow the circumference to be adjusted. Skirts may be made adjustable by adding overlapping extensions on the entire length of the skirt. In Kadison's[31] invention, the left and right front skirt edges were extended at center front. When worn, the skirt sides overlapped in front and were held in place by a series of buttons and buttonholes. In this design, the garment circumference is controlled by the waist. As such, as the waist circumference increases, so does the circumference of the entire skirt. This concept is more commonly identified as a "wrap skirt." A similar concept is seen in a Diane Von Furstenberg 1970s wrap dress.[32] In this instance, both left and right fronts are extended, and a long tie is patterned that is sewn onto the end of each extension. The garment is secured at the desired fit by wrapping the ties around the body (the underlapped tie emerges through a slit in the side seam) and securing them at the front waist.

Other waist extension concepts have focused on adjusting only the waist of the garment. Gaines[33] proposed that the waist be adjusted by means of a cord running inside a fabric channel stitched to the interior of the pant waistband. The cord would be pulled and secured with some type of fastener to fix the waistband at the desired circumference. Excess fabric would be gathered onto the cord. This concept is more commonly identified in the current times as a "drawstring waist." Keller[34] further improved upon this drawstring waist concept by making the cord a continuous loop so it could not become lost inside the waistband, and providing openings to tighten the drawstring at the front, back, or either side. The wearer would pull the excess string out of the hole of his/her choice and then tie it in a knot to secure the pants. In both of these concepts, the patternmaker makes the pant waist at least as wide as the hip and then creates an additional pattern piece for the drawstring channel.

Cantil[35] proposed to allow for the waist of trousers to expand by having a single deep pleat on each side of the waistband, continuing down the trouser leg. Stylistically and pattern-wise, this is similar to a basic pleated trouser style. What made it adjustable was that the pleat was held in place by a large hook and then a series of large eyes. Lampowitz[36] also proposed deep pleats, which were held in place with a button tab (Figure 7.3). This system additionally included elastic inside the waistband to control the fit. In a maternity support band sold some time prior to 1972,[37] waist adjustment is provided through lacing at the side of the garment.

June 12, 1956   P. LAMPKOWITZ   2,749,556

ADJUSTABLE ELASTIC WAIST FOR TROUSERS AND OTHER GARMENTS

Filed Feb. 12, 1954   2 Sheets—Sheet 1

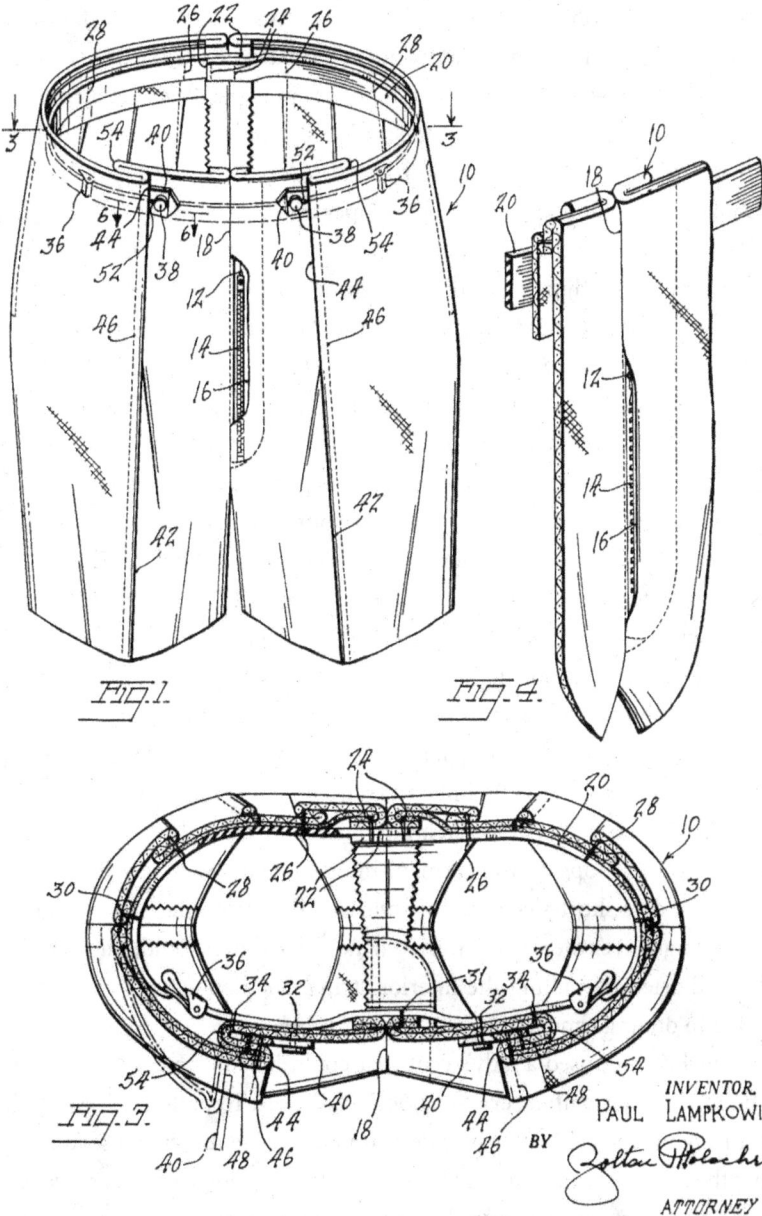

Figure 7.3 Method for waist circumference adjustment. Patent 2,749,556. Adjustable elastic waist for trousers and other garments. Paul Lampkowitz, New York, NY.

Reardon[38] proposed a triangular extension over a pant fly with a hook-and-loop or multiple button closures to allow the expansion of the garment at the waist. The triangular extension could be added to the pattern of the overlapping side. In a 2009, patent assigned to Destination Maternity Corporation, Gardner[39] describes an invention for an adjustable waist. This design allows for several inches of expansion of the waist. It does not allow extension of the lower portions of the garment (as with the wrap skirt). The main concept is that a triangular panel is sewn behind a zipper. Thus, the zipper may be more or less unzipped to control the waist circumference. Furthermore, there is a long tab with a buttonhole on the end of one side of the zipper opening and four buttons on the opposite side, allowing the wearer to secure the opening at the desired position. To use this type of adjustment, the pattern could be drafted as usual for the desired skirt or pant style, then the patternmaker would simply have to make additional patterns for the triangular panel and the tab.

Another waist adjustment strategy seen in garments is to simply pattern the waist larger than needed and adjust the fit with a belt. For example, belts are commonly seen across the back waists of men's pants to adjust fit. One example is the late-nineteenth century vest included in our analysis.[40] In this instance, the patternmaker would add two patterns for the left and right belts and the means necessary to attach the belt buckle. A similar adjustability feature was found on a woman's white cotton lab coat. The belt could be adjusted by placing the button on one extension in one of three buttonholes on the opposite extension.[41] To control circumference, Erickson[42] proposed a drawstring in a casing sewn over the back waist of a shirt. The casing has an opening at the center back. The strings can be pulled to the desired amount and secured by tying in place.

Keller[43] patented a system for creating removable pleats by drawing a string though a series of loops on the garment interior (Figure 7.4). The invention is demonstrated on a short-sleeve raglan style top. The raglan sleeve was patterned with extra length over the shoulder. The garment neckline, shoulder, and armhole could be adjusted by pulling the interior string. Such an adjustment could be applicable to other garment areas, such as waistlines.

Padernacht[44] proposed a lady's coat that could be adjusted at the side seam and underarm seam with a series of hooks-and-eyes. To pattern such a design, extensions would be added to the side seam and sleeve underarm seam. When wearing the garment with minimal extension the extensions would lap over each other and be secured in the desired position with a series of hooks-and-eyes.

Stuart et al.[45] proposed a way to lengthen the pants portion of children's all-in-one footed pajamas (Figure 7.5). To the garment pattern, extra length was

Jan. 15, 1957   C. KELLER   2,777,130

ADJUSTABLE SIZE GARMENTS

Filed June 14, 1954   2 Sheets—Sheet 1

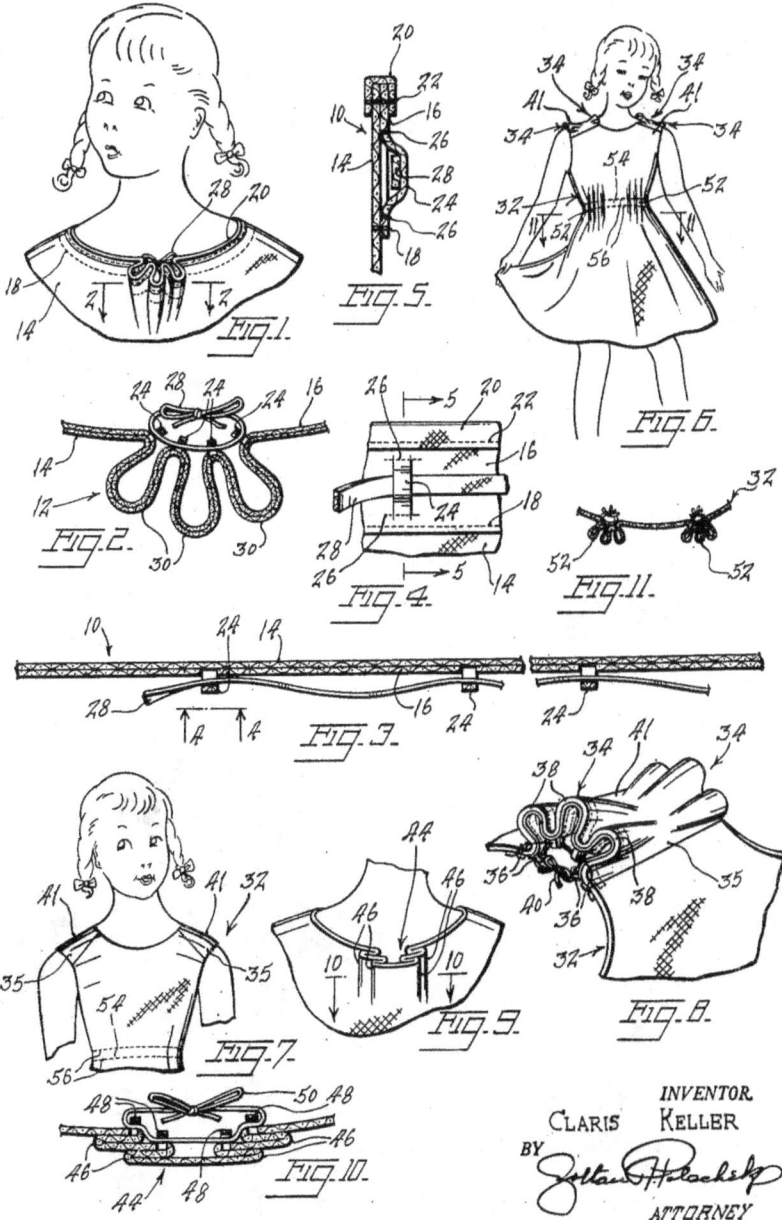

Figure 7.4 Method for changing the neck and shoulder dimensions of an upper body garment. Patent 2,777,130. Adjustable size garments. Claris Keller, Union, NJ.

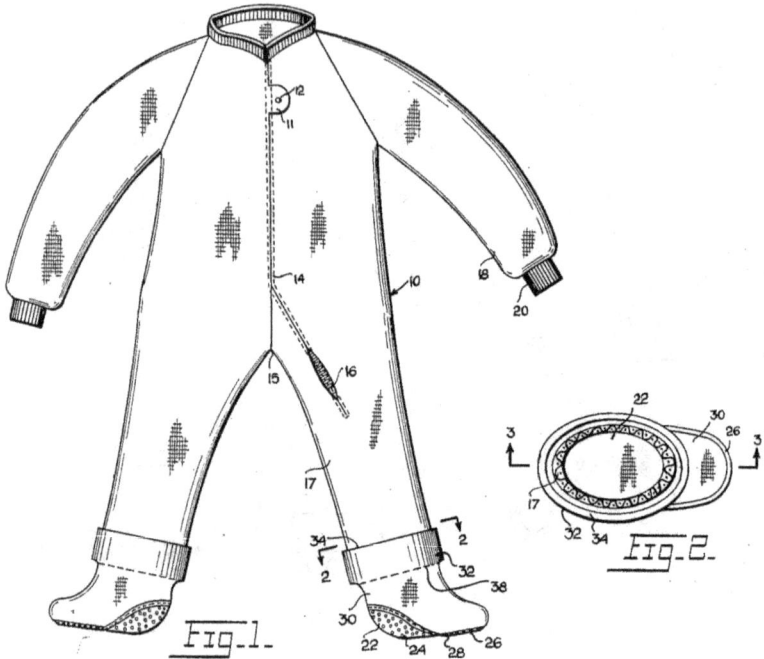

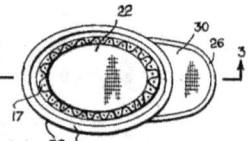

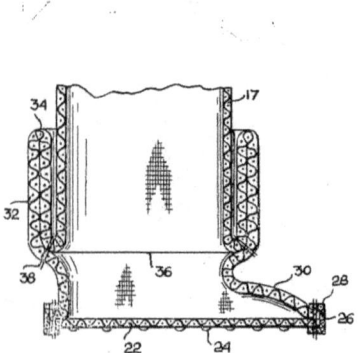

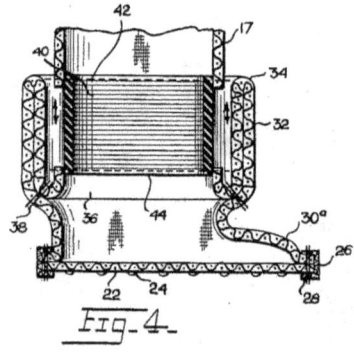

Sept. 29, 1959   A. STUART ET AL   2,905,944

ADJUSTABLE SLEEPING GARMENT

Filed May 1, 1958

INVENTORS
ALLAN   STUART
HAROLD   DRACHMAN
BY

ATTORNEY

Figure 7.5 A method for lengthening pant legs in children's pajamas. Patent 2,905,944. Adjustable Sleeping Garment. 1959. Alan Stuart, Roslyn Heights, and Harold Drachman, Forest Hills, NY.

added in the leg of the pant. This extra length was then folded and stitched into a horizontal pleat on the exterior of the garment above the ankle, resembling a cuff. As the child grew taller, the stitching could be removed to release the pleat and lengthen the leg portion of the pajamas. This type of garment adjustment is easy to pattern; however, is reversible only if the garment owner can re-sew the fold. This type of garment length adjustability is commonly seen in current times inside the sleeves and pant legs of children's winter outerwear.

Conclusion: current and future applications of historical patternmaking practices to make garments adjustable

Historically, garment patterns have been adjusted in a number of ways to allow the garment to be size-adjustable. Garment size-adjustability is an application of the product adaptability type of adjustable design.[46] Garment size-adjustability has the potential to increase the lifespan of garments that would otherwise become unusable due to body-size change. Thus, size-adjustable garments may decrease apparel consumption and improve sustainability.[47,48] Further, size-adjustable garments may allow more consumers to obtain well-fitting garments. Human bodies vary widely in the proportions of body parts.[49] This makes it difficult for many customers to obtain garments that fit their proportions. Further, bodies that have the same circumference measurements (e.g. bust, waist, and hip) may vary in the distribution of that measurement in the front or back of the body, creating a need for a differently shaped garment.[50] As bodies gain weight, there are differences in where the weight is carried, magnifying differences in body shapes and therefore necessitating differences in garment shapes to fit those bodies.[51] Lack of appropriate sizes is a major source of clothing dissatisfaction for plus-size women.[52] If apparel manufacturers could include ways to adjust the garment size and shape in the garment design, more consumers could more easily obtain well-fitting garments.

Applications of patternmaking size-adjustability methods to garment types and locations

One area not well addressed in terms of patternmaking for garment size-adaptability is the hip. This is unfortunate given that lower-body fit is one of women's major areas of fit concern.[53] This concern indicates that current sizing systems do not provide good fit for all of the variations of waist-to-hip proportions found among human bodies. Providing desired fit in the hip and waist, particularly for bifurcated garments is a complicated undertaking of getting the correct combinations of body measurements, body shape, and desired ease.[54] If garments had hip adjustability, such issues could more easily be resolved, providing more customers with well-fitting garments.

Applications of patternmaking size-adjustability methods to garment circumference and length

We found a number of methods to adapt garment patterns to make garments adjustable in both circumference and length. However, fewer options were found for adjusting other overall body circumference areas.

Circumference adjustments were seen primarily in the waist and chest areas. Waists were adjusted through the addition of extensions, which could be closed to varying degrees with a range of closure types. Waists were also adjusted by gathering excess fabric with a belt or drawstring. All of these patternmaking strategies for garment size-adjustability are successful and should continue in current and future use. The ability to adjust the waist circumference of a garment increases the chances of selling ready-to-wear garments to a wider range of consumers with varying waist-to-hip proportions. A consumer simply has to find a garment that fits his/her hips, and then may adjust the waist to fit. These waist-adjustability strategies are reversible in nature, making it possible to continue to wear a garment during weight gain or loss. Many garments, such as skirts and pants are anchored to the body at the waist circumference. It is therefore, an important area for garment size-adjustability because if a skirt or pant is too large to stay at the waistline, it cannot be worn. There are limitations to the usefulness of waist size-adjustability without corresponding hip size or total garment size-adjustability, in terms of an overall increase in body circumference.

Concepts were seen for adjusting garment circumference at the hip through wrap skirts or dresses with large center front extensions. Yet, no historical methods were found for changing circumference of pants at the hip area. Further, wrap designs are limited in their scope of adjustability to the front. As the back does not adjust, the side seam can quickly be moved out-of-alignment. Skirts may still fit and function fairly well with side seam misalignment. However, for upper-body and full-body garments, side seam alignment can cause fit problems of the armscye and sleeve. The one method found for side seam adjustment used a very large number of hooks and eyes. Lower cost and easier to use strategies are needed for whole-body circumference adjustments. This is an area ripe for development in future patternmaking research. If the whole-body circumference could be more easily adjusted, consumers could adjust the garment parts needed to make the garment fit their particular proportions. This way, more consumers would be able to obtain well-fitting garments. Further, consumers would achieve a longer wear life with their garments, as they could make the garment smaller or larger as needed for weight gain or loss.

Adjustments to garment chest circumference were seen primarily in bras and were accomplished through overlapping extensions of the bra band. Such concepts have been long-standing in use and may continue as a garment size adjustability method. The fit of the chest band is important for holding the bra in the correct location and in turn, functioning as intended. Chest band extensions have the potential to increase garment wear life through size-adjustment and also to increase garment sales. Bras with adjustable bands allow consumers within a small range of cup size to band size proportions to purchase the same size bra. Methods were not found to adjust bra cup size. This is an area for future potential bra patternmaking innovation. Adjustability in bra cup size is important for those not served by the current sizing system, as well as for body-size changes. Bras are sold in a limited number of bra size and band combinations. Some consumers are not served by the current bra sizing system because their breast cup size is smaller or larger than what is available on the market with the bra band size that fits her body.[55] Further, many women experience breast volume changes with their monthly menstrual cycle.[56] Women that are lactating experience changes in breast volume multiple times per day, as their breasts produce and deliver milk to their babies.[57] Wearing a bra cup size that is too small for swollen breasts is painful. Adjustable cup sizes would allow women to obtain the fit they need to have comfortably supported breasts at all times.

Many strategies were found for making garments size-adjustable in length. Length adjustability was primarily created by patterning an extension of the entire garment width at the hem. The length was controlled either through a removable horizontal pleat running the garment's circumference, by folding and securing excess fabric inside the garment, or by removing (either permanently or temporarily) lower garment extensions. Strategies to increase garment length are particularly applicable in the childrenswear market. Children becoming taller is an undeniable fact of life. Garments that may increase in length as the child grows certainly have the potential to increase garment lifespan, reduce waste, and improve sustainability. Upon reaching adulthood, the need for increases in garment length typically stops. Therefore, length adjustments are less of a concern for this market. However, garments with length adjustability (particularly for floor-length garments, such as pants or gowns) could increase garment sales. Consumers vary widely in height for their size, as evidenced by the need for petite, regular, and tall-sized clothing. If consumer-friendly length-adjustability methods were incorporated into more ready-to-wear garments, retailers may increase their garment sales, while carrying a smaller number of sizes. A number of the strategies seen within the historic garment patents for controlling garment length by securing the excess fabric inside the garment would create unsightly bulk. Care is necessary in selecting the method for securing the fabric. Apparel designers should investigate ways to incorporate control of garment length either through removable hem portions or through horizontal pleats. The challenge with removable hem portions is that it usually creates a horizontal line or lines at that garment part. Designers may experiment with ways to make this less noticeable or more aesthetically pleasing. The removable horizontal pleat is a patternmaking strategy for garment adjustment seen in childrenswear but rarely for adult apparel. For lined pants, this strategy could be easily incorporated. Designers may also consider how removeable horizontal pleats may be aesthetically incorporated into adult garments.

Garment length adjustability was also found in strategies for strap length adjustment. Strap patterns were elongated and then the adjustment was controlled through folding under with a sliding buckle or overlapping extensions and securing with a closure. Such adjustments provide size-adaptability for the upper-body. Human bodies vary in upper-body length proportions. As such, the ability to adjust strap length is a useful and important size-adjustability strategy, allowing more consumers to purchase the same garment. Upper-body garment length adjustability strategies are also relevant for the childrenswear market as they may allow the garment length to increase in accordance with a child's height. Interestingly, these upper-body length adjustment strategies were primarily seen only in women's undergarments. Designers may investigate how these strategies may be incorporated into a wider range of garments so that people of varying upper-body proportions can obtain better fit. This adjustability is particularly important for garments with a seamline that should be correctly aligned on a body landmark, such as an empire seam. The empire seam should sit directly under the bust. However, if the upper-portion of the garment is too short, the seam may instead fall in the middle of the bust. Integrating upper-garment length-adjustability into childrenswear would also improve garment wear life by enabling the upper-part of the garment to increase in length as a child grows.

Opportunities for future applications and improvements of patternmaking size-adjustability methods

Many historical methods for creating patterns for size-adjustability were found. Most of these concepts continue to have applicability today and into the future. There is potential for these concepts to be applied in different garment locations or for different markets. Means of adjusting garments may be applied to solving design problems with other types of garments or worn products as well. Areas where options for garment size-adjustability are lacking still exist and represent opportunities for future garment patternmaking innovations.

Home Sewing Transformed: Changes in Sewing Pattern Formats and the Significance of Social Media and Web-Based Platforms in Participation

Addie Martindale

This chapter brings the story of sewing and patternmaking communities into the twenty-first century by exploring how the internet has contributed to a resurgence in home sewing, interpersonal exchanges of information about garment creation, and the impact of digital technologies on sewing pattern format and dissemination. While Chapters 1, 2, and 5 all discuss ways in which sewing and patternmaking information were shared in the nineteenth and twentieth centuries (namely through in-person interactions and printed texts), this contribution explores the impact of digital communication on home sewing, patternmaking, and pattern acquisition. Addie Martindale explores how the internet provides easy, twenty-four-hours-a-day access to free and low cost sewing and patternmaking training, inspiration sources, and a community of makers willing to lend support at any time of day. The author expands the discussion of community and information sharing by exploring the phenomenon of independent pattern designers who largely sell and disseminate their patterns in PDF format. Martindale notes that these small independent businesses have changed how patterns may be accessed (from home, via digital download) and have also created the opportunity for relationships to flourish between patternmakers and home sewers, as many independent pattern designers are actively engaged and involved with their customers and provide pattern support for technical issues and answers to questions about their patterns. Thus, this focal point within the chapter provides a modern take on "The Tailor's Voice" by demonstrating how modern pattern drafters strive to share their innovations and refinements with the public at large.

Home sewing is any type of sewing that is completed in the home as an activity to create apparel, crafts, or home décor.[1] Home sewing was once an essential task for most women.[2] Home sewing has been transformed many times throughout history by economic and technological changes with the most significant happening in the nineteenth and twentieth centuries.

The home sewing industry is the sewing-related segment of the overall craft industry including fashion sewing, quilting, and sewing for home décor. This industry sells fabric, notions, equipment, and instructional materials such as patterns and books to home sewers.[3] For apparel sewing, home sewers typically require a pattern, fabric, and related notions (e.g. buttons, zippers) to complete the garment. A home sewing pattern is a "guide for cutting pieces of a garment sold by a company."[4]

In the nineteenth century, home sewing was impacted by both the introduction of a variety of sewing publications and commercial sewing patterns and the sewing machine.[5] The availability of commercial sewing patterns allowed women to sew more complicated garments without advanced training and the sewing machine greatly reduced the time needed for garment construction.[6] Commercial sewing patterns that women could purchase to sew garments for themselves and their families began to emerge on the market in the 1860s.[7] These patterns were initially sold in general stores, where women would traditionally buy their fabric, or by mail-order. Four main sewing pattern companies were established around that time, thereby creating the home sewing pattern industry: Butterick, McCalls, Vogue, and Simplicity. These companies are still selling patterns today in fabric stores and online.

In the twentieth century, home sewing was significantly impacted by the availability of ready-to-wear clothing, although its availability was quite limited until 1920. The increased availability of ready-to-wear slowly began to cause a decline in home sewing, as women of higher income levels were able to purchase ready-made clothing instead of sewing it.[8] Despite this, many women continued to sew throughout the 1960s and 1970s due to the high cost of ready-to-wear and concerns with quality.[9] The gradual price decrease of ready-to-wear finally reached a critical point by the middle of the 1980s when it became more expensive to sew clothing than to buy it.[10]

Here in the twenty-first century, the technological advancement that has most impacted home sewing is the internet. The internet provides easy access to free and low-cost sewing training to anyone with an internet connection, thus lowering entry barriers to home sewing participation. The internet has also changed the landscape of the home sewing industry. Numerous online businesses selling fabrics, patterns, and notions have emerged. This has impacted the format in which sewing patterns are delivered to consumers. The internet serves as a tool to help the home sewer decide which of an ever-widening array of sewing patterns to purchase and use. We have also seen changes in who has the ability to design and sell sewing patterns, and the relationship that the patternmaker has with the home sewer. All of these factors have worked together to support a resurgence in home sewing. The purpose of this chapter is to provide the reader with information regarding the resurgence in home sewing, the impact that the internet has had on the growth in participation, and changes we are seeing in the home sewing industry, particularly in sewing pattern format and development.

Information sources

This chapter weaves together information from three main sources to help the reader understand the resurgence in home sewing, the impact that the internet has had on the growth in participation, and changes we are seeing in the home sewing industry, particularly in sewing patterns. Existing literature, both academic and industry-related, forms the foundation of the discussion. Findings of my recent study of women's current sewing motivations and practices illuminate the impact of the internet on home sewing participation as well as home sewers' pattern preference and use.[11] Finally, I collected new data for this chapter on independent designers of PDF print-at-home home sewing patterns including their training and motivations for participating in this market.

Method: study of women's sewing motivations and practices

One of the pieces of qualitative research discussed in this chapter was part of a larger grounded theory[12] study regarding the reasons why women choose to sew clothing for themselves. The study used a purposive sample of fifteen English-speaking female home sewers from ethnically diverse backgrounds who were recruited from Facebook sewing groups. Semi-structured in-depth interviews were conducted with each of the women to ask questions regarding the benefits received and reasons for their personal garment sewing. The transcribed interview audio from the fifteen interviews was analyzed. The present research focuses on findings within two themes from the larger study: cognitive investment, and empowerment.

Method: independent sewing pattern designers

The second qualitative research question discussed in this chapter took a netnographic approach[13] to seek to learn more about the independent sewing pattern designers. To get a list of designers, I chose to use a popular independent sewing pattern designer list from a large independent PDF pattern sewing fan group with over 80,000 members.[14] The list contained over 200 independent pattern designers that sold patterns in PDF format online. All designers who did not have business websites with "About" pages were eliminated because there was not sufficient data for analysis of these designers. Many of the designers on the list sold their patterns exclusively through their Etsy store, which does not provide much information about the designers. Sixty-one of the designers had business websites with "About" pages containing information regarding the designer that included information pertaining to his or her educational background or patternmaking training and motivations for designing sewing patterns. Each of the "About" pages was coded for recurring themes that related to educational background or training and motivation for designing sewing patterns.

Background: the home sewing participation resurgence

Since the last decade of the twentieth century into the beginning of the twenty-first century, there has been a resurgence in home sewing participation. This renewed interest is part of a resurgence in handcraft participation that has occurred as part of the overall do-it-yourself movement which started in the 1990s.[15] Increased sewing participation has been connected to changes in the stability of the economy. The renewed interest in sewing started to see growth around the time of the dot.com crash when many women found themselves out of work and renegotiating their careers. Then after 9/11, sewing participation interest further grew as did domestic crafts altogether as individuals began to desire activities that brought them closer to home.[16] It has been presented that the renewed interest in domestic crafts was further fueled by a frugality-based ethos that began when the US economy worsened in the late 2000s as a result of the great recession.[17] The downturn of the economy resulted in lost jobs and a rise in unemployment. These factors in turn caused individuals to have more available time to participate in sewing and created a desire to be productive and save money.[18]

Although the economy's impact on the renewed interest in craft cannot be denied, there have been other societal reasons that have sparked women to return to sewing especially since, in many cases, the cost to make an item is more than the cost to purchase it.[19] Many women in the late 1990s and early 2000s found themselves overeducated, underpaid, and in a cubicle. These women sought ways to express their creativity and find personal fulfillment that was not found at work.[20] Handcraft became a way to deal with frustrating bosses, unfulfilling jobs, and boring work environments.[21] These women found themselves working to produce nonmaterial products all day and felt that, at the end of the day, they had nothing to show for their work.[22] Participating in handcrafts as a hobby provided a creative outlet, an escape from their monotonous lives, and a way to make tangible objects that they could be proud of.[23] The resurgence has also been attributed to a do-it-yourself shift in consumer ethos to have more control over the consumption process.[24]

The growth of the sewing resurgence is not estimated to stop anytime soon. There are steady growth predictions through the end of 2019.[25] American sewing industry professionals have estimated that 20 percent of all US households are now participating in some form of home sewing.[26] These different types of sewing include fashion sewing of garments and accessories, quilting, home décor, and other craft sewing.[27] The Craft and Hobby Association of the United Kingdom found that in 2014, 3.5 million people in the UK were involved in making their own clothes.[28] With the most interesting finding revealing that many of these home sewers were new to the practice of sewing.[29] It has also been revealed that the growth in sewing interest is tied to an individual's desire to mend and upcycle clothing that he or she already owns.[30] An increase in home sewing participation has also been credited to the popular television shows *Project Runway* and *The British Sewing Bee* which increased awareness and sparked interest in the activity.[31] In addition, the popularity of sewing blogs and the sharing of sewn items on social media has been given much of the credit.[32]

The impact of the internet on twenty-first century home sewing participation

The internet has been noted as a key factor in the growth of all types of craft participation including sewing. Some have argued that the internet holds the craft world together. The internet removes all geographic barriers and allows individuals from all over the world to connect.[33] Online craft forums, websites, Facebook groups, and blogs provide ways to communicate ideas and share stories.[34] This social engagement that craft participation provides online has been identified as a significant factor that has drawn individuals to make instead of purchase items.[35] It also offers crafters, as well as artists, new ways to collaborate and contribute to larger works.[36] Various craft sharing websites for all types of crafts have opened up places for people to share what they are making and see what others are making as well.[37]

Findings regarding home sewers' use of the internet

While exploring women's motivations to sew, the important role that the internet played on women's sewing participation was revealed.[38] All of the women expressed that the internet had an impact on their continued sewing participation. Several of the women exposed that it was women sharing their sewing projects on the internet that inspired them to learn to sew.

Lowering home sewing participation entry barriers: easy internet access to sewing training

The internet provides easy access to free and low-cost sewing training to anyone with an internet connection, thus lowering entry barriers to home sewing participation. The impact of the internet on interest in home sewing can be found in the participation of individuals in online platforms and the growth in availability of online classes and tutorials. These internet-based learning opportunities are much more cost-effective than in-person classes and offer those wanting to sew low-cost or no-cost learning opportunities.[39] For example, Craftsy.com, which caters to all types of crafts from sewing to baking, offers over 150 sewing classes that start at $14.99 and can be viewed an unlimited number of times by the purchaser.[40] Other online sites, such as PatternReview.com[41] and BurdaStyle.com[42] are exclusively tailored to fashion sewing including garments and accessories. Both of these sites offer a wide range of low cost garment sewing classes that start at only $7.00 a class, while they also offer many free tutorials. Each of these sites provides free membership and also offers their potential members a free class or pattern when they sign up.[43] Each of these platforms has a very large community of sewers. PatternReview.com has close to half-a-million members[44] and BurdaStyle.com[45] has close to one-and-a-half million members. Each of these sites gains hundreds of members a day and BurdaStyle.com reported their online community membership increased 47 percent in 2012 alone.[46] Users of these sites interact with other users by sharing their sewing projects, recommending patterns, sharing tips, and commenting on other users' projects.

In addition to sewing websites, there are a plethora of personal sewing blogs that share free advice on sewing with their readers. Most blogs are run by sewing enthusiasts who share what they are making and typically provide instructions and tips for their readers. A Google search for sewing blogs generated over a million options that sewers can visit to learn sewing skills for no cost. Popular sewing blogs have reported having close to a half-a-million page views a month.[47]

Sewing knowledge

All of the women in the study indicated that use of the internet was essential to their process of learning to sew. A few even started their sewing with a Google search, as evidenced by the comment, "I would just kind of Google 'beginning sewing project's or . . . basically [a] beginning sewing project, that's what I started with." Even the women who did not initially learn how to sew using the internet shared that it was used frequently to advance their sewing skills. When discussing the theme of sewing knowledge, the women shared the specific web-based platforms most frequently used: YouTube, videos, Facebook sewing groups, sewing blogs, and social media.

YouTube videos were frequently mentioned by the women as a preferred way to learn needed sewing skills. The women expressed that whatever technique they needed for the project they would search for videos to teach them. One participant expressed after being given a sewing machine she "just started watching YouTube videos." The importance of YouTube was captured well in this comment: "When I come across a problem, I go to YouTube. YouTube is my best friend when it comes to sewing."

Facebook groups were used frequently by all of the women with many of them sharing they were active within multiple groups. The women disclosed that they used the groups to find help in solving sewing problems and to improve needed skills. The women shared remarks similar to "They are very very good for troubleshooting" and "It's a lot easier than having to Google tips." One participant expressed how she used the groups this way, "I like the Facebook groups because they're there, willing to help you with it if you have any issues." The women especially liked that Facebook groups allowed them access to assistance from sewers all over the world, which provided for twenty-four-hour assistance. For example, one sewer noted, "I know that in any of my sewing groups, someone's up and sewing at all times. So, you can post and have an answer in like ten minutes." While another shared "You can literally pull up, type a question, and somebody is gonna be there to answer."

All of the women indicated that they followed sewers on Instagram and Pinterest, and read sewing blogs to attain or improve their sewing skills. Two of the women even indicated looking at sewing blogs is what made them want to learn to sew. The blogs provided them an opportunity to gain sewing information and interact with other sewers by commenting on a blog post. Instagram was revealed to be mainly used to watch what sewing peers were sewing and to share their "makes." The use of Pinterest was also discussed; sewers utilized it primarily to find sewing patterns and instruction links. One woman who shared how she used Pinterest said, "On Pinterest, they have these little pictures, and then right next to it is like a basic pattern kind of concept."

Sewing together: the internet as a community building and decision-making tool

The internet has changed the way that sewers connect and has affected how they make their sewing-related purchases. The internet serves as a tool to help the home sewer decide which of an ever-widening array of sewing patterns, fabrics, and notions they can now access to purchase and use. Pinterest, Instagram, and Facebook have also proven to be popular in the sewing decision process as well as places where the sewer can become part of a community.[48] A search on Pinterest for sewing tutorials revealed countless options of projects that sewers can choose from, ranging from beginner to advanced apparel sewing and pattern drafting. Instagram is a place where sewers can look at the photos of other sewers and share their own photos as well. Sewers can find other sewers to connect with using hashtags. The popular social media hashtag "#sewing" currently has over two million posts on Instagram alone. Sewers use Facebook somewhat differently from other platforms by forming and joining Facebook groups. These groups become sewing communities for sharing projects and asking questions regarding sewing problems. Many Facebook sewing groups, like Sewing Inspiration and Tutorials, have over 45,000 members.[49]

Sense of community

The internet provided these women so much more than a place to learn to sew and share their sewing achievements. A sense of community among sewing participants was a theme expressed by all of the women interviewed. Participation in online communities allowed the women to connect with others across the globe who enjoyed the same hobby of sewing.

Each participant had a slightly different experience but the involvement of all the women in the study in online communities positively influenced their sewing. Many women commented how the online community kept them participating in sewing. "I've made some pretty good friends all around the world that share the same interest as me and I can bounce ideas off of and there's just a lot of support." For most of the women, these online communities served as their primary source of support related to sewing. Several women disclosed how they did not personally know anyone who sewed, commenting "I don't know people personally who do sew," while others shared how their in-person friends were not interested in sewing. One woman said, "I'm pretty young; my friends don't have any interest in sewing." These groups provided the women with opportunities to interact with like-minded people with whom they would not have otherwise interacted. For example, one woman said, "I've been able to meet a lot of people who share the same passion for sewing and creating as I do." Although for some of the participants the group involvement was just sewing-related support, many of the women in these groups had found a circle of very close friends who provided support beyond sewing. One woman explained: "I think some of the best friendships I have are through the sewing community. So many questions get answered. I get to answer so many questions. I feel useful. As a stay-at-home mom, I go crazy with no adult interaction."

Selecting what to sew

Interactions and observations online were found to impact what the women chose to sew. This impact came from three sources. The first was the observations of what others were sewing and posting about. The second was the recommendations from other sewers. The last factor impacting what they sewed was reading online pattern reviews.

For many of the women, the most frequent inspiration for making a garment came from their observations of their sewing peers' garments. The women used several sources to acquire this information but social media including Facebook played a key role. The women discussed how they would "browse for pictures online, like on Pinterest or Instagram." The women disclosed that they looked for peer sewers to express positive sewing experiences. A garment became more interesting for the women to sew the more they saw their peers successfully sewing the garment. One woman shared that a factor in her selection of a garment to sew was, "I'll see a lot of versions of a pattern sewn up on Instagram." Another woman explained, "I get a lot of ideas looking at what others have sewn and the fabrics they've used." Peer influence also came from receiving recommendations. One woman discussed a garment she had made, saying, "I have a friend who sews as well, and she said she really liked it, so I went with it." The sharing on social media of photos of what others were sewing also influenced these women's selections of what to sew. All of the women read sewing pattern reviews, but a few relied heavily on pattern reviews written by their peers reading many pattern reviews before they purchased.

Home sewing patterns in the twenty-first century: the impact of the internet

Where once sewing patterns were only available in a store or by mail order, they can now easily be purchased over the internet. Sewers now have more choices in the availability of sewing patterns that include commercial sewing patterns and independent designer sewing patterns. In the United States, commercial sewing patterns are produced by the companies Butterick, McCalls, Vogue, and Simplicity and are commonly referred to by sewers as the big four. The majority of these patterns only come in a hard copy paper pattern that can be used to cut out a garment right away. With independent designer sewing patterns, a sewer can choose from thousands of companies that typically only sell their patterns online in a print at home format.

Changes in home sewing patterns: format and content

Print at home portable file document independent sewing patterns

The print at home portable file document (PDF) has impacted the format in which sewing patterns are delivered to consumers and the relationship that the patternmaker has with the home sewer. PDF sewing patterns are quite different from traditional commercial paper sewing patterns. With commercial patterns, the designers of the patterns are not easily accessed by the consumer. Independent PDF patterns are different in that the designer is available to answer questions and this availability is part of the selling point for the pattern. They make themselves available to their customers via email and Facebook groups.

The PDF sewing pattern format allows home sewers instant access to the patterns they have selected because the tiled format can be printed on home printers. This capability allows home sewers access to new sewing patterns at any time of the day. PDF sewing patterns can be accessed immediately by anyone with a home computer, tablet, or smartphone and a home printer. This technology provides home sewers with access to sewing patterns anytime of the day or night. There is no waiting for a pattern to be shipped or going to the fabric store to purchase a pattern.

A comparison of commercial patterns and independent sewing designers PDF patterns revealed several key differences. The independent (indie) designers' instructions read more like an electronic book (eBook) of the sewing process that is filled with pictures or illustrations of each sewing step accompanied by in-depth instructions that traditional fold out paper pattern instructions do not include. The indie designer included measurements and cutting instructions in both metric and standard measurement to accommodate sewers around the world. The instructions discuss each step of the sewing process providing many details for each step. Unlike traditional commercial patterns, the independent designers do not assume that the sewer of the pattern has any previous experience sewing when writing their instructions. Designers also include additional information for the sewers, such as pressing reminders. The directions are written so that sewing terminology is explained for a novice sewer; details such as the stitch length is provided when a basting stitch is needed. The instructions also include images for each step in the instructions and in some cases will provide multiple images if needed. They also include many images of other sewers' versions of the garment for inspiration.

Unique to this sewing pattern platform is the changing role of the pattern designer. Unlike traditional paper pattern designers, PDF pattern designers are also the individuals promoting and selling their patterns. They are engaged and actively involved with their customers and provide pattern support for issues and questions about their patterns through Facebook groups and other social media such as Instagram. The success of a PDF sewing pattern is largely dependent on members of the sewing community sharing and recommending their patterns through social media, sewing Facebook groups, blogs, and other web-based sewing platforms.

Findings on independent PDF sewing pattern use

As part of my research to better understand the motivations that women have for sewing their own clothing[50] participants were asked questions regarding their use of sewing patterns. The use of independent designer PDF sewing patterns among the participants was found to play a significant role in their sewing participation. All of the women in the study had purchased and regularly used independent designer PDF sewing patterns. Many of the women disclosed that they exclusively used independent designer PDF sewing patterns. It was revealed in the women's description of their pattern use that there were several reasons for their preference for PDF sewing patterns. One participant spoke of her pattern choice like this: "I think paper patterns are incredibly confusing." Two women who recently learned to sew admitted that they had yet to purchase or sew a commercial sewing pattern. The reasons described by the women were related to clear instructions, availability of pattern sewing assistance, ease of access, and testing newly developed patterns for independent pattern designers.

The most popular reason indicated for using independent PDF sewing patterns was the way that the instructions for cutting and sewing were written. Participants indicated that PDF independent sewing patterns instructions are written in a more approachable manner that is easier for sewers of all skill levels to understand. They revealed that this pattern type includes more photos and drawings than commercial patterns and uses terminology that is much easier to understand. A few women in the study even revealed that the PDF instructions were "how I taught myself to sew."

Another emergent theme in the preference for independent PDF sewing patterns was the sewing and pattern alteration assistance. The majority of the women in the study valued the option that you have with this pattern format; you can ask questions to other sewers who have used it and in most cases the pattern designer can be queried. As one participant noted of an independent PDF sewing pattern, "you have the person who designed it and drafted it to help you versus with a paper pattern I don't even know if that's possible."

Although not all participants mentioned it in their interviews, the ease of access to the independent PDF sewing patterns clearly had an impact on their decisions to use them. The women mentioned how they could access the patterns at any time of day whenever they were ready to sew and there was no need to leave their homes. As one participant put it, "I can print at home." This pattern format allowed the participants who were not close to sewing retailers an option to sew patterns instantly without a shipping delay.

Another aspect of independent sewing pattern use that was revealed was the ability to be chosen as a pattern tester for these designers. The women found it very appealing to be part of the pattern development process by providing feedback to designers regarding their opinions of how the pattern sewed and fit as well as the clarity of instructions. They also liked that the designers show off the garments they have made. One woman shared, "half the fun of pattern testing is having your patterns featured."

Changes in home sewing patterns: who has the ability to design and sell

The "About" pages of sixty-one designers selling patterns in PDF format for download through their own websites revealed only eight designers indicating patternmaking experience or an apparel design education. Seven of the designers stated that they all had several years of apparel industry experience in positions related to apparel design. The designers' experience was varied and included experience in childrenswear, womenswear, and Broadway costume design. One of the designers included in the study currently works designing custom formal wear in addition to selling his PDF sewing patterns. The "About" pages of these designers focused mainly on their training, industry experience, and highlights of how their patterns were designed.

Analysis of the other fifty-three designers' pages (those who did not indicate any patternmaking training or apparel industry experience) found that the "About" pages did not focus on the designer's experience, education, or highlights of what their patterns offered. Most of the designers without formal training indicated that they were "self-taught" while most shared that they felt it was the next step for their hobby because sewing was a "passion" for them. Only one designer disclosed that she took classes for Adobe Illustrator to gain the skills she needed to make quality sewing patterns. All fifty-three of these designers were women. In their "About" page, the women told their story of the motivation they had to be a PDF designer and the flexibility that this type of work provided them. Some of them disclosed their previous employment type or educational background. Among them were a school teacher, a chemist, and a business analyst. The motivations for these women to learn how to make and sell PDF patterns related to being a stay-at-home mom, loving sewing as a hobby, and blogging about sewing. The majority of the women (72 percent) wrote about how being a stay-at-home mom influenced them to become PDF pattern designers. Many of the women disclosed how becoming a PDF pattern designer gave them something productive to do while being a stay-at-home mom. One designer shared she was a "stay-at-home-mom who loves to sew." A few of the women mentioned the extra income that it generated or how it allowed them to make money in a way that was flexible to their family's schedule. The second emergent theme of motivation to design PDF sewing patterns was that sewing was a hobby they loved. This love of sewing motivated them to start making their own sewing patterns which they could also sell to other sewers. The length of time that sewing had been a hobby for the women varied from twenty years to less than a year. Lastly, revealed within the theme of motivation, was how blogging about their sewing endeavors lead to their interest in PDF pattern design. The positive feedback received from their blog posts encouraged them to make patterns of their own. Additionally, a few of these women were motivated by a lack of pattern selection in niche segments such as breastfeeding tops and dresses.

Conclusion

There have been significant technological changes that have impacted women's sewing participation with the internet being one of the main driving forces. Most of the barriers that kept sewing education and developing sewing patterns limited to a restricted few—those with the correct formal training and monetary resources, have been lifted. Sewing blogs provide very low-cost ways for sewers to share their sewing with others. Social media platforms such as Facebook, Instagram, and Pinterest are free ways that sewers can connect and help each other in their sewing endeavors. Additionally, the low barrier to entry into designing and selling PDF sewing patterns and the interest of home sewers to purchase this type of pattern can have serious implications for those in the commercial sewing pattern industry who have for over 100 years controlled the market. Additional larger scale research is needed to better understand how these sewers have changed the dynamics from relying on the industry-trained professional to working together and financially supporting each other to gain the sewing knowledge and materials that they desire.

Part Three

Creative Diversity: Multicultural Approaches to Pattern Creation

Creolized Patterning: A Jamaican Perspective

Elli Michaela Young

In this chapter Elli Michaela Young explores the practices of three dressmakers from Kingston, Jamaica—their techniques, their motivations for designing and making, and the expressive quality of their work are situated in the context of people of the African diaspora searching for a way to create a sense of self. Young notes that creativity and innovation have always been an important part of the daily experience of Jamaican life and explores a specific manifestation of these impulses by examining a unique methodology of pattern production that has developed on the island: freehand dressmaking. Young defines freehand dressmaking as an approach in which makers either draw patterns directly onto the fabric without the use of a fully-drafted pattern, or in the case of very skilled makers, simply cut the fabric by eye. Young reveals that freehand dressmakers may draw inspiration from across the globe to incorporate into their style, but the final product manifests a uniquely Jamaican style. This discussion of freehand dressmaking serves as an interesting counterpoint to the discussion of tailoring systems in Chapter 5 and the discussion of computer-aided patternmaking in Chapter 6. Young's work reveals that codifying all of the intricacies of patternmaking is not the only approach to pattern design in the twenty-first century and that the "eye" of the garment maker remains an important aspect of patternmaking that is passed from teacher to student just as it was in the earliest recorded history of this craft.

The Caribbean island of Jamaica is unlikely to be the first place that comes to mind when one is thinking about fashion and dress histories. Yet Jamaicans have a long and important relationship with dress. Fashion has been intimately tied to the ways in which the people of the African diaspora have produced identities. Professor Paul Khalil Saucier, in his article, "Cape Verdean Youth Fashion: Identity in Clothing" describes this relationship as a fundamental aspect in the construction of African diasporic identities: "Over the centuries, fashion has been one of the ways in which people of the African diaspora have created their sense of self, sense of community, and sense of place. Bodily practices have been almost as important as political manifestos in the struggle for freedom, agency and identity."[1] Jamaica's history is one intertwined with a history of European imperialism that was integral in the remaking of the island that we know today. First colonized by the Spanish in the fifteenth century, then by the British in the seventeenth century, Jamaica remained a British colony for over 300 years until its independence in August 1962. Despite a history of slavery and colonization, Jamaicans have been "proactive bearers of culture, not mere zombies—passive receptacles of the will of the enslaving other."[2] Creativity and innovation have been part of the daily experience of Jamaican life, a manifestation of which is reflected not only in the ways that Jamaicans have adorned their bodies, but also the methods of production that developed on the island.

Dress has been intimately tied to the construction of identities in Jamaica. From the point of arrival on the island, clothing has been for enslaved Africans intimately tied to surviving the traumas of the New World. Steeve Buckridge has highlighted the importance of dress in Jamaica pointing out that it has been used as a tool of resistance, as a marker of difference, an expression of social mobility, to communicate political messages, and Bakare-Yusuf has argued for its use by working class women in Jamaica to challenge dominant normative ideas of beauty.[3] Dress practices have been integral to working through ideas of self in both colonial and postcolonial Jamaica. As a visually-accessed form of discourse it was especially important in the absence of a shared language, culture and/or religion. Dress is a powerful resonant non-verbal form of communication that can be used to combat hegemonic discourse, thereby creating its own discourse based on commonalities such as race and ethnicity.[4] Jamaicans have produced and consumed fashion in ways that have necessitated a level of innovation and creativity to simply keep pace with the ever-changing demands of Jamaican consumer tastes. Their often-original use of dress has created an aesthetic that has found expression in a unique Jamaican style narrative. Refusing to play by global fashion rules, Jamaicans wear what they want, when they want, and how they want. They may draw inspiration from across the globe to incorporate into their style, but the ways in which they adorn themselves manifests in a uniquely Jamaican way, making Jamaica's relationship with fashion as complicated as its history.

In this chapter I show some of the ways that Jamaican makers have employed creative and innovate practices in the production of Jamaican fashion. Taken from a much larger research project, the information provided here is only a small sample of the information that has been gathered. Focusing on Jamaicans who lived and worked in Kingston, Jamaica's capital, I first show how makers utilized a technique called "freehand dress making" to create their clothing in colonial Jamaica. I then move on to a designer, dressmaker, and teacher working in contemporary Jamaica to consider the continued importance of dressmaking and show how patternmaking techniques have evolved. This evolution is informed by a Jamaican creolized way of being that informs the ways in which Jamaicans think and approach fashion production and the construction of identities.

The complex societal structures that have emerged from Jamaica's complicated colonial history affect how someone engages with dressmaking practices. A consideration of the full implications of class and race (for example) on freehand dressmaking practices is beyond the remit of this chapter. Therefore, the focus here is on working class African-Jamaicans and their everyday clothing. Dressmaking was a characteristic cultural and social feature of Jamaicans, practiced by diverse racial groups. It was a means of socialization for the middle classes, but a necessity for the working classes.[5] I use the term working class here, however, it is not a term that any of the respondents used during interviews. The ways in which Jamaican social classes are defined are extremely complex and are understood and articulated through understandings of race, underpinned by the historical narratives that informed understandings of difference within their colonial context. While this chapter only provides a small sample of a vast, diverse Jamaican experience, I hope that by examining clothing worn and made by Jamaican dressmakers I can show the important contribution of freehand dressmaking in the construction of Jamaican style. In the process I will also show that the making and wearing of fashion in Jamaica was not only creative and innovative, but also a collaborative process among designers, makers, and consumers.

One need only take a cursory look at Jamaican fashion (past or present) to acknowledge that Jamaicans have and continue to engage with fashion in complex ways. Jamaicans do not necessary follow seasonal fashions, as I said they wear what they want, when they want, how they want. One of the methods of production that is manifested in the complex landscape of colonial Jamaica was freehand dressmaking. Building on the work that has been undertaken by Carol Tulloch and Davinia Gregory in relation to dressmaking and freehand dressmaking in Jamaica and the Jamaican diaspora, I show it as an important creative practice that was used by many Jamaicans because it allowed for individual expressions of identities in diverse and intricate ways.

Freehand dressmaking

Freehand dressmaking is a technique in which makers either draw patterns directly onto the fabric without the use of a fully drafted or commercial pattern, or in the case of very skilled makers, simply cut the fabric by eye. I use the term freehand dressing here to describe both the process of making patterns and also the making of clothing using the same technique. Dressmakers approached the technique in different ways; some dressmakers sketched out their designs on paper, while others would make those calculations mentally, bypassing paper and going straight to the fabric. Unlike the dressmaking systems of the nineteenth century, the only tools utilized in the patternmaking process for many Jamaican dressmakers were pencils or chalk, paper, measuring tape, and scissors. Freehand dressmaking requires an extensive understanding of the garment-making process and provides makers with the opportunity to express greater levels of creativity and innovation in the process.

Divinia Gregory's description of Dee Davis, a freehand dressmaker from a rural community in Clarendon, provides detailed insight into the process. Davis was able to "cut and throw together a perfectly fitting garment without measurement or pattern."[6] Anella James, a freehand dressmaker interviewed by Carol Tulloch described the technique as the creation of individualized designs inspired from a variety of sources, and not predetermined by a paper pattern.[7] The explanations of both Gregory and Tulloch describe a technique that required not only detailed measurements, but an extensive understanding of garment construction. The dressmaker needed to know how the different elements of production worked together in order to get the best fit, but also required a level or creativity and innovation that allowed the maker to adapt patterns to her needs.

Freehand dressmaking was taught, usually informally, to many young women learning dressmaking. In her article, Gregory describes this informal training in detail. She describes an informal school run by a dressmaker for her local community.[8] However, two of the dressmakers discussed in this chapter both learned their skills through family networks. In the case of Mrs. Lewinson, she was taught by female members of her family, while Mrs. Graham learned first by watching a local dressmaker who made school uniforms, then learned by working as an assistant once her skills had begun to develop. The popularity of dressmaking as a profession in Jamaica is detailed by Tulloch in her article, "No Place Like Home. Home Dressmaking and Creativity in the Jamaican Community of the 1940s and 1960s." As she explains, there were thousands of independent and professional dressmakers to be found on the island, with over 3,000 in

Kingston alone.[9] However, I believe that this number would only account for those who considered themselves to be "professional dressmakers," and it is likely there would have been a significant number of "non-professional" dressmakers, who were not reflected in this number. Many of the women in Jamaica who trained as dressmakers either made their own clothes or used their skills to develop a client base, providing them with economic independence in the process. There is a longstanding history of dressmaking in Jamaica that has been identified by both Gregory and Tulloch, who suggest the practice could have been a continuation of West African traditions.[10] As a creole society it has been argued that enslaved Africans incorporated Western African practices and traditions with European practices and traditions, as well as the know-how of other cultures in the creation of something completely new.

It is not clear at this stage of my research how freehand dressmaking evolved in Jamaica. However, if we consider the technologies of garment making before dressmaker and tailor drafting systems were properly introduced, there are enough similarities that it is possible that some of these techniques influenced the freehand dressmaking practices that were developed in Jamaica. Enslaved Africans would have had limited time to learn complex tailoring and patternmaking techniques, and with access to only meagre resources, any system they developed would have necessitated adaptations that would allow them to produce clothing that suited their tastes. To recreate garments that they saw, but which they would have had limited access to, they had to develop a particular way of thinking to replicate or create similar garments. The ability to think in ways that relate to space, area, size, and position rather than in standardized units of measurement, became the way in which makers thought about, understood, learned, and passed on freehand dressmaking techniques. The techniques used by professional tailors and those used by enslaved Africans could not have been exactly the same. They would not have had access to the same equipment, or the same level of training and experience, or the same amount of time to dedicate to making personal clothing. It is therefore likely that these gaps were filled with ways of making that were transported from Africa, which they may have preferred or of which they may have had an intimate knowledge. Therefore, with a few adjustments it would not be unrealistic to suggest that Jamaican freehand dressmaking techniques emerged as part of the same creative innovative dialogue that produced creolized ways of being.

As indicated earlier freehand dressmaking was a widely used method of production in Jamaica. It has provided a way for Jamaicans to engage with creative practices and construction of clothing that reflected one's individuality while also challenging dominant colonial narratives. The first two dressmakers I examine for this chapter are Mrs. Hazeline Lewinson and Mrs. Gloria West. Mrs. Lewinson used the practice to construct clothing that reflected her sense of self and tested the boundaries of her sexuality. She was not interested in replicating styles that she saw in style books and magazines. She wanted to create outfits that were unique to her. Gloria West, working in Jamaica at the same time as Mrs. Lewinson, in the mid-twentieth century, had a different approach. She replicated the clothing that she saw, and her close replication was informed by her understanding of class and respectability. However, while her outfits were copies of the garments she saw, there were other adaptations that she made, which were not as obvious as the adaptations made by Mrs. Lewinson. The final maker I examine is Mrs. Andrea Graham, a designer, maker, and teacher working in contemporary Jamaica. While she does not use freehand dressmaking techniques in the same way as Mrs. Lewinson or Gloria West, her technique highlights the ways in which patternmaking has developed within Jamaica; informed by techniques she learned during a period of study in one of Jamaica's fashion schools and that she developed in order teach students with little or no dressmaking experience.

Miss Cherry

Mrs. Hazeline Lewinson, known to her family and friends as Miss Cherry, was born in Kingston in 1936. Born into a family of dressmakers, she received no formal training in fashion design, patternmaking, or dressmaking, nor did she work full time as a dressmaker, which is perhaps why she did not describe herself as a professional dressmaker during our interview. Her dressmaking skills were learned informally from her grandmother and the women around her. Miss Cherry not only made her own clothes, she had regular clients, and often assisted her sisters with finishing clothing for their clients. However, as she explained, this was only done when it involved a finished method she enjoyed. During an interview she explained freehand dressmaking was the only technique she was taught and that she had never learned to use commercial patterns. When asked about the availability of commercial patterns her response was: "I had a friend called Joyce who bought a pattern and made a dress. But I didn't understand head nor tail. So, I made my clothes without."[11] Miss Cherry went on to explain that paper patterns were readily available in Jamaica, but she never learned to incorporate them in her practice. Miss Cherry's frustration with commercial patterns is not surprising. They restricted her creative process. Her rejection of paper patterns also suggests that she had developed a particular way of thinking about constructing garments that made it difficult for her to incorporate someone else's design and understanding of construction, into her own thought processes. When attempting to explain the freehand dressmaking technique, Miss Cherry had difficulty articulating it in any detail, possibly because it had now become second nature to her or simply because she had never been asked to describe the technique in any detail before. "You just look at something and then you make it"[12] was the only way that she was able to articulate the process, even when pressed for more detail about her process and thinking.

Miss Cherry had the ability to look at a garment, deconstruct it, and reconstruct it in her mind in order to bring together elements that would suit her style. It is here that one sees the importance of understanding garment construction in her practice. Without an extensive understanding of the process, Miss Cherry would not have been able to mentally take the garment apart so easily or understand how and why particular styles worked. While thinking about the garment's construction, she would already be thinking about the types

Figure 9.1 Mrs. Lewinson, "Miss Cherry," depicted in Kingston, *c.* 1950. In this image Miss Cherry is wearing a white off-the-shoulder blouse, which she matched with a plain calico skirt, which is decorated with hand-painted flowers. Flowers were painted by a local artist (artist unknown).

of fabrics that would work best with her intended style. Miss Cherry designed and made the entire garment in her head before beginning the cutting and making of a garment. In addition, she planned which accessories would work with the outfit, and of course where she would be wearing her new creation. Miss Cherry used catalogues and magazines for inspiration, but making her own adaptations of particular garments allowed her to engage in the design process. Tulloch has pointed out the manipulation of commercial designs to create something new tested the boundaries of copyright[13] but the refusal to conform intrinsically also says something about the identity of the maker. Adapting designs to one's personal tastes can also be understood as a rejection of standardized dressmaking techniques, a rejection of commercial patterns, and standardized measurements—a position that challenges dominant narratives about what is and what is not deemed fashionable.

For Miss Cherry, the ability to adapt and redesign these mass-produced styles in ways that were specific to her was crucial in the construction of her identity and an expression of her taste and creativity. Speaking about designing in the 1950s she noted: "Then they had a book called *Lana Lobel* style book. I would look into it and take parts of a dress and find a back out of my head to go with it. Especially if it didn't look that hot. Sometimes, you know, they would show you the back and the front of the dress."[14] Miss Cherry used the practice to push the boundaries of what was acceptable and appropriate dress for a woman in Jamaica. Her dress was an expression of her sexuality. She said: "I used to cut it down low, just to there. Cut it down low, so when I have on my dress that is cut just two inches from the waist, you don't see no bra. Oh yes low, very low."[15] She went on to explain that when her clothing was cut in this way it required adaptations to her underwear, the display of which would have spoiled her overall look.

Freehand dressmaking allowed Miss Cherry to exercise her creativity without restrictions, but also allowed her to create one-off unique designs. She made a deliberate choice not to make two garments that were the same. The ability to create an individual outfit was important for Miss Cherry, and freehand dressmaking gave her the freedom to do this. She explained that it was important for her to create one-off outfits in order to attract customers. If someone liked what she was wearing they would ask her to make it for them. Interestingly, despite using her creations as a way to attract customers, she refused to replicate any of her designs for her clients. She might make something similar, but it was never exactly the same. It was important for her that others did not have access to her style. Miss Cherry did not stop at individualizing her clothes; she would often have accessories, such as shoes, made to match specific outfits.

Being a freehand dressmaker was not simply about necessity for Miss Cherry. Miss Cherry's one-off designs openly challenged standards of morality when she wore them on the streets of Kingston and spoke to her individuality.

Gloria West

Gloria West was born in Whitfield Town, in Kingston between 1924 and 1925. She was a dressmaker in Kingston in the 1940s before immigrating to the United Kingdom in the 1950s. Gloria was also a freehand dressmaker, but her practice included the sketching of designs onto paper before drawing the pattern onto the fabric and then cutting. I have been unable to confirm where and how Gloria learned the process, as she died several years ago. Much of the information about Gloria and her family history was taken from interviews with her brother, but it is known that her younger sister was not a dressmaker. Gloria's mother died when she was young, and she was raised by her father, so it is likely that Gloria may have sought out a woman/or women in the local area to learn the technique. In comparing her style to Miss Cherry, her dressmaking appears not to have been as adventurous or innovative. She did not modify her clothing in the same ways as Miss Cherry. However, Gloria's decision to closely replicate the things that she saw did not in any way reflect an inability to create innovative designs.

Standing at almost six feet tall, Gloria was able to utilize her dressmaking skills to both make her own clothing and ensure a proper fit, but also to earn extra money by making clothes for others. Dressmaking was a popular way for many Jamaican women to earn additional income because it could be undertaken at home, in the hours that suited the maker, providing women like Gloria, the freedom to control her labor and finances. In this image (Figure 9.2) she is wearing a pair of loose-fitting trousers that taper at the ankle, and a loose-fitting shirt, an outfit her brother confirmed she made herself. Tulloch's (1999) argument that a dressmaker's clothing carried an element of prestige by avoiding the stigma of wearing something that was ill-fitting is important here, because of Gloria's above-average stature. Like Miss Cherry, Gloria had difficulties understanding commercial paper patterns. Visiting her home as a child, I would often encounter paper patterns strewn across her small sewing room and it was never clear why such delicate papers were discarded in this way, but interviews with Miss Cherry revealed the level of frustration commercial patterns would cause a freehand dressmaker. They confused her way of thinking about the making process, so instead of cutting outfits directly from the paper she would

Figure 9.2 Gloria West, depicted in Kingston, Jamaica, *c.* 1950. Gloria was a freehand dressmaker and made all her own clothes; a practice that she continued after emigrating to the United Kingdom.

simply copy the shape freehand onto the fabric before cutting. This for Gloria was the compromise she found between freehand and commercial patterns. Using them as a source of inspiration then discarding them at the moment they interfered with her creativity.

Looking at a photograph of her brother, Barrington Young (Figure 9.3), taken in the same location by the same photographer there are similarities in the ways in which they styled themselves. Standing on a neatly manicured lawn in front of a building that looks like a church with stained glass windows, the clothing that both Barrington and Gloria are wearing is too casual to suggest that they are attending church, so the location choice adds another layer to the way in which they were constructing their identities. Gloria's trousers are almost exactly the

Figure 9.3 Barrington Young, depicted in Kingston, Jamaica, *c.* 1950.

same as Barrington's but made more feminine by adding a belt and a tapered ankle. There are also similarities with the shirt and blouse, both of which have a wide neck, but the shirtsleeves are of different lengths. However, in another photograph of Barrington, he is wearing a similar short-sleeved shirt in a different color. In an interview with Barrington, he explained that growing up he and his siblings shared clothes and shoes, because they were (as he described it) "poor."[16] Barrington and Gloria were the same height and build, so it could be possible that memories of sharing as children influenced her styling. A closer examination of her shirt shows that it buttons left-over-right, which could suggest that she sought inspiration from Barrington's clothing for her own. It also suggests that adhering to gendered clothing was not as important for Gloria as controlling the way in which she constructed her identity. Her style choices offer the possibility to consider the use of gendered signifiers in the expression of her femininity as a way of pushing the boundaries of fashion and style. The willingness to adapt clothing, and how far those adaptations would go, were ultimately tied to Gloria's ideas of class and ideas of respectability. Women and men in colonial Jamaica followed the social etiquette of the period, thus stepping outside of these boundaries could have implications for the ways that one was viewed in the community. As Barrington explained in an interview, if one was not appropriately attired it would negatively impact on his or her reputation.[17] Barrington reinforced the importance of clothing made by dressmakers and tailors, explaining that during the 1940s and 1950s ready-to-wear clothing was not fashionable in Jamaica. A suggestion that reinforces Tulloch's (1999) argument that clothing made by dressmakers had far more cachet than other clothing. The concept of "appropriateness" of attire suggests that there were specific rules that needed to be followed and that he understood the importance of sartorial practices within colonial Jamaica. Gloria challenged these ideas with her sexuality and by using masculine signifiers in the construction of her identity. Her dress suggests that she may also have been uninterested in fashioning herself within the limited parameters of gendered respectability—an issue that raises questions about gendered clothing in Jamaica and which merits further in-depth research.

Being able to produce unique designs was one of the reasons that freehand dressmaking remained popular in Jamaica, despite on-going technological advances in dressmaking and tailoring that were happening outside of the country. Dressing-up and creating style narratives that reflected one's own understanding of social position within colonial Jamaica was an important aspect of fashioning self. Clothing was not merely something that covered bodies; it was an aesthetic expression of self. It allowed Jamaicans to challenge dominant narratives, reflecting their understandings of Jamaican sartorial practices within complex colonial constructs. However, one of the problems of freehand dressmaking is that it is difficult to quickly replicate a garment, which is necessary if you want to compete in a market that is flooded with imported mass-produced goods. Not only was it difficult for Jamaican dressmakers to compete in this arena, the perceived status of the clothes made by them was also in decline—they had lost their appeal with the new generation of Jamaicans growing up in an independent Jamaica.

In the post-colonial period, there were changes in tastes among Jamaican consumers. In addition, in the 1960s, the Jamaican government made a concerted effort to develop a Jamaican fashion industry that could compete on a global stage. The professionalization of the industry saw the launch of an organization called the Jamaican Fashion Guild at this time. The Guild comprised a group of Jamaican designers whose remit was to design and produce clothing that was instinctively Jamaican. Designers such as Ivy Ralph, Annie Lopez, Daphne Logan, and Trevor Owen set out to change the face of Jamaican fashion and market it to an international audience. Dressmakers were no longer running their own businesses but working behind the scenes producing designs for the new generation of Jamaica's fashion industry.[18] However, as with many things, there is a cycle and in contemporary Jamaica, while freehand dressmaking may be less popular than it once was, this kind of dressmaking has recently seen a rise in popularity.

Mrs. Andrea "Anniegee" Graham

Mrs. Andrea "Anniegee" Graham, a designer, dressmaker, and teacher, regularly runs classes teaching dressmaking skills at her Fashion Institute on Constant Springs Road, in Kingston. Anniegee has been teaching patternmaking and dressmaking for almost twenty years and had seen the interest in dressmaking diminish. However, this is now beginning to shift with a marked increase in interest since September 2016; an increase that she attributed to a television program called *Mission Catwalk,* a television program that showcases young Caribbean fashion designers. Anniegee believes the program has encouraged a future generation of Jamaican designers,[19] many of whom may attend Anniegee's school and learn her patternmaking and dressmaking techniques.

Born in 1962, the year of Jamaican independence, Anniegee learned to sew at a young age, and by the age of six or seven she was assisting a family helper make school uniforms. After leaving secondary school she decided to study fashion design and attended LaFont School of Fashion in Jamaica. She continued to develop her skills through various technical workshops and training seminars both in Jamaica and abroad. She explained that her training at LaFont School of Fashion included the traditional methods of garment designing including flat patternmaking and draping.

Anniegee currently uses a form of flat patternmaking to teach her students. In a discussion about patternmaking she said, "You have some persons who just go directly to the fabric and cut, but I still think they are using patternmaking because you still need to construct an informal pattern on the paper, or on the fabric that doesn't have any guarantees to fit. When you do patternmaking it is more structured, so you are guaranteed a fit."[20] A garment that fits well and is finished to a high standard is important to Anniegee. She noted, "You are not supposed to be able to look at a garment and know that it was made by a dressmaker."[21] Anniegee runs her classes as drop-in sessions, so students are often at different levels and at different places in a project when they attend classes, and are working at their own pace. While this may be unusual for a standard college course, this flexibility is important to Anniegee because she understands the everyday pressures that her students encounter which may make it difficult for them to attend fixed sessions. The course is not only practice-based, it also comprises a written module developed by Anniegee, which the students undertake as an additional way to enhance their understandings of techniques and equipment.

In describing her technique, Anniegee explains that she has broken the process down into simple steps. Once a student has taken necessary body measurements, he or she will be able to construct a pattern in less than two minutes.[22] It was necessary for her to develop this process because her courses are only ten weeks long and many of her students come from Kingston's poorest urban areas. She also found that many of her students had difficulties understanding the complex calculations required for standardized pattern-making. Figures 9.4 and 9.5 are photographs taken during one of her drop-in

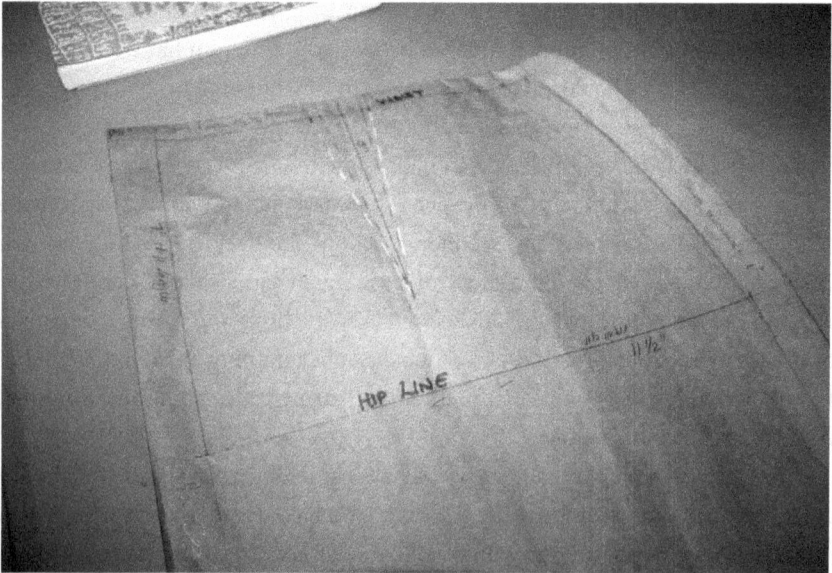

Figure 9.4 An example of the flat pattern technique used by Anniegee in her regular dressmaking class at Anniegee's Fashion Institute in Kingston, Jamaica.

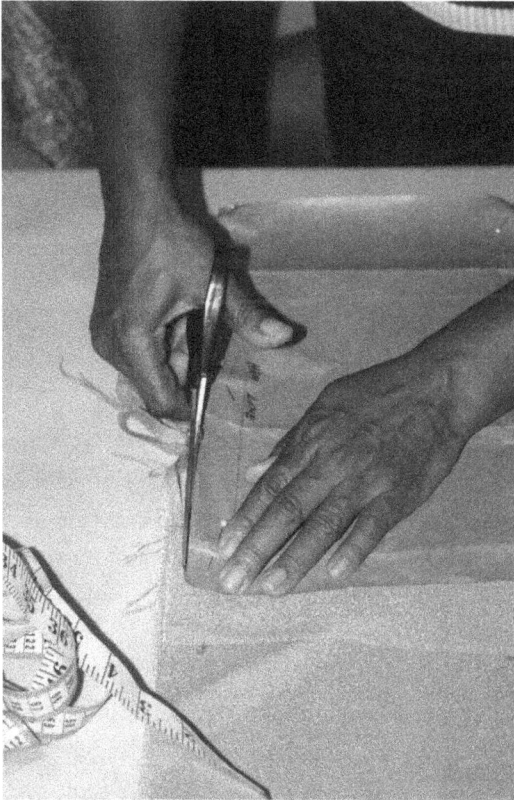

Figure 9.5 An example of the flat pattern technique used by Anniegee in her regular dressmaking class at Anniegee's Fashion Institute in Kingston, Jamaica.

classes and show the basic method taught to students. Anniegee's technique first requires accurate body measurements to be taken; the body is broken down into specific sections, which are translated into an exact paper pattern. Anniegee explained, "It fits in exactly the same way if you would have used a flat pattern without the need for any understanding of fractions or complicated mathematical calculations."[23] What is interesting about Anniegee's technique is that while it is more accurate than the freehand dressmaking technique, there are elements from freehand that she draws on in her technique. By reducing the number of calculations and breaking the body down into specific parts, she is training her students to think about their garment construction in a way that is similar to freehand dressmakers. Anniegee incorporated the spatial thinking that is required in freehand dressmaking within her method because she recognized that teaching students the standard flat pattern technique takes much longer for the students to understand. Making the process easier for the students to understand is an important element of the course. Despite the short length of the course, Anniegee insists her students will be able to utilize the skills they learn within Jamaica's garment industry. After ten weeks students must be able to construct several different styles of skirts, pockets, sleeves, collars, blouses, and jackets. Students must meet her exacting standards in order to finish the course and compete in the market.

Conclusion

Jamaicans were and continue to be very particular when it comes to fashion. The decisions that they make in relation to their clothing reflect the complex terrain of Jamaican society, which they have learned to navigate. Fashion sense and individuality were important drivers of the freehand dressmaking market and dressmakers and tailors filled this important role by producing garments specific to their client's needs. Dressmakers like Miss Cherry and Gloria were able to use their practice to express their identities in ways that ready-to-wear clothing would not have allowed. They challenged dominant fashion rules by creating garments that spoke to their identities. In an independent Jamaica, there were very different ideas about fashion and the way it could be utilized in the expression of identities. The Jamaican government sought to professionalize its fashion industry and market Jamaican fashion on a global stage. However, despite the changes in fashion there are elements or threads that connect these periods. Regardless of the difference in geography, location and time, there are similarities between Anniegee's school and Dee Davis's school. For example, Dee's sewing school provided supplementary skills from which to build economic security, a tradition that Anniegee continues by providing her students with the skills to enter the Jamaican employment market, or by simply providing others with the ability make clothing for themselves or family members. There are also clear differences in the teaching methods of each of these dressmakers. Anniegee modernized dressmaking by incorporating more formalized patternmaking into her techniques. However, there is an element of the spatial awareness and understanding of garment construction that remains. She has creolized patternmaking, making it more suitable and accessible for her audience. The industry may have moved on and the techniques may have changed, however, fashion production has remained an integral means by which Jamaicans communicate a sense of self.

Re-Make, Re-Model, Re-Define: Fashioning a Nation's Identity

Anthony Bednall

In this chapter, Anthony Bednall begins by exploring how Chinese rulers and regimes have engineered fashion or clothing to represent aspects of politics and nationality, and he demonstrates how political change has resulted in the adoption and dismissal of sartorial conventions including imperial garb and Western dress. This detailed back-story thus facilitates an exploration of a communist-era patternmaking book that provided specific instructions for remaking outmoded dress styles that were anathema to Communist ideology. Bednall argues that the re-cutting of old clothes in a sense symbolized the cutting of ties with foreign, capitalist legacies and functioned as an assertion of a new Chinese identity. This notion that the cut of clothes is evocative of national and personal identity picks up a theme that was developed in Chapter 9 with regards to Jamaican identity. In addition, this chapter considers how in the late 1950s patternmaking and the individual hand crafting of clothing became the necessary method of constructing garments for the majority of the population due to inadequate textile and apparel resources. The author reveals that both natural and political phenomena created privations that could only be addressed by recycling apparel (according to government instructions). Thus, this chapter shares a central theme with Chapter 4, which explores the re-working of apparel by civilians to offset shortages during the Second World War.

For most of the twentieth century, China has searched for cultural and national uniqueness as it negotiated the end of the longstanding imperial dynasty and responded to global, political and social volatility. A common and accepted identity is the paradigm for both individuals and nations in their search for safe ground in disturbed times, and consecutive Chinese rulers or regimes have engineered fashion or clothing to represent and symbolize order, national and bureaucratic codes, modernity, functionality, gender, and cultural significance.[1] It would be an understatement to say China has been through disturbed times in both its immediate past and its more distant history; it continues to be a complicated, diverse, and unique country with a contemporary population firmly rooted within its broader historical characteristics. It is a nation still attempting to define and contextualize its uniqueness within a national and global environment.

There is a compelling argument regarding the progressions of individual and collective dress in China. Dress practices have represented generative and thenceforth re-generative stylistic norms by being cyclically dismissive of existing sartorial conventions, and in doing so, formatively and radically remaking, redefining, and remodeling the nation's identity. This chapter considers how in the late 1950s patternmaking and the individual hand crafting of clothing developed in China and became the necessary method of constructing garments for the majority of the population.

The context of this was in direct response to political doctrine, inadequate resources, and previous interventions surrounding dress reform, modernization, Westernization, and the recognition of clothing as not only cultural capital but as a characteristic of social standing and a representation of external influences. To support and inform individual garment construction on a mass scale, the Communist Party sponsored publications that acted as instructional guides on remaking garments from existing clothes as well as economizing on fabric usage. The publications illustrate stylistically acceptable modes of dress and align the content and audience with the prevailing political landscape. This particular period bookends a complex and long historic narrative of regulation, craft, and symbolism, and is a reflection of the socio-economic temper of China as a nation during the early years of Communist rule.

There have been extensive research projects, exhibitions, publications and commentaries regarding the history of Chinese dress.[2] What is relevant to this chapter is the cut and silhouette of traditional Chinese garments and how Western design and tailoring techniques ultimately came to inform urban clothing styles. This Western influence impacted dress of the late Qing dynasty and supported the modernization of dress codes in China under a new Nationalist government after the 1911 revolution. The modernization of dress in China could be interpreted as the Westernization of China and undoubtedly dress styles were influenced by large influxes of Western inhabitants who brought access to international media, global information, trade and manufacturing. As China came under Communist rule post 1949, capitalist doctrines and practices were renounced and many newly developed and adopted Western clothing styles were abandoned. These Western styles were representative of previous political and moral excesses and conflicted with the philosophies of Mao's New China and the population's desire to associate, through clothing, with the new regime's sartorial icons and culturally significant heroes and heroines.

Edicts, status, fabrication, and cut

To understand the significance of the dress practices of the late 1950s and how pre-owned garments could be remodeled, it is important to understand the traditional dress practices that were interpreted and reworked over a significant timeline. These practices, which cover some 600 years, inform the journey of individual garments whilst contributing to the process of change, in terms of both patternmaking and cultural significance. As early as the founding of the Ming dynasty by the Han leader, Zhu Yuanzhang in 1368, Chinese authorities imposed a system of clothing regulations on its court and on its population in order to create a well-defined social hierarchy, which not only regulated an individual's activities, but established a stable society under the close control of the state.[3] These regulations which were in place for the entirety of the Ming dynasty, instituted a clearly identified system of classifications, primarily reinstating Han style dragon robes as conventional wear, for noblemen and officials.[4] Image-based adornment (either woven or embroidered) referencing birds and animals was also established for these robes, with specific creatures representing levels of standing and power.[5] Centuries later, when China came under the rule of the Manchus in 1644 and the Qing dynasty (1644–1912) was initiated under the Emperor Kang Hsi, further adaptations and refinements surrounding attire were constituted and an official document entitled the *Chin Ting Ta Ching Hui* was produced in 1694.[6] This extensive and detailed manuscript not only defined the ceremonial laws and procedures of the Qing dynasty, but specified initial edicts regarding individual grades of costumes that could be worn in the imperial court, as part of a demarcated hierarchy. For men, the Manchu robes that were identified as being representative of the new ruling class were not a radical departure from the existing garments worn by the Han majority population during the Ming dynasty. They were, however, less voluminous and incorporated details such as front and back vents rising vertically from the hem, and a curved, over-lapping right front opening and fastening, which clearly reflected on the Manchu legacy and heritage as nomadic horseman.[7]

Hierarchical organizational structures continuously adhered to the symbolism of, and association with, the eminent leaders within a bureaucracy, so it is difficult to distinguish differing male styles of the Qing period, as they increasingly dressed alike. However, Manchu and Han Chinese women, although borrowing styles from each other, wore markedly differing styles of dress. In simplistic terms, the Manchu women wore a long robe with a curving front side fastening whilst the Han Chinese wore a three-quarter length robe similar to a jacket with a pleated skirt and trouser underneath. Final specificity surrounding the regulations pertaining to Manchu dress were published in the most significant document of the period entitled, *The Illustrated Regulations for the Ceremonial Paraphernalia of the Imperial Court (Huangchao Liqi Tushi)* commissioned in 1748 and completed in 1759.[8]

The impact of this publication and its subsequent elaborations and distinctions regarding wardrobe, to this particular scholarly narrative, is timeline and cultural endurance. The cut of the robes, identified within the *Illustrated Regulations* ostensibly remained in place, albeit with minor nuances, until the dawn of the twentieth century. Innovations in terms of patternmaking and tailoring were minimal, as the emphasis throughout this early period of Chinese dress was on decoration and ornamentation—as hierarchical position constituted superior garment elaboration and fabrication techniques. An understanding of some of these long-lived garments is fundamental to comprehending Communist Party initiatives of the mid-twentieth century.

Among the garments that endured across this 200-year span was the *Chaofu*, the most formal of the robes. The *Chaofu* had a kimono-style upper body with long, close-fitting sleeves that terminated in a "horse's-hoof" shaped cuff and a closely fitted neckband, which was worn over a detached collar distinguished by wing-like tips that extended over the shoulders.[9] The "horse's-hoof" cuff was designed to reflect upon the Manchu riding heritage and represented protection of the fingers when on horseback. The lower section of the garment, attached to a set-in waistband, was a full, pleated, or gathered skirt.

The *Jifu*, or "dragon robes" (*longpao*) bore direct relation to the robes of the Ming dynasty. The dragon robes became the semi-formal robes worn by the scholar-officials during the Qing dynasty. The robes were full-length, cut loose in an A-shaped pattern with no shoulder seams. Male robes had slits on the bottom of the front, back, and sides to facilitate riding with a side front opening consisting of two overlapping parts secured with fabric loops, and textile or metal buttons. The hem of the *Jifu* cleared the ground to permit easy walking and the extra side slits were the only feature that distinguished the *Jifu* of men below the rank of emperor from the *Jifu* of their wives. All robes were elaborately patterned against an immensely complex set of regulations, but it is the consistency of the shape and its future (albeit minor) chronological and morphological development, which becomes synonymous with both ancient and modern Chinese dress.

The *Changpao*, a garment for informal activities, which was sometimes worn with a riding-style shorter jacket named a *Magua*, was a plain, long robe worn by all classes. The men's was cut in the style of the *Jifu* and was usually made of loom widths of monochrome patterned fabric, whilst the female version had wide, loose sleeves edged with especially designed decorative sleeve bands. Existing examples of untailored dragon robes show the width of the bolts of silk lengths to be generally consistent and the pattern pieces of individual garment styles to be constrained by the width of the loom that they were woven on.[10]

These existing examples show that the selvages, or finished side edges, of the silk are located at the center-front or center-back of the garment and at the end of the connected sleeve head. The sleeves are not attached to the body in the shoulder area, but the upper part of the sleeves are cut in one piece with the body in a T-shaped orientation. This cutting style removes the requirement for a shoulder seam and allows the garment to be folded along the shoulder line. The side seams, which narrow at the top of the body, give the loosely-shaped A silhouette, whilst the lengths have already been attached along the central front and back selvages in order that the embroidery can be completed over the seam joins.[11] This shape and cut feature as a significant resource when versions of the style are opened up and re-cut in line with the conventions of the mid-twentieth century. This is possible, due to the fact that there are no fit elements, such as darts or fitted sleeves; all the constructions rely on square shapes, wrapped fastenings, and some elements of pleating, thereby making the most economical use of the fabric produced.

In contrast to these Chinese patternmaking techniques and regulatory codes, seventeenth-century European tailors were beginning to articulate the concepts of fit, cut, and construction through publications that included methods of technical instruction and patternmaking guidance. These concepts approached the patternmaking and construction of garments from a diametric position to the Chinese. Juan de Alcegas' book of the practice of tailoring, measuring, and marking-out (1580) (*Libro de geometria practica y traca*) is one of the earliest surviving publications regarding patterns and their purpose. Alcegas' defined goal was to instruct tailors to cut pattern pieces that were economically efficient and adhered to body shape.[12] Other tailors produced further publications both in Spanish and in French but the first English language publication was *The Tailor's Complete Guide,* devised by the Society of Adepts and produced in 1769, only ten years after the dissemination of the *Illustrated Regulations for the Ceremonial Paraphernalia of the Imperial Court.*[13] The English publication was considered rudimentary by later scholars and lacking in accurate measuring systems, as it relied on the "rock of eye" method of cutting, whilst the Chinese regulatory publication outlined a distinctive and authoritative visual narrative of the Chinese court and its codified costume.[14] Notwithstanding these differences of approach, these documents show clear evidence of parallel sartorial systems, which were ultimately destined to collide, as the industrialization and globalization of the world was embraced by some nations and imposed by others. China, throughout the Qing dynasty, continued to maintain its values and symbolism through dress but was, by the mid-to-late-nineteenth century, becoming more aware of the external factors about to challenge its cultural identity and propagate the onset of modernism.[15]

Modernization, Westernization, and the breaking of traditions

As already noted, there was a significant timeline of stylistic continuity, in terms of Chinese dress, particularly with respect to the layering, cut, and silhouette of garments. External Western influences upon clothing in China were initially inconsequential but the presence of Westerners (living in China to conduct trade) would have at least fostered discussion and debate, amongst the Chinese elite. Foreigners would most certainly have been viewed as figures of curiosity, who approached garments and the cut of clothing from a radically contrastive position. Through trading, eighteenth and early nineteenth century Europeans embraced *chinoiserie.* The Brighton Royal Pavilion, built by King George III, and completed in 1808, is a particularly ostentatious example of this impulse in architecture. Conversely, European influence, *europerie,* impacted China, as European goods were prized and European architects were commissioned by Emperor Qian Long to create baroque pavilions in the Summer Palace, just North of Beijing.[16] However, these initial interactions and cross-cultural acceptances of the creative arts could be considered nothing more than a somewhat superficial Eastern and Western fascination with the exotic and the new.

It was not until the middle of the nineteenth century, when foreign powers operating under the guise of trade, attempted to aggressively exploit and dominate the country. This led to a diverse cultural collision and Western styles and tastes subtly assumed the role as cultural influencer. In 1842, at the conclusion of the first Opium war of 1840, foreign expansion into China began in earnest. The first ports were opened-up through a treaty system that established the principle of extra-territoriality and granted Britain "most favoured status" as a trading partner.[17] Pressure from America, France, and ultimately Japan, to engage with the treaty port system meant that the foundations had been located for the multinational penetration of China.[18] Indeed, Chinese commentators themselves recognize 1840 as marking the beginning of the nation's modern history.[19]

Initially, the foreign nations' ambition was to open up the huge Chinese nation for trading purposes, however as post-industrial nations, they were more militarily powerful than China and arrogant enough to resent any opposition that challenged their financially-driven view of the world. Conversely, Chinese intellectuals and conservatives from the Scholar-officials were rooted in a history of heritage and believed (that as often happened in Chinese history) any reforms could be managed successfully through the restoration of Confucian values and institutions.[20] Clearly, they underestimated the complexity of the foreign aggression and its far-reaching potential impact on China. A series of uprisings and military actions cemented foreign enclaves, improved and extended the scope of international treaties, and enforced what was effectively a semi-colonial environment.[21]

By the latter half of the nineteenth century, greater accessibility to ports such as Shanghai, Tianjin, and Guangzhou facilitated the development of foreign communities, leading to multi-faceted topographical and socio-cultural characteristics. For example, by the early twentieth century the city of Tianjin included a local Chinese-administered section, as well as nine foreign concessions or areas, with differing administrations and newly constructed architecture, each of which reflected the lifestyle of the individual countries of origin. Within the immigrant communities specialized service industries developed. Importantly, this included tailoring services to satisfy the *émigrés'* stylistic needs. Invariably the foreign tailors hired local Chinese as apprentices or workers and taught them the techniques of western cutting and patternmaking.[22]

The local Chinese tailoring practices that made the traditional robes and jackets were known as the Ben Bang tailors, whilst the new foreign-trained tailors who also learnt the craft of repair for Western-style garments, became known as Hong Bang tailors.[23] The Hong Bang tailors were introduced to darts and cutting lines and the concept of modeling on a stand, which must have been revolutionary concepts as a contrast to the flat square shapes, devoid of fit, which constituted the construction methods of the Qing styles.[24] The Chinese population, across all levels of society, must have been unsure of how to respond to the foreign interventions and the influx of foreign communities with radically different dress codes and beliefs. The Chinese viewed themselves as a highly developed civilization, organized through clear sartorial dictates, with a supreme authority in the form of the Emperor. However, its survival as a socio-political entity, and even as an independent state, was in the balance, given its inability to repulse military or political incursions and further "unequal treaties" as defined by foreign nations. Anti-traditionalism, which dismissed China's cultural heritage and embraced Westernization became a notion among the Chinese modernizing elite, and would contribute alongside foreign aggression to the collapse of the Qing dynasty in 1911 and the establishment of a republic by Sun Zhongsan (Dr. Sun Yat-Sen) and his revolutionaries.[25]

Significantly, when Sun Zhongsan presided over the official ceremony to launch the provisional Republic on January 1, 1912, this collision of clothing as cultural capital was apparent. Western-style frock coats and top hats were the outfits of choice for the guests, denoting that the previous sartorial extravagance of imperial costume amongst a ruling elite had been quickly dismissed and superseded in the search for a modern China. In the initial years of the twentieth century leading up to the 1911 revolution, Chinese urban populations' dress styles for both men and women had gradually become neater and more streamlined. Sanctioned by the imperial government in 1902 the Chinese military was re-imagined and modernized stylistically under German and Japanese guidance and inadvertently became the vanguard of vestimentary change.[26] Military schools became prominent when the old examination system was abolished and new curricula, including physical education, were implemented. This change meant there was no place for the traditional long robe and school uniforms became directly modeled on military uniforms. Men's styles began to follow the global trend for greater simplicity and sobriety with a trimmer fit, and although Western suits on non-Westerners were rare at the outset, Western hats became prominent and popular fashion accessories. For women, the cut of clothes also shifted from wide to narrow, colors changed to darker more restrained tones, and high collars emerged as a feature in both men's and women's design, indicating a symbiosis of the relationship between military and civilian dress.[27] The rise of the collar evolved in the years after the new military schools gained popularity and men in uniform gained "handsome" status by Chinese women.[28] Ultimately, after centuries of no collars on garments, the stand-up collar became a definitive visual statement of self-representation and national identity across political and cultural environments for both men and women in China. With the onset of the new Republic came a confusing transitional period in China as its population shifted its role from imperial subjects to nation's citizens. The Republican Senate issued edicts in 1912, within an illustrated regulatory booklet, which ironically offers comparisons with the 1759 *Illustrated Regulations for the Ceremonial Paraphernalia of the Imperial Court,* in that it specified in some detail, official formal attire and the expectations on the appearance of the new male Republican leaders and government officials and administrators. The regulations defined within the booklet illustratively identified a set of dress styles deemed appropriate for a modern government, although some of the illustrations indicate that there was a degree of experimentation with a new hybrid style of garment, in which the design takes reference from both Western and Eastern styles. However, the reality was such that the Senate accepted that the adoption of Western formal wear would align the new Republic globally and situate its leaders as conforming to international standards of dress.[29]

The regulations were a significant departure from the previous long-standing imperial dress codes and their alignment with western dress included the Western frock coat and trousers with top hat for high formal wear and either a Western-style suit with bowler hat or homburg or traditional-style *Changpao* and *Magua* jacket with a bowler hat or homburg for formal day wear. The *Changpao* and the *Magua* retained the cut and length of previous traditional Chinese garments although there were new stipulations surrounding fabrication and color of both styles: black for formal wear, shades of gray and blue for men's daily wear, as opposed to the bright silks and patterning of the imperial Qing period. The illustrated regulations went as far as describing shoe styles, to be worn with respective outfits. The Western-style suit would eventually become prominent within urban society as it acted as a leveler not only for its functionality but also for its association with new values and modernization.[30]

There was a perception amongst the Chinese population and amongst commentators of the time that modernization meant Westernization and despite the apparent need in the post-imperial period to understand, explore, and apply Western ideas of the state, law, and democracy to China, Chinese Confucian traditions embedded within the culture for many centuries proved incredibly resilient and more flexible than it had first appeared. Chinese tradition was therefore not totally removed stylistically and there remained an appetite within the populace for a creative approach to clothing styles that would help to re-define how China was represented culturally and globally without the loss of any sartorial uniqueness.

Sun Zhongsan (Sun Yat-Sen) the provisional president had been photographed in a variety of styles ranging from full Prussian military plumage, to military uniforms and Western lounge suits, but it was in 1920, as part of the creation of the Guomingdang (Nationalist) party, he first appeared in the Zhongsan Zhuang (Sun Yat-Sen suit), which captured the spirit of revolution and redefined Chinese style for men. The suit is believed to have been based on a Japanese military uniform, possibly a Meiji-period student uniform (a Japanese school uniform based on a sailor's outfit) and a Western tailored suit. This became a significant garment; it was worn as official dress for civil servants, and was worn and modified by intellectuals as a clear statement of a break from the previous autocratic imperial regime. Undoubtedly, Mao and the fledgling Communist Party of the early twenties would have worn the garment when it was introduced and his later modifications would, in turn, become China's national dress and become pseudonymous with Mao and the Communist Party itself.

The new Republic had specific dress codes for men and only one form of dress was specified for women. This was a basic embroidered jacket and skirt, which to all intents and purposes was a continuation of the Han style. The Republican period was however characterized by greater freedom of expression for women, as they were able to pursue education and employment, and many urban citizens seized that opportunity to embrace modernization and find their own stylistic voice. The emancipation of dress for women, which was in line with these greater freedoms, was to be even more radical than the changes in men's dress and came in the shape of a dress known as a *Qipao* (Mandarin) or *Cheongsam* (Cantonese).[31]

Qipao translates as banner dress, due to its resemblance to a square-cut hanging banner, so it could have its origination in the long Manchu style robes with the curved opening on the right side of the garment which were worn throughout the Qing dynasty. The *Cheongsam* in Cantonese translates as "long gown" and there is speculation that the garment could have been developed from the male *Changpao*, whilst its high collar almost certainly echoed military styles. The Hong Bang tailors, who were initially constructing the garments with their new-found Western pattern cutting techniques, would almost certainly have understood that darts would contribute to the reduction of volume between the hip and the waist. The darts and cutting lines would give the pattern a more body conscious and feminine manifestation. The abolition of foot binding in 1911 and breast binding in 1928 ensured the *Qipao* very quickly became women's standard wear. Not only was the *Qipao* distinctively Chinese and imbued with a new social narrative of personal mobility, of femaleness and of modernism (through new fabrication and shape) but, it reflected the transformation of women's bodies.[32]

Much of the urban populations had embraced or accepted change; some of the port cities had thrived as commercial centers attracting rural urban immigrants as opportunities for both trade and work developed. Shanghai became the most prominent port and by 1920 was the sixth busiest in the world, and arguably one of the most decadent. The most successful ports were not only gateways to China but became trade and manufacturing hubs as well as locations for large numbers of entrepreneurial Chinese who embraced capitalism.[33] The end of the imperial dynastic period, the influence of Western nations through semi-colonialism and the birth of the new Republic may well have given China a distinct legacy surrounding clothing and dress, in terms of cut, silhouette, representation, socio-cultural relevance, and positioning within global communities. It did not, however, bring stability. Instead, it ushered in a series of conflicts that tore China apart. Regional centers led by warlords competed for power. Furthermore, the First World War was a catalyst to foreign powers to relinquish their claims to Chinese ports and territories as well as an instigation of mass anti-foreign protests.[34] The anti-communist campaign of 1929–33, the anti-Japanese war of 1937–45 and the civil war of 1946–9 all meant that, as 1949 came to a close, a new revolutionary party, the Communists, came to power. For the majority of the population this was a huge relief after more than thirty years of conflict and invasion. Mao Tse Tung, the new leader, had connected with the populace and he was more than aware of the power of dress and identity as a representation of a nation and a political paradigm.

Identity, economy, and practicality

After 1949 our production of fabrics and silks increased considerably as did the quality of life and expectations of the people. Increased production of fabric however is not enough alone to meet the people's needs. We should therefore not just increase production to meet demand but look at how we can use and save fabric. One of the important and practical ways to increase fabric saving is to change old clothes into new clothes. It seems such a waste that there are so many large mountains of old clothes that are stored in cases and homes so if we could change old clothes into new clothes we could meaningfully save large amounts of goods (raw materials) for the country and also save spending on fabric.

This is a section of the introductory statement from a patternmaking and clothing construction publication from October 1957 entitled *New Clothes from Old Clothes.* The publication was produced by the Shanghai Cultural Department in conjunction with the Shanghai Government Group (Apparel) and provided practical examples of how to re-work and re-model existing garments. The main introduction not only defines the context of the publication but also describes two fashion events in early and mid-1957, held in Shanghai, which introduced the public to the concept of reconstructing, or in contemporary terms up-cycling, old clothes into new clothes. The final selection of designs included within the instruction manual are cited as being inspired by the most popular garments displayed within the events. In line with the final designs, the Shanghai Government Group produced commercial paper patterns, which could be purchased individually by the public, and which related directly to the construction techniques defined within the publication. The printed instructions indicate clear processes of construction for the dressmaker, measurements, and methods to unpick existing garments.

The introductory statement also poses a number of pertinent questions with regards to: the lack of raw materials for clothing production, a failure by the fledgling government to meet the basic needs and expectations of its growing population, and the excessive number of used garments now considered redundant both stylistically and politically.

Figure 10.1 The Yu family portrait taken in Beijing in 1930 illustrates the diversity of clothing influences on affluent Chinese of the period and the types of garments that could be re-modeled at a later date.

Significantly, the front cover of the publication portrays a character that is markedly in contrast to the general Western perception of China's language of dress during the 1950s. The key image of the woman and the surrounding illustrations are embedded with layers of conflicting narratives. The main image recognizes and positions a well-manicured, sophisticated, educated, urban inhabitant, which suggests a deliberate message from the publishers to promote the acceptance of a certain notion of "style"; that of an urbanized population positioned within an accepted, political paradigm. This image seems to conflict with the realities of the time. In the early years of the regime, in the years after the peasantry fought the civil war, the Communist Party began to construct and manage a new society. With a population of 600 million and a philosophy of utopianism implemented from a centralized control system, the new and inexperienced regime was destined to encounter difficulties.[35] Poor crops in the mid-1950s, workers' unrest in the form of strikes opposed to pay reductions, and lessening support from the USSR meant that the initial seeds of growth post-1949 had by 1956 largely failed. Food shortages grew due to climate failure, poor distribution, and resistance to the collective farm system, whilst factories were unable to meet their targets and construction work slowed.[36] Sartorially, the population lacked the finances, resources, and the desire to deviate from the expectations of a party philosophy that rejected the past, and who's leader, was both anti-Western and anti-imperialist.

The image taken in 1930 of the Yu family in Beijing, captures a range of styles that would have been rejected by socialist doctrine as they contained the remnants of Qing dress styles (re-fashioned to be acceptable by the Republican Senate), alongside Western styles of formal and casual wear. It is these styles that likely would have populated the "mountains of old clothes" identified in the publication, that would be suitable for re-purposing.

The younger women at the rear of the image all sport contemporary versions of the high-collared *Qipao* as well as fashionable bobbed style haircuts of the time, whilst the more elderly women in the foreground are wearing the early versions of the *Qipao,* which had a much wider cut, were less body conscious and were based more closely on the Qing dynasty banner dresses. The majority of the men are in *Changpao* and *Magua* jackets with only one male, in a Western three-piece suit, implying that for more formal activities, such as a family portrait, there was a retentive link to traditional wear.[37] These choices are testament to the fact that the population continued to wear clothing that identified culturally with China's stylistic heritage, particularly eminent families such as the one pictured.

Figure 10.2 Pattern and construction book entitled *New Clothes from Old Clothes*, produced by the Shanghai Cultural department in 1957. The text encourages and gives instruction to the population to up-cycle existing garments.

Although the Communist Party rejected previous styles of dress, unlike both the imperial dynasty and the Republican Senate, they did not issue edicts regarding appropriate types of clothing that defined association or social standing within the regime. They did, however, develop a complex system of visual coding that was delivered and continually reinforced to the population, through posters, the media, novels, plays, and films. This method of disseminating information had been established by the Soviets who used artistic representations of muscular state heroes and radiant heroines as powerful propaganda.[38] The Communist Party used similar methods of visualization (which was important, considering much of the population was still illiterate) to reinforce political doctrine and define dress within a new sartorial landscape that shifted the emphasis from the individual to the collective.

Collectively, men abandoned Western styles and sought association with cultural and military heroes and political leaders. Mao had modified the *Zhongsan Zhuang* (the Sun Yat-Sen suit) and appropriated it to symbolize the new China, whilst the civilian cadres (officials), workers, and technicians readily accepted the *Zhifu,* which was a version of the military jacket, except made of dark blue cloth. Gray versions were worn by administrative staff, who had slightly higher status within the ruling systems.[39] Many women also donned the same or similar garments as the men, and patriotic dress became not only utilitarian and practical but represented clothes for the masses whilst being ideologically symbolic.

Information regarding specific details surrounding clothing practices during this period of Chinese history remains somewhat scant, as this topic would not have been of much cultural significance. The fact remained that clothing the population was an enormous task. It is only by the collecting of individual narratives through a series of interviews that we can gain an illustration of the period and details of the broader collectivization of clothing, responses to visual codification, and a clear understanding of the role of the handmade in the production of garments.

Ordinary residents such as Yuming Lu, who was living in Shanghai when the Communist Party took control in 1949, when interviewed regarding his relationship to clothing, recalled that he did not particularly care what he dressed in. Rather he just wanted to look the same as everyone else, as to differentiate himself through his clothing or hairstyle would have brought trouble upon himself.[40] Trouble could be incurred by standing-out, by being individual, and therefore by being noticed by the authorities.

Zhao BaoXun, a Beijing resident in the late 1950s, when asked about how clothing was procured during this period, recalled how popular the *Zhifu* and the *Zhongsan Zhuang* were, as they represented the new China and bore resemblance to the revolutionary military uniform. He also recollected that the actual military uniforms were the most prized to own but were difficult to acquire if one was not in the army. Nevertheless, if one could get second-hand military buttons then that would finish off a homemade jacket more stylishly.[41]

The most significant garment for men of this period was the *Zhongsam Zhuang* and the book (Figure 10.3) gives clear instruction on how to construct one through deconstructing a *Changpao,* by opening up the side seams and laying the garment fully flat to accommodate the newly purchased commercial pattern pieces. With no shoulder seams, there is sufficient length within the deconstructed garment to allow for a pants pattern to fit readily through the body section, whilst the wrap opening provides the fabric for the two-piece sleeve pattern. The information in the upper left-hand box of the page contains the length, waist, and sleeve length measurements of the *Changpao,* whilst the lower box contains the measurements for the length of the jacket, the jacket

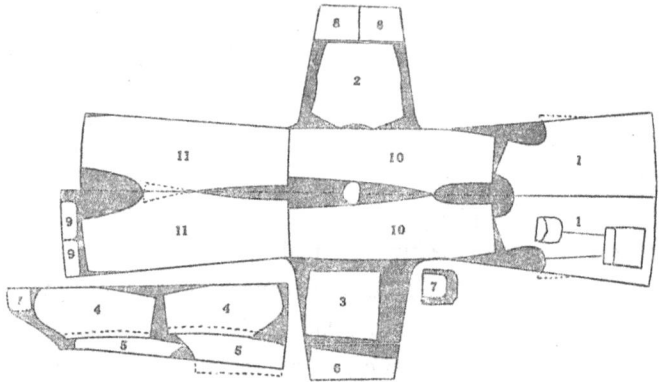

（二） 長衫改制中山裝一套 排料圖之二

Figure 10.3 Specific instructions on how to construct a modified *Zhongsam Zhuang*, or as its more commonly known the "Mao Suit" from a traditional floor length men's garment known as a *Changpao*.

waist, and jacket sleeves measurements. In addition, the box contains the length of the pants, the pants' waist measurement, and the distance around the hem of the pants. Further information in the main box identifies and names the pattern pieces and information about fixing holes including previous button plackets in advance of re-making. Within the booklet there are clear instructional guides that apply to all the styles, providing both general information and specific cautions. These include detailed information on a range of processes, including how to unpick the existing garments and how to press them flat before placing the pattern pieces. The primary deviation from these military-rooted styles occurred within women's apparel. Femininity was essentially abandoned as women embraced the basic shirt and trouser ensemble or "people's dress" and initially adopted the Soviet-style Lenin suit, which represented solidarity with China's Soviet allies and empathy for the spirit of revolution. As the Soviet influence diminished in China, around the time of this particular publication, female versions of the *Zhongsam Zhuang* and *Zhifu* worn by male cadres (officials) were developed. A number of these styles are identified within the patterns and clarify this stylistic evolution.

The *Liang Yong Shan* jacket, which translates as the two-function top (Figure 10.4) is a female version of the *Zhangsam Zhuang*. The collar pattern is open at the neck and turned down flat, in contrast to the men's version and the two breast pockets, common in the men's style, are removed to make the fit more suitable for the female body. The label "two-function" refers to the design being both suitable as a light coat for summer or as a layer underneath heavier jackets in winter, dependent on the fabric used for its manufacture. The garment pattern uses astute reconstruction techniques from a previous Western style, the male suit jacket. This includes incorporating the original pocket and fit lines into the design with no deconstruction required, and creating a clever fit through a style line across the top of the bust. The smaller cut of the women's jacket allows the center-front buttonholes to be omitted and the internal jacket facings to be utilized. From the early 1950s, Western suits were viewed as remnants from the old society and associated with capitalism and foreign intervention. They were often re-modeled into *Zhifu*-style uniforms, which were inexpensive to reconstruct as labor was cheap, and stylistically they were recognizable as a mark

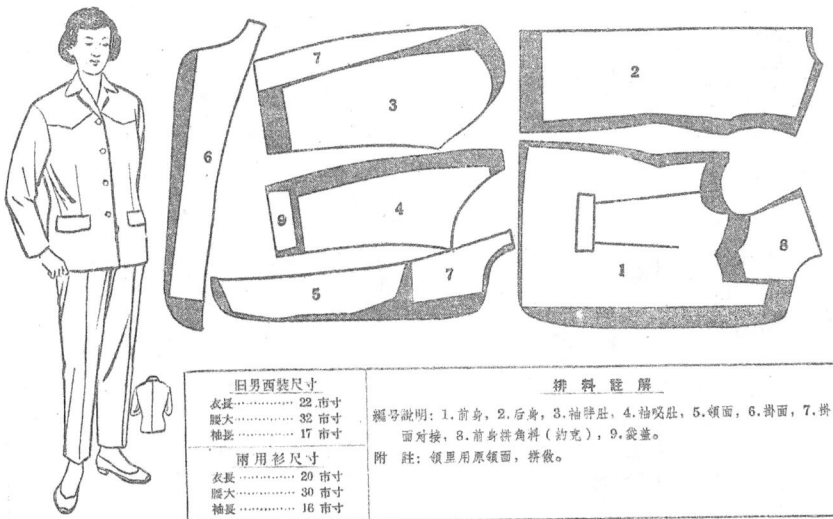

（五十一）　男西裝改制女式两用衫一件　排料圖

旧男西裝尺寸	
衣提	22 市寸
腰大	32 市寸
袖提	17 市寸
两用衫尺寸	
衣提	20 市寸
腰大	30 市寸
袖提	16 市寸

排料詮解

編号說明：1.前身，2.后身，3.袖肆肚，4.袖吸肚，5.領面，6.掛面，7.拼面对接，8.前身拼角料（約克），9.裂蓋。

附　註：領里用原領面，拼做。

—— 57 ——

Figure 10.4 This pattern shows how the popular *Liang Yong Shan* jacket for women (translated as the two-function jacket) can be constructed from a Western man's tailored jacket. This could be purely pragmatic or a political gesture empowering both women and the regime.

of a progressive state employee who followed the sartorial model set by Chairman Mao himself.[42]

Figure 10.5 gives clear instruction on how to deconstruct a *Qipao* and to re-make it into a light, convenient, casual top. As previously noted, the Qipao had become a significant garment worn by the majority of women in urban locations and there would have been extensive amounts of previously worn garments to reconstruct. For this particular pattern there is not enough fabric provided by the original garment and the additional pieces are required from other sources. Importantly, this is noted in the instructions within the page. Many garments during this period were patched or constructed from more than one type of fabric, so this would not have been seen as unusual. Symbolically, the Qipao represented Western influence and sexuality and was at odds with the political environment so it is surprising that there are also instructions on how to construct a *Qipao* from a man's *Changpao*, within the publication. The instructions indicate that from a *Changpao*, a long-sleeved or short-sleeved *Qipao* can be fashioned, as well as a pair of pants, but only if the person for whom the garments were created was small in stature. Notably the *Qipao* was

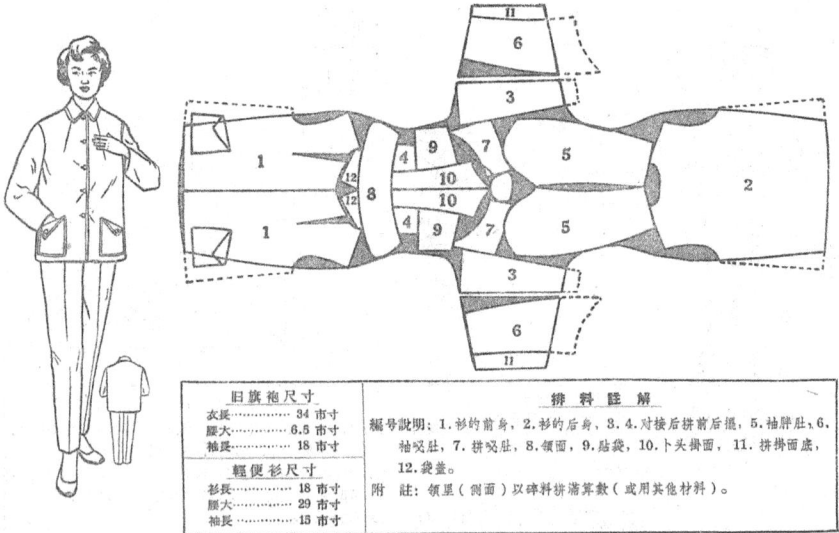

Figure 10.5 The *Qipao* went from being the most popular female garment in China pre-1949 to being redundant by the late 1950s. This pattern reworks a *Qipao* into a more functional and culturally appropriate jacket.

out of fashion with the majority by the time this publication was produced, so it is unlikely that this style of garment would have been re-made from other garments. *New Clothes from Old Clothes* may be considered as part of a broader political statement addressing the issue of clothing within the population by encouraging an engagement with the art of construction. There are ninety-one styles identified within the text, each cleverly cut to maximize fabric usage, previous styles of garments, fit and shape lines and details. There are garments for men, women, and children, well-constructed from patterns with expertise that seem to be responding to appeals from both the government and the population itself to improve its sartorial representation, particularly with respect to its urban populations. There was a brief attempt to address the drabness of the nation by the Ministry of Culture that had been made through the short-lived Dress Reform campaign of 1955–6. The campaign included the development of new garment styles and textiles prints that were featured in fashion shows and in the media; an effort that may well have positioned clothing, albeit briefly, on the social agenda, possibly opening up a broader debate around national identity, self-perception and socio-cultural associations.[43] There was certainly a considerable show of interest from the public in the major urban conurbations, as fashion events during this campaign displayed new styles and fabrics and this method of engaging the public in the development of new garment styles may well have been the precursor to the patternmaking book identified here.[44] The development of the garments featured in *New Clothes from Old Clothes* may have been inspired by the Dress Reform Campaign, however it is more likely to have been a pragmatic exercise in re-using existing materials and reinforcing frugality due to the wider economic and political scenarios. Notably, that campaign and the publication itself are framed within the same timeline (1956–7) of the Hundred Flowers movement, which was also meant to give a voice to the people but ended as a tool of retribution.[45] Inevitably though, the tightening of government control and the purging of individual ideas after the Hundred Flowers movement alongside disastrous policies such as the Great Leap Forward, contrived to ensure that whatever ideas had been formulated around dress in relation to visually re-affirming the success of the Communist Party's doctrine as a symbolic and representational illustration of a global power were decimated.[46] As a result of poor management, ineffective policies, famine, and the lack of resources on a gargantuan scale, by 1960 sustaining the basic needs of a large population, including clothing, became impossible.

Frugality and rationing had been put in place in the mid-1950s and by the end of the decade covered the majority of products including shoes and fabrics, so in order to clothe themselves the population had no choice but to revert to making and re-making. Shuzhen Zhang, interviewed about her relationship with clothes during the 1950s and 1960s, recalls working together with her local community in Shanghai, to share knitting and making techniques, as well as using commercial paper patterns for making shoes, as well as clothes, both of which became a common practice. She also recalled sharing annual ration coupons for fabric (normally four-and-a-half feet per person) with neighbors.[47] Propaganda in the form of posters, mass media, and further patternmaking publications remained vibrant internally throughout this period in China, but externally the country began to retract behind its borders as internal politics and desperate living conditions led to the chaos of the Cultural Revolution in 1966. Clothing and dress remained low on individuals' hierarchy of needs and garments were continually patched, recycled, and home-constructed as a matter of necessity until the late 1970s after the death of Mao and the commencement of China's engagement with an outward facing global "opening-up" policy.

The Ottoman Kaftan: Designed to Impress

Gozde Goncu-Berk

In this chapter, Gozde Goncu Berk explores how dress that was worn in the Ottoman Empire carried significant meanings associated with the rank and the profession of an individual. Berk notes that distinct differences among high-ranking officials, courtiers and the public could be expressed through textiles and colors but also through the way in which clothing was cut. In this chapter, the author investigates how the pattern, cut, and construction details of sixteenth through eighteenth century Ottoman *kaftan* communicated layers of meaning. Berk's study provides the reader with yet another way to consider the importance of patternmaking by highlighting how design features found in the cut of apparel may have specific communicative effect. Thus, Berk's work opens up the discussion of the expressive potential of patterning that was considered in light of personal expression in Chapter 9 "Creolized Patternmaking: A Jamaican Perspective" and explored as a form of national expression in Chapter 10 "Re-Make, Re-Model, Re-Define; Fashioning A Nation's Identity." These chapters, considered as a unit, show how specific attention to patterning facilitates new perspectives in dress studies.

The Ottoman Empire (1299–1923) was a transcontinental and multi-cultural empire controlling a large territory in Asia, Europe and North Africa. The Ottoman state began as one of many small Turkish states that emerged in Anatolia (Asia Minor) during the breakdown of the empire of the Seljuk Turks. The Ottoman period spanned more than 600 years and came to an end in 1922, when it was replaced by the Turkish Republic and various successor states in southeastern Europe and the Middle East. The first period of Ottoman history was characterized by almost continuous territorial expansion, during which Ottoman dominion spread out from a small northwestern Anatolian principality to cover most of southeastern Europe and Anatolia. Some scholars and historians state that the golden age of the Ottoman Empire was reached in the sixteenth century under the reign of Suleiman the Magnificent. In contrast, the period after that is considered an era of stagnation. Halil Inalcik, a respected Turkish historian of the Ottoman Empire, notes that the failure to control the vast territorial and financial resources of the centralized empire and Europe's new military technology contributed significantly to the transformation of the Ottoman Empire by the beginning of the seventeenth century.[1] The fall of the Ottoman Empire in the First World War triggered the rapid collapse of the empire and the birth of the modern Turkey as a secular and democratic republic in 1923.

In the Ottoman Empire, dress had significant meanings associated with the ranking and the profession of the individual in the social system. Ottoman dress showed distinct differences among courtiers and the public settled in Anatolian and Rumealian (the possessions of the Ottoman Empire in the Balkan peninsula) villages. Textiles, colors, and cuts used in the court dress were forbidden for the public. Court dress also showed variations depending on where and when they were worn. Ceremonial dress and dress worn during military expeditions were different than casual attire. Dress of the non-Muslim public was also set by regulations showing distinctions among different religions. In addition, the military uniforms of Janissaries, an elite Ottoman army unit, was standardized so that they could be differentiated from the public. Therefore, design details such as pattern and construction, in addition to the quality and embellishment of the textiles, functioned as a visual language conveying meanings of status in the Ottoman Empire. Although there exist many studies on the textiles used in Ottoman court dress including its fiber, construction details, embroidery and print characteristics,[2,3,4] and the socio-cultural history of Ottoman dress,[5,6,7,8,9] research on pattern design, cut, and construction details of Ottoman dress especially in the English language is very limited. This study investigates the pattern, cut, and construction details of sixteenth through eighteenth century Ottoman court dress and is based on close readings of the literature and observations held in the Topkapı Palace Museum Collections. The study specifically focuses on *kaftan*, a front-opening coat usually reaching to the ankles, with long or short sleeves. *Kaftan* patterns worn at the Ottoman court are analyzed in detail focusing, specifically on the overall silhouette, collar and neckline, sleeve, and pockets. Construction details such as seam finishes, linings, and facings are also explored.

The earliest resources of information about Ottoman dress to this date are the Ottoman miniature paintings, the diaries and travelogues of foreign visitors, and examples of court dress in the Topkapı Palace Museum. All royal clothing was made at the palace workshop, which at its height at the end of the sixteenth century employed close to 700 tailors.[10] The Topkapı Palace Museum, in Istanbul, houses many court *kaftan* and other clothing items thanks to the Ottoman tradition of preserving the Sultan's and his immediate male relatives' clothing in sealed bundles in the treasury after their deaths.[11] According to Fikret Altay, the author of *Caftans*, the Topkapı Palace Museum houses twenty-one *kaftan* that belonged to Mehmed II (Mehmed the Conqueror, 1432–81), seventy-seven that belonged to Suleiman I (Suleiman the Magnificent, 1494–1566), thirteen that belonged to Ahmed I (1590–1617), thirty that belonged to Osman II (Young Osman, 1603–22) and twenty-seven that belonged to Murad IV (1612–40).[12]

The ancestry of the founders of the Ottoman Empire goes back to a nomadic Turkish tribe named *Kayı* who had entered Anatolia from Central Asia. The dress of the Ottoman Empire had its roots in this Central Asian nomadic culture. The nomadic lifestyle, based on constant traveling in diverse climates and horse-riding, required comfortable loose trousers (*shalwar*) that eliminated chafing, dressing in layers, and long, front-opening coats mainly known as *kaftan*.[13] Dressing in layers was one of the most significant characteristics of the Ottoman dress. A typical Ottoman ensemble was composed of three layers of clothing: the inner layer included *don* (underpants) and a *gömlek* (an ankle-length top directly worn over the skin); the mid layer was an *entari* (gown); and the outermost layer included a *kaftan* as well as other additional robes.[14] Dress of the Ottoman Empire showed a strong resemblance to this style for 600 years until the mid-nineteenth century. Starting from the mid-nineteenth century this style has changed drastically with Western influences.[15]

According to the dress historian Charlotte Jirousek, the layering of clothing in Ottoman culture did not mean merely wearing clothing items on top of one another, but the layers were designed and arranged to create a "sumptuous effect" and to "muffle the body form" to look taller and larger.[16] Jirousek further defined this characteristic as a spiritual concept tied to Islamic decorative arts where layering of the patterns was a metaphor for the divine order. Thus, to fully understand *kaftan* and the way it is cut, it is important to define other clothing layers worn with it. *Don* (sometimes termed *çakışır*) was a knee- or ankle-length foundation garment usually made of cotton, linen, silk, or wool. While women wore the *don* alone, men usually wore them under their *shalwars*. *Don* were cut wide at the top with large crotch gussets, the legs tapering to the ankles or to the knee to an opening just wide enough to get the foot through. The opening was tightly cut to prevent them from riding up during movement. The ankle-length *don* was cut long at the back to accommodate bending forward and sitting cross-legged. *Uçkur* was used as the fastening sash that gathered the waist. *Gömlek* were another foundation garment worn as a full-length top. They were T-shaped cut, kimono sleeved, pull-over style tops with a slit opening from collar down to the waist. The mid-layer *entari* was a gown worn for hundreds of years by the Ottomans underneath *kaftan* or sometimes by itself.[17] *Entari* opened at the center front and were either collarless or had small mandarin collars. They were fitted at the waist and flared through the skirt with godets on the sides. Compared to *kaftan*, *entari* were made of plain, lighter silk-blend fabrics.[18] The inner *entari* were usually secured with an embroidered or jeweled sash. The outermost layer of clothing, *kaftan*, had its roots in Mesopotamia where it was usually worn by men.[19] Robes similar to *kaftan* were depicted in the palace reliefs of ancient Persia dating to 600 BCE. By the thirteenth century, the style had spread into Eastern Europe and Russia, where *kaftan* styles provided the basis for a number of different basic garments into the nineteenth century.[20] Since the time of the Anatolian Seljuks, *kaftan* had been used as an outer garment and remained unchanged in the Ottoman Empire period.[21] *Kaftan* as the outer layer were one of the most significant clothing articles for the Ottomans. This outerwear item was worn by women, men, and children alike. However, *kaftan* were particularly elaborate in the imperial wardrobes of the sixteenth-century Ottoman Empire. The most commonly used fabrics for *kaftan* were silk, silk satin, silk brocade with gold and silver thread, satin, cotton, wool, mohair, velvet, and velvet brocade. Depending on its style, *kaftan* took different names; *kaftan* with lining were called *kapama*, short-sleeved *kaftan* were called *salari*, short-hemmed overdress *kaftan* were called *çekrek*,[22] sleeveless, fur-lined ceremonial *kaftan* were called *kapaniçe*. The Sultan and his courtiers might layer two or three *kaftans* with varying length sleeves for ceremonial functions.

    Kaftan especially functioned as a symbolic clothing item indicating the power and the estate of the Sultan. They were ranked based on the color, the number of woven cordings, and the button closures. The quality of the fabric used, the amount of fabric yardage, and number of *kaftan* layers worn by an individual all signified wealth, power, and rank. The *hil'at* (robe of honor) was the valuable *kaftan* that the Sultan presented to statesmen and foreign ambassadors to bless and honor them.[23] They could be presented at court ceremonies, at religious festivals, and at the beginning of new military expeditions or to show general appreciation, to reward a service, and at an instatement, and were presented to the receiver with great ceremony. *Hil'at* were woven with a certain color and level of quality depending on the ranking of the receiver and the degree of honor to which it was presented.[24] The color, the style, and the number of buttons and amount of cording on the chest would signify the ranking of the *hil'at* receiver or the importance of his service. Although differences in *kaftan* style and its materials conveyed information regarding rank, the distinction between men's, women's and children's *kaftan* was not obvious except for the size, color, and the amount of embellishment.[25]

Kaftan construction

There were many government regulations on design and manufacturing of fabric in the Ottoman Empire and the limits to conspicuous consumption in public were set by the Sultan. For example, only the Sultan (or at his express orders one of the viziers) could wear cloth of gold. Most textile ateliers located in Istanbul were associated with the palace, which would allow them to manufacture fabric using gold and silver thread and execute the prints and patterns designed by the palace artists called *nakkaş*.[26,27] There were laws regulating the thread and dye quality and the amount used in production of the fabric. The fabrics that did not meet the regulations were collected and ateliers were shut down.[28] Hülya Tezcan, curator of the Sultans Costumes and Textiles section of the Topkapı Palace Museum, described the regulations related to weaving:

> The numbers of silk thread in the warp and the basis weight of the silk thread that determine the quality of fabric were set by regulations. Those ateliers that weave with fewer amounts than regulated were fined. Gold and silver strings used in weaving were manufactured in *simkeşhane*[29] under government control and were required to have a control seal. Finishing treatments for the woven fabric was conducted by the government. And finally fabrics were measured and stamped to allow their sale in the market.[30]

The quality of the Ottoman fabric started to decline in the eighteenth century parallel to the stagnation and the period of decline of the Empire. The number of the warp threads and the basis weight of threads were decreased. Un-patterned fabric and fabric with small floral patterns were manufactured in contrast to earlier fabric with rich motifs.[31]

Commonly used fabrics in *kaftan* construction are described as below:

1. *Seraser* is defined as the richest type of all silk brocade fabric in the sixteenth century, primarily used for ceremonial *kaftan* and *hil'at*. The weft was silk

and silver and/or gold strings, the warp was silk and it was woven with double strands of warp.[32]

2. *Kemha* is described as heavy, rich, and stiff silk brocade fabric. Both the warp and the weft of *kemha* were of silk, and either gold or silver gilding reinforced the top row of the fabric.[33]

3. *Dibâ* is described as a high-quality *atlas*[34] that was overlaid with metallic thread and patterns.

4. *Çatma* is a fine type of brocaded silk velvet with either flat or raised pattern style, sometimes woven with metal threads.

Kaftan had a simple T-shaped cut with mostly rectangular and triangular pattern pieces. *Kaftan* patterns were created, laid out, and cut using the strategy of minimizing the waste of precious and expensive fabrics. Therefore, *kaftan* included design elements like godets, gores, gussets, and minimal sleeve and armhole shaping to match the available fabric length and width. In addition, it has been observed that symmetry of the shape of gores and godets on the left and right of the *kaftan* was not sought after, and gussets were broken down to even smaller pattern pieces. The waist was fitted with additional pattern pieces on both sides when the width of the fabric was not enough to cover the waist circumference. It also has been observed that fabric motif continuity was only sought for large-scale motifs and patterns but was sacrificed in smaller pattern pieces like the under-arm gussets and small pattern pieces of the waist and smaller godets on the skirt hems. The simple rectangular pattern cut on the front and back bodice of the *kaftan* also allowed the display of intricate brocade motifs which distinguished the Ottoman court dress from public dress with their delicacy and symbolic meanings related to power and sovereignty. From the fourteenth century through the seventeenth century, fabrics with large motifs were used in *kaftan* construction. One of the most famous of these designs was the *çintemani*[35,36] motif, composed of three balls and a wavy line. Other frequently displayed motifs in the Sultan's *kaftan* included floral motifs, celestial motifs such as moon, star, sun, and clouds, and an interpretation of a crown motif adopted from Italian weaving which were all well suited to the imperial image.[37]

The cut of Ottoman clothes had the ability to show power and prosperity. *Kaftan* were flared at the skirt with the help of godets called *peş*.[38] *Peş* was a significant design element for *kaftan* and other Ottoman clothing. Garments that included this design element were named "*peşli*" meaning with godets. *Peş* were applied to the center front and two sides of the skirt at the front and at the back to create a voluminous effect down to the hem using the narrow-width

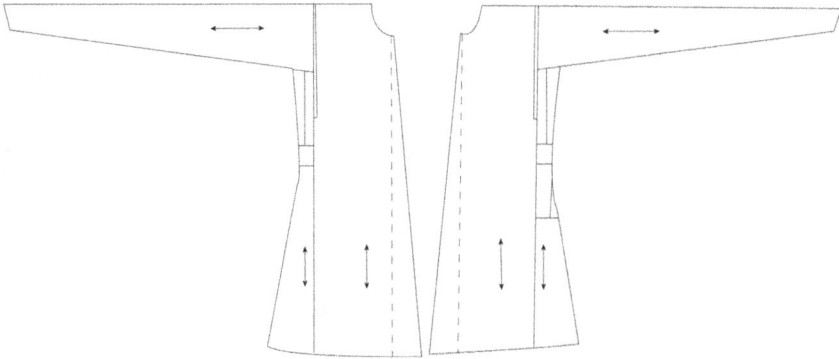

Figure 11.1 Example of asymmetrical pattern piecing on the left and right front sides of a seventeenth-century *kaftan*. *Kaftan* in the collection of the Ottoman Palace Museum, Istanbul.

hand-woven fabric.[39] *Peş* added to the center either started from the neckline or the waist; *peş* added to the sides of the skirts were also broken down to smaller pattern pieces to save fabric in some cases. The Ottoman court dress was designed and cut to give the wearer a grandiose appearance. Austrian ambassador Ogier Ghiselin de Busbecq (1555–62) defined Ottoman dress in his letters as a loose and full-length silhouette which made the wearer appear taller and larger, unlike Western dress which was tight fitting, revealing contours of the body.[40] The layering of different full-length clothing articles, decorated headgears, and voluminous cuts with the help of added *peş* were used to make the Sultan look taller and larger than his actual stature. As the Ottoman Empire entered economic and political decline in the eighteenth century, the decline observed in the quality of textiles and change in the cuts of the *kaftan* were also evident; *kaftan* had a more form-fitting look with smaller *peş* patterns.

The cut of *kaftan* was also related to its functionality. *Kaftan* had vents at the side seams or at the center back which, together with extra volume added to the skirt by the use of *peş* and the center front opening, were significant functional design elements in Ottoman dress. First, the horse was the most important means of transportation for travel, military expeditions, and hunting for the ancestors of the Ottomans, and the tradition of horse-breeding and horse-riding continued in the Ottoman Empire. Second, sitting cross-legged on a padded, raised dais, which was covered with fine carpets was another custom Ottomans took over from their nomadic ancestors who lived in tents. Many miniatures show the Ottoman Sultan traditionally sitting in a cross-legged position while accepting foreign visitors. The center front opening, and the side and center back

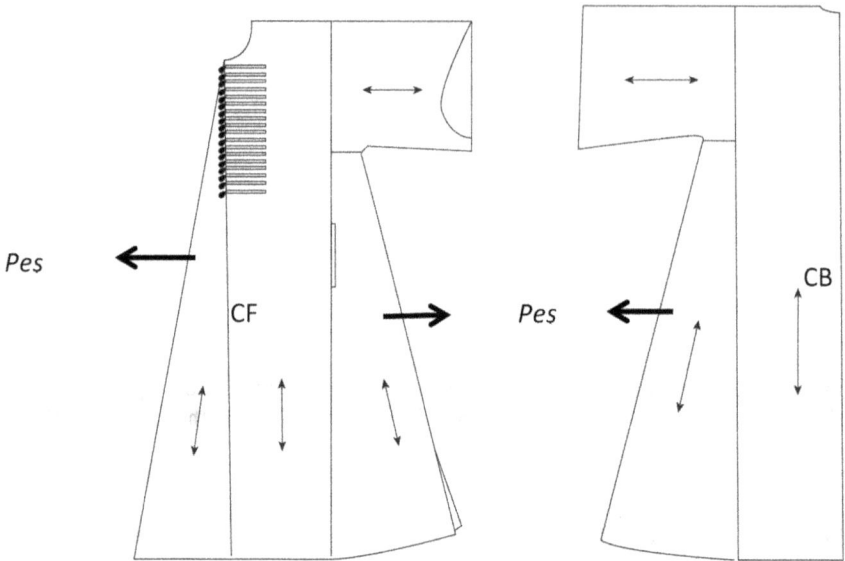

Figure 11.2 A visual representation of a seventeenth-century *kaftan* that belonged to Murad IV. *Kaftan* in the collection of the Topkapı Palace Museum.

vents as well as the flares added with *peş* to the skirt allowed for a comfortable riding position and a cross-legged sitting position. Finally, this structure of the *kaftan* allowed the wearer to show the glamour of all the fabrics worn as under-layers inside the *kaftan*. Especially, the *entari* worn underneath *kaftan* had an embroidered sash around the belt used to carry and display the valuable daggers and other weapons which were all made visible by the help of the center front opening of the garment.

The cut of clothing could also show the expense and complexity of a wearer's wardrobe. *Kaftan* came with different varieties of sleeve cuts and sleeve types. The Sultan and his court would generally wear a *kaftan* with short sleeves and an inner layer of *entari* with long sleeves so that contrasting fabrics could all be visible and admired.[41] The basic *kaftan* would have short, kimono-style sleeves, but the sleeve and the bodice were not a single piece like in a typical kimono sleeve pattern. The sleeve was cut as a straight or curved rectangular pattern and attached to the bodice with a straight seam. Gusset-like patterns were sometimes used to curve the under-arm area. The straight short sleeves were sometimes cut in a curved shape at the hem, which allowed the sleeve length to shorten down to the elbow joint in the front to provide ease of movement in bending the elbow. This curvature of the sleeve hem on the front also made the rich contrasting lining fabric and the sleeves of the inner layers visible adding an extra glamour to the Sultan's appearance. Some short-sleeved *kaftan* had extra detachable sleeves or false sleeves, which were buttoned to the *kaftan* to make it even more splendid for the court gatherings.[42] The extra pair of long sleeves that would attach to the *kaftan* could also be used for warmth. The detachable long sleeves would have an angled hem that was longer on the over arm and shorter on the under arm. The hem would widen with a small curve towards the wrist and open with a small slit at the under-arm region of the wrist including two or three buttons and loops. This way sleeves could be partially detached to display the under-sleeves.

The cut of clothing could also indicate the degree of formality or use of a *kaftan*. Long sleeve *kaftan* were observed at different lengths ranging from extra-long sleeves reaching the ankles to sleeves a few inches longer than the arm. Ceremonial *kaftan* had extra-long sleeves reaching the ankles and slits at the shoulders to put the arms through.[43] The very long sleeves were not worn, but instead thrown back over the shoulder hanging freely. This type of *kaftan* would usually be worn as the outermost level over another short sleeve *kaftan* and a long sleeve *entari*. Another type of long sleeve observed in Ottoman *kaftan* had a slit at the elbow on the front, which allowed either wearing the garment as long-sleeved or as short-sleeved by putting the arm through the slit. This type of long sleeve included buttons and loops in the hem to make the sleeve tight fitting when needed. The extra-long sleeves with arm slits were worn by the Sultan during ceremonies to add extra glamour to his looks. Another interpretation of the function of extra-long sleeves available in the literature is about the tradition of kissing the Sultan's hand to express servitude and respect. However, this tradition was banned after Murad I was assassinated by a foreign soldier who, during a war in 1389, had been admitted into the Sultan's tent to show his respects

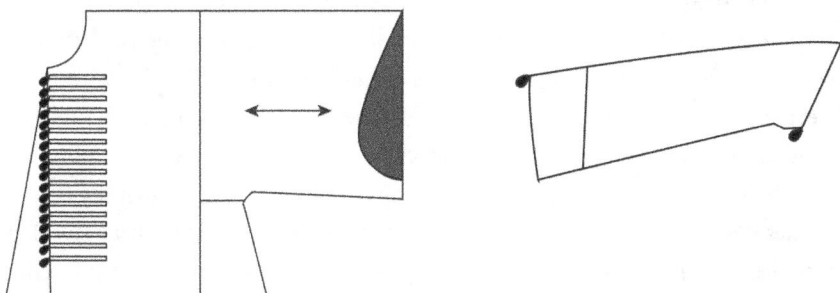

Figure 11.3 An illustration of a curved sleeve hem from Murad IV's seventeenth-century *kaftan* and an example of a detachable sleeve. Garments in the collection of the Topkapı Palace Museum.

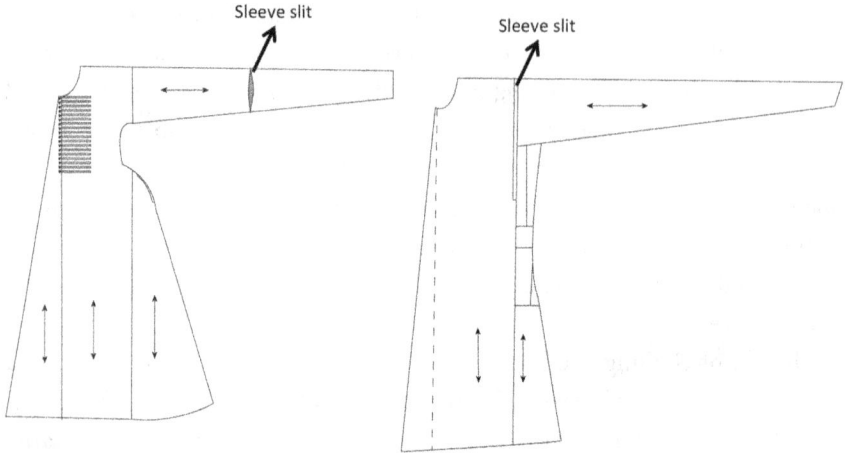

Figure 11.4 Example of a mid-sleeve slit and shoulder sleeve slit from Ahmed I's seventeenth-century *kaftan*. Garment in the collection of the Topkapı Palace Museum.

and had killed him. Kissing the hem of an Ottoman Sultan's *kaftan* instead of his hand became a protocol for foreign visitors. Some sources say that the very long sleeves of the Sultan's *kaftan* were designed for being kissed. Later, the concept these of extra-long hanging sleeves also translated into European fashion as sleeve extensions called tippets.[44]

Some *kaftan* had long sleeves just a few inches longer than the arm which could be folded back like a cuff. Long sleeves were cut in a fitted pattern shape with a slit at the under-arm seam with buttons and loops to fit the sleeve below the elbow. Inside this slit a contrasting, solid-colored fabric could be seen that gave the sleeve a wide, unfitted style when the slit was unbuttoned. The slit was usually decorated with bias binding or trims, and the fabric inside the slit was cut shorter than the actual sleeve hem to add an extra visual element.

The cut of *kaftan* had the special ability to reveal the hidden luxuries within a garment. Winter *kaftan* and ceremonial *kaftan* were commonly lined or trimmed with furs or leather. Winter *kaftan* named *kapaniçe*[45] were lined inside with sable, beech martin, squirrel, or ermine fur.[46,47] There were regulations about who could use which type of fur as well as when to wear a fur-lined *kaftan*. D'Ohsson described the Ottoman traditions regarding fur-lined *kaftan*, "When the Sultan decides it is time (which would be a Friday before going for the Friday prayer) to stop wearing the fur-lined *kaftan*, a palace officer would let the grand vizier know and the whole palace community would take off their fur lined *kaftan*."[48] According to Jirousek, by the fourteenth and fifteenth century Western fur-lined coats displayed a strong resemblance to Ottoman *kaftan*.[49] Winter *kaftan* could also be filled with cotton and quilted with straight line quilting, creating an illusion of a striped pattern on an otherwise solid color fabric.

The inside of the Sultan's *kaftan* was visible while walking, sitting cross-legged, or riding on horseback since it was open in the center front and generally had vents at the sides. Therefore, *kaftan* displayed additional aesthetic qualities with detailing used in the linings and facings. *Kaftan* were finished with facings at the neckline, sleeve hem, skirt hem, vents, and the center front opening and were fully lined. Linings were lightweight cotton fabric while facings were bright atlas and taffeta in contrasting colors. Collarless *kaftan* would be finished with bias binding around the neck with the same fabric as the *kaftan* itself. Lining patterns were attached together and to the bodice with tack stitching. Facings were attached to the lining with overcast stitching and to the bodice with tack stitching. In some *kaftan* examples, thin silk twist cording or narrow woven trims were attached on the seam between the lining and facing using overcast stitches. Square-shaped corner appliques with *rumi*[50,51] motifs were observed to decorate hem of the *kaftan* at the facing and lining intersection. Two kinds of applique techniques were employed in *kaftan*; *oturtma* and *kakma oturtma*. The *Oturtma* technique involved stitching solid color fabric to a base fabric to create the motifs, while *kakma oturtma* involved cutting away layers of fabric to form a motif.[52] *Kaftan* without linings were decorated with narrow woven trims to finish the seam allowances. It could be interpreted that the additional facing and lining decoration at the hem of the Sultan's *kaftan* could be due to the fact that

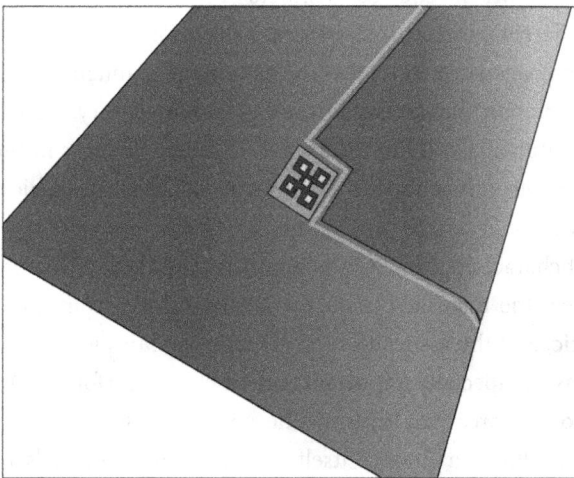

Figure 11.5 Example of facing and lining decoration detail at the skirt hem of Osman II's *kaftan*. Garment in the collection of the Topkapı Palace Museum.

hems of the *kaftan* were visible to public when the Sultan was sitting and horse-riding, and during the hem kissing ceremonies. In addition, it was noted that the hems of *kaftan* were tucked up into the *entari* sash to display both linings and the under layer clothing worn beneath.[53]

Like its other features, *kaftan* closures held symbolic meanings related to power. *Kaftan* had closures and fastenings at the center front and sleeve hems. *Çaprast* (meaning diagonal) was a decorative form of closure used on the chest of *kaftan*. It was a thin strip running from the collar to the waist of a *kaftan* on both sides of the center front opening where it ended with buttons on the right side and loops on the left. The number of *çaprast* strips on *kaftan* denoted rank and the Sultan's *kaftan* would have the largest number of *çaprast*.[54] The Sultan's *kaftan çaprast* would be embroidered with precious stones and enamels. *Çaprast* stripes were woven either by hand-braiding or using the *çarpana*[55] (card weaving) technique. Buttons and *çaprast-like* horizontal band closures were observed in European fashion in the sixteenth century while comparable examples on *kaftan* were seen in the fifteenth century; before this date, brooches and pins were the most common closures seen in Western dress in the Medieval period.[56]

Conclusion

The origins of the Ottomans can be traced back to the steppes of Eastern Central Asia, to nomadic Turkic tribes who were horse riders following their herds. The nomadic lifestyle, which required members of the tribe to be on the move and exposed to different climates, necessitated a dress form with loose trousers and front opening coats worn in layers. The Ottomans maintained this dress style unchanged for centuries. Starting in the eighteenth century, increasing contact between the Ottomans and Europeans accompanied changes in the traditional dress. In the nineteenth century, the Ottomans adopted the fashions of Europe discarding traditional clothes like *kaftan*.

Significant characteristics of Ottoman dress were the layering of garments in a way to reveal the materials of all the layers, simple geometric cuts to save precious fabric, and the association of garment qualities with rank and power. The *kaftan* was an especially important and timeless dress for the Ottoman court that served to reinforce and transmit the power and wealth of the Sultan, his court, and the Ottoman Empire itself. From the royal officials to the Sultan himself, *kaftans* of increasing quality and splendor were worn. Study of the dress of the Ottoman Empire, which occupied a large territory and lasted for more than 600 hundred years, has been quite limited compared to the literature available on Western dress of the same period. This chapter aimed to illustrate the associations of *kaftan* construction details with symbolic meanings.

The study of Ottoman dress history has usually been encapsulated within the royal costumes and textiles, while neglecting dress of ordinary people. Future research could extend beyond the imperial court and focus on the dress in different geographical regions of the Ottoman Empire. New research on links between Ottoman dress and Western dress could be conducted.

Notes

Chapter 1

1   Dorothy Burnham, *Cut My Cote* (Toronto: Royal Ontario Museum, 1973), 3–4.
2   Anne Van Buren, *Illuminating Fashion: Dress in the Art of Medieval France and the Netherlands* (New York: The Morgan Library and Museum, 2011), 3–4.
3   Katherine Barich and Marion McNealy, *Drei Schnittbücher: Three Austrian Master Tailor Books of the 16th Century* (Kennewick, WA: Nadel and Faden Press, 2015), 5.
4   Ibid., 133.
5   For an example of this see Barich and McNealy, pages 206–9.
6   See pages 169 and 157 of Barich and McNealy for examples.
7   Kevin Seligman, *Cutting for All: The Sartorial Arts, Related Crafts, and the Commercial Paper Pattern* (Carbondale, IL: Southern Illinois University Press, 1996), 3 and Edward Giles, *The History of the Art of Cutting in England* (New Delhi, India: Isha Books, 2013), 75–6.
8   Giles, 76.
9   Ibid., 77.
10 See Seligman 4 and Giles 80, respectively.
11 Giles, 73.
12 Ibid., 72.
13 Claudia Kidwell, *Cutting a Fashionable Fit* (Washington, DC: Smithsonian Instituion Press, 1979), 1.
14 Ibid., 47.
15 Ibid., 50, 77.
16 Ibid., 16.
17 Joy Spanabel Emery, *A History of the Paper Pattern Industry* (New York: Bloomsbury Academic, 2014), 21, 11.
18 Ibid., 40–1.
19 Ibid., 100.
20 Ibid., 50–1.
21 Ibid., 86.
22 Ibid., 61, 104.
23 Ibid.,13.
24 Elizabeth Hawes, *Fashion is Spinach* (London: Forgotten Books, 2012), 38.

25 Christian Dior, *Dior by Dior,* Trans. Antonia Fraser (London: V&A Publications, 2007), 120.

26 *The Pictorial Guide to Modern Home Needlecraft* (London: Odhams Press Limited, 1946), 207.

27 Johanna Chase, *Sew and Save* (Glasgow: The Literary Press Ltd., n.d.), 25.

28 Maggie Wood, *"We Wore What We Got" Women's Clothes in World War II* (Warwickshire, England: Warwickshire Books, 1989), 28.

Chapter 2

1 Joy Spanabel Emery, *A History of the Paper Pattern Industry: The Home Dressmaking Revolution* (New York: Bloomsbury, 2014), 8.

2 Clive Ashwin, *A History of Century of Art Education* (London: Middlesex University, 1998), 29.

3 Arthur Efland, *A History of Art Education* (New York: Teachers College Press, 1990), 122–3.

4 A Century of Art Education Exhibition 1882–1982 was held at Middlesex Library, London, March 1982.

5 E. Sheila MacEwan, interviewed by Peter Green, August 4, 1981, MacEwan Papers, Hornsey College of Art Archive, transcript.

6 Peter Green, "Obituary Miss Sheila McEwan: Artist and Teacher," Hornsey Journal (London), June 14, 1982.

7 Ashwin, *A History of Century of Art Education*, 32.

8 D.F. McKenzie, *Bibliography and the Sociology of Texts* (Cambridge: Cambridge University Press, 1999), 19.

9 Valarie Holman, *Print for Victory: Book Publishing in England 1939–1945.* (London: The British Library, 2008), 82.

10 Claire Squires, "Britain from 1914," in *The Book: A Global History*, eds. Michael F., Suarez S.J. and H.R. Woudhuysen (Oxford: Oxford University Press, 2013), 313–4.

11 F.R. Morris, *Ladies' Garment Cutting and Making* (London: The New Era Publishing Co. Ltd., 1950), v.

12 W.H. Hulme, *The Practice of Garment-Pattern Making* (London: The National Trade Press, 1946), vi.

13 Cheryl Buckley, *Designing Modern Britain* (London: Reaktion Books, 1990), 125.

14 Holman, *Print for Victory*, 249.

15 Amy Flanders, "'Our Ambassadors': British Books, American Competition and the Great Book Export Drive 1940–60," *The English History Review* 125, no. 515 (2010): 909.

16 E. Sheila MacEwan, *Your Pattern Cutting* (London: The Sylvan Press Ltd., 1950), preface.

17 Elsie G. Davenport, *Your Handweaving* (1948), *Your Hand Spinning* (1953), *Your Yarn Dying* (1955). Betty Dougherty: *Your Leatherwork* (1947), *Your Linocraft* (1949). J.P. McCrum: *Your Toymaking* (1951), *Your Light Furniture* (1952). E. Sheila MacEwan: *Your Pattern Cutting* (1950), *A Handbook of Your Children's Crafts* (1950). Helen Brooks: *Your Embroidery* (1949).

18 Margaret Owen, foreword to *Your Leatherwork*, by Betty Dougherty (The Sylvan Press Ltd., 1947), 7.

19 Betty Dougherty, *Your Leatherwork* (London: The Sylvan Press Ltd., 1947), 8; Betty Dougherty, *Your Linocraft* (London: The Sylvan Press Ltd., 1949), 18. Elsie Davenport, *Your Handweaving* (London: The Sylvan Press Ltd., 1948), 9.

20 Paul Greenhalgh, "A History of Craft", in *The Craft of Culture*, ed. Peter Dormer (Manchester: Manchester University Press, 1997), 21.

21 Ibid., 37.

22 Rozsika Parker, *The Subversive Stitch: Embroidery and the Making of the Feminine* (London: I.B. Tauris & Co. Ltd., 2010), 5.

23 Emery, *A History of the Paper Pattern Industry*, 194.

24 Christopher Breward, *Fashion* (Oxford: Oxford University Press, 2003), 58.

25 Ibid., 57.

26 Helen Reynolds, *Couture or Trade: An Early Pictorial Record of the London College of Fashion* (Phillimore & Co.: London, 1997), 25.

27 Christopher Breward, "Fashion's Front and Back: 'Rag Trade' Cultures and Cultures of Consumption in Post-War London *c.* 1945–1970," *The London Journal* 31 no. 1 (2006): 36.

28 Emery, *A History of the Paper Pattern Industry*, 1.

29 MacEwan, *Your Pattern Cutting*, 122.

30 Marge Garland, 'Artifices, Confections, and Manufactures,' in *The Anatomy of Design: A Series of Inaugural Lectures by Professors of the Royal College of Art*, ed. R Moynihan (London: The Royal College of Art, 1951), 83.

31 Hazel Clark, "SLOW + FASHION—an Oxymoron—or a Promise for the Future . . .?" *Fashion Theory* 12 no. 4 (2008): 443. Kate Fletcher, "Slow Fashion: An Invitation for Systems Change," *Fashion Practice* 2, no. 2 (2010): 262.

32 Breward, *Fashion's Front and Back*, 20.

33 MacEwan, *Your Pattern Cutting*, 4.

34 Ibid., preface.

35 The Womens' Craft Department "trained students for the dress industry as designers, cutters and graders and skilled operatives, embroideresses, or as artists" and lists classes in "Pattern Cutting and Modelling" alongside "Tailoring for Ladies, Children and Men" which included "preparation of basic blocks and their use in cutting jackets, skirts, coats, trousers, riding breeches, shorts etc." 16–17, Hornsey College of Art and Crafts Prospectus 1955/6, Hornsey School of Art Archive, Middlesex University, London.

36 MacEwan, *Your Pattern Cutting,* 7.

37 Ibid., 22.

38 Ibid., 12.

39 Ibid., 239.

40 Ibid., 54.

41 Ibid., 7.

42 Ibid.,121.

43 Amy de la Haye "Court Dressmaking in Mayfair from the 1890s to the 1920s," in *London Couture 1923–1975: British Luxury,* eds. Amy de la Haye and Edwina Ehrman (London: V&A Publishing, 2015), 11.

44 MacEwan, *Your Pattern Cutting,* 28.

45 Ibid., 8.

46 The National Archives. "Currency Converter: 1270–2017," The National Archives. March 6, 2018. Accessed June 9, 2018. http://www.nationalarchives.gov.uk/currency-converter

47 MacEwan, *Your Pattern Cutting,* 125.

48 Ibid., 38.

49 Alexander Palmer, "Virtual Home Dressmaking: Dressmakers and Seamstresses in Post-War Toronto," in *The Culture of Sewing: Gender, Consumption and Home Dressmaking,* ed. Barbara Burman (Oxford: Berg, 1999), 213.

50 Kevin L. Seligman, *Cutting for All!: The Sartorial Arts, Related Crafts, and the Commerical Pattern Industry: A Bibliographic Reference Guide for Designers, Technicians, and Historians* (Carbondale: Southern Illinois University Press, 1996), 62.

51 MacEwan, *Your Pattern Cutting,* 4.

Chapter 3

1 *The Work of the American Red Cross in the World War: A Statement of the Finances and Accomplishments for the Period July 1, 1917–February 28, 1919* (Washington, DC: American Red Cross, 1919), 23.

2 *The Work of the American Red Cross in the World War,* 23.

3 ARC 400-3 Man's Slip on Sweater, Sleeveless (US Navy), September 1964 printing, Folder 494.1, Box 776, Series 4 1947–64. Record Group 200, American National Red Cross Central Decimal Files, 1947–64, National Archives at College Park, Maryland. This pattern was reprinted for the last time in 1964.

4 *American Red Cross Annual Report for the Year Ended June 30, 1965.*

5 *American Red Cross Annual Report for the Year Ended June 30, 1918,* ARC 501, February 15, 1919: 60.

6 Burges Johnson, "Mars Invades the Campus," Red Cross Magazine, December 1917, 580.

7 "Art Needlework," *Dry Goods Economist*, August 11, 1917: 91.

8 Anne MacDonald, *No Idle Hands: The Social History of American Knitting* (Random House Publishing Group. Kindle Edition), loc. 4220.

9 Marian Moser Jones, *The American Red Cross from Clara Barton to the New Deal* (Baltimore: Johns Hopkins University Press, 2012), xiv, 122, 137–41, 157–63; Julia F. Irwin, *Making the World Safe: The American Red Cross and a Nation's Humanitarian Awakening* (New York: Oxford University Press, 2013), 5–6.

10 Jones, *The American Red Cross*, 117.

11 Letter from J.M. Hansen to Minneapolis Chapter of the Red Cross, May 10, 1917. Box 1, Folder 3. American National Red Cross. Northern Division, Red Cross Northern Division records. Minnesota Historical Society.

12 Letter from J.M. Hanson to Minneapolis Chapter, May 10, 1917.

13 *American Red Cross Annual Report, 1918*, 60.

14 Minutes of the Woman's Advisory Committee, June 13, 1917, 1. Folder 118.922, Box 112, Series 2 1917–34, NACP.

15 Minutes of the Woman's Advisory Committee, June 13, 1917: 1.

16 Minutes of the Woman's Advisory Committee, June 13, 1917: 4.

17 Minutes of the Woman's Advisory Committee, June 13, 1917: 4–5.

18 "Instructions for Knitting" contains several patterns that are either identical or almost identical to patterns issued by the Navy League Comforts Committee, another organization that ran a knitting program for sailors. Both the Wisconsin Historical Society and Winterthur Museum, Gardens, and Library have copies of these patterns.

19 Ida C. Clark, "Red Cross," *American Women and the World War* (New York: D. Appleton and Company, 1918). Digital Edition at the World War I Document Archive. https://net.lib.byu.edu/estu/wwi/comment/Clarke/Clarke11.htm

20 Minutes of the Woman's Advisory Committee, July 24, 1917: 11.

21 Telegram from National Headquarters to Minnesota Chapter of the Red Cross, August 16, 1917. Folder 1, Box 1, ANRC. Northern Division, MHS.

22 "ARC 400: Instructions for Knitting," Woman's Bureau of the American Red Cross, August 11, 1917 printing.

23 Jane Eayre Fryer, *The Mary Frances Knitting and Crocheting Book: Or, Adventures Among the Knitting People* (J.C. Winston Company, 1918), 265–70.
   "Hurry Up Knitting for Our Soldiers," *The Touchstone*, October 1917, 105–6, 213.
   "Instructions for Knitting," *Alaska Railroad Record*, February 5, 1918, 13, 102.
   Reah Jeannette Lynch, *"Win the War" Cookbook* (St. Louis County Unit, Woman's Committee, Council of National Defense, Missouri Division, 1918), 157–61.

24 Special Meeting, Minutes of the Woman's Advisory Committee, December 3, 1917: 63.

25 Documents 58–66, Folder 118.922, Box 112, Series 2, NACP.

26 *The Pittsburgh Chapter of the American Red Cross* (Pittsburgh: Pittsburgh Printing Company,1922), 96.

27 Letter from General Manager to Division Manager, "Discontinuance of Further Knitting by Chapters," December 23, 1918, Folder 422.1 Box 421, Series 2, Record Group 200, NACP.

28 *American Red Cross Annual Report for the Year ended June 30, 1919*, 82.

29 *American Red Cross Annual Report for the year ended June 30, 1920*, 19.

30 This department had a number of different names between 1921 and 1965, Production, The Production Corps, Production and Supply Service, and Production Service. For brevity, I refer to this department as Production.

31 Jones, *The American Red Cross from Clara Barton to the New Deal*, 175.

32 Knitting Report from June 1, 1918 to October 1, 1919, Box 2, Folder 8, ANRC. Northern Division, MHS.

33 James Fieser to Mabel Boardman, August 31, 1925, Folder 422.4, Box 421, Series 2, NACP.

34 NH 338 Volunteer Service, Folder 422.4, Box 658, Series 2, NACP.

35 NH 113, Suggestions to Knitters, Folder 494.1, Box 472, Series 2, NACP.

36 NH 113, Revised November 1925, Folder 494.1, Box 472, Series 2, NACP.

37 Isabel Chamberlain to Grace Reames Street, July 11, 1928, Folder 494.1 ARC-D, Box 711, Series 3, 1935–46, NACP.

38 The History of the ANRC The History of Volunteer Special Services, 126, Box 767, 494.2. Series 3, NACP.

39 James Fieser to Area Managers, March 8, 1941, Folder 403.4, Box 651, RG 200, Series 3, NACP.

40 James Fieser to Area Managers, March 8, 1941, Folder 403.4, Box 651, RG 200, Series 3, NACP.

41 The Citizens Committee for the Army and Navy reported receiving letters from commanding officers asking about a possible knitting program throughout 1941. When the Red Cross came into conflict with this group over their Million Sweater program, they pointed to these requests.

42 Norman Davis to Frank Knox, September 27, 1941, Folder 422.4, Box 658, RG 200, Series 3, NACP.

43 Lists of Articles needed for Able-Bodied Army Stations between 1941 and 1944, Folder 403.4, Box 651, Series 3 NACP.

44 Joy Homer, "Present Arms," *The Red Cross Courier*, November 1941, 9.

45 Letter from Frank Knox to Norman Davis, quoted in letter from Horace Sprague to Don C. Smith, February 25, 1942, p. 2 Box 658, RG 200, Series 3, NACP.

46 ARC 467: *Production Service*, American Red Cross, 1964 printing, Folder 494.1, Box 781, Series 4, NACP.

Chapter 4

1 Margaret Bubolz, "Home Economics and Home Sewing in the United States, 1870–1940," in *The Culture of Sewing,* ed. Barbara Burman, 303–25. (New York: Berg, 1999), 313.

2 Ibid., 306, 313.

3 Maggie Wood, "*We Wore What We Got": Women's Clothes in World War II* (Warwickshire, England: Warwickshire Books, 1989), 21.

4 Wade Laboissonniere, *Blueprints of Fashion: Home Sewing Patterns of the 1940s,* 2nd edition (Atglen, PA: Schiffer Publishing, 2009), 25.

5 "Remodeling of Cast-Off Clothes to Conserve Material is Taught," *The New York Times* (March 9, 1942), 11. www.timesmachine.com

6 "Salvage Sewing Unit of America Bundles Will Open 2-Day Fashion Fair Tuesday," *The New York Times* (June 14, 1942), 78. www.timesmachine.com

7 "Relief Recipients Trained for Jobs: Welfare Department School Teaches Household Skills to 100 Women All over 50," *The New York Times* (September 27, 1943), 16. www.timesmachine.com

8 Helen Reynolds, "'Your Clothes are Materials of War.' The British Government's Promotion of Home Sewing During the Second World War," in *The Culture of Sewing,* ed. Barbara Burman (New York: Berg, 1999), 336.

9 Wood, 29.

10 Raymond Daniell, "British People Demand Greater War Effort," *The New York Times* (September 27, 1943), 3. www.timesmachine.com

11 "More Home Sewing Urged," *The New York Times* (April 7, 1942), 25. www.timesmachine.com

12 "Revival of Home Sewing Brings a 40% Rise in Yard Goods' Sale," *The New York Times* (February 20, 1943), 16. www.timesmachine.com

13 "Sewing Kit's Value in War Stressed: Woman's Outfit Made From Man's Old Suit Among Raiment on Display," *The New York Times* (June 11, 1942), 22. www.timesmachine.com

14 "Bank for Savings Promotes Sewing," *The New York Times* (December 6, 1945), 29. "Salvage Fair Planned: Garments Made From Odds and Ends to Be Shown Next Month," *The New York Times* (May 26, 1942), 18. www.timesmachine.com

15 Wood, 24–5.

16 Joanna Chase, *Sew and Save* (Glasgow: The Literary Press Limited, n.d.), 15.

17 "Thrift Shops are Short of Goods Due to Mounting Demands of War," *The New York Times* (March 28, 1942), 28. www.timesmachine.com

18 "Push Cotton Bags for Home Sewing," *The New York Times* (September 22, 1946), 105. www.timesmachine.com

19 "AWVS Sewing Classes: Remaking of Clothes Will Be Taught Twice a Week," *The New York Times* (June 1, 1944), 12. www.timesmachine.com

20 Vogue Pattern Service, *Vogue's Book of Smart Dressmaking* (London: Vogue Pattern Service, n.d.), 3.

21 *Make Do and Mend* (Ministry of Information: United Kingdom, 1943), 19.

22 Chase, 21.

23 *Make and Mend for Victory* (Spool Cotton Company, 1942), 9.

24 "WPB Fixes Rules for Women's Wear," *The New York Times* (April 9, 1942), 22. www.timesmachine.com

25 "Pattern Industry Gains as Home Sewing, Through WPB Order, Has Renaissance," *The New York Times* (July 16, 1942), 14. www.timesmachine.com

26 "Patterns to Save Fabric," *The New York Times* (May 27, 1943), 22. www.timesmachine.com

27 "Home Sewing Gain Blamed on Prices," *The New York Times* (August 3, 1948), 34. www.timesmachine.com

28 "Leaflet Gives Aid on Remaking Suits," *The New York Times* (November 30, 1942), 16. www.timesmachine.com

29 *Make Do and Mend*, 19.

30 *Make Do and Mend*, 21.

31 *Singer Make-Over Guide: Ideas and Instructions for Renewing-Altering and Restyling Clothing and Fabric Furnishings* (New York: Singer Sewing Machine Company, 1943), 34–5.

32 *A Bag of Tricks for Home Sewing* (Memphis, TN: National Cotton Council, 1945), 3.

33 Chase, 23.

34 Chase, 29–30.

35 Chase, 38.

36 "The Complete Book of Sewing. By Constance Talbot," *The New York Times* (July 11, 1943), 58. www.timesmachine.com

37 Jonathan Walford, *Forties Fashion: From Siren Suits to the New Look* (New York: Thames and Hudson, 2005), 131.

38 "Revival of Home Sewing Brings a 40% Rise in Yard Goods Sale," *The New York Times* (February 20, 1943), 16. www.timesmachine.com

39 *Singer Make-Over Guide,* 2.

40 "Relief Recipients Trained," 16.

41 Reynolds, 33.

42 "Pattern-Maker for Home Sewing Aids Fitting of Sizes from 4 to 46: Stencil-Like Guide Lends a Professional Touch to Amateur Tailoring—Other Devices Assist in Rennovation," *The New York Times* (July 31, 1943), 16. www.timesmachine.com

43 Wolford, 126.

44 Dominique Veillon, *Fashion Under the Occupation*. Trans. Miriam Kochan (New York: Berg, 2002), 55.

45 Veillon, 59.

Chapter 5

1 Susan Lee and Peter Passell, *New Economic View of American History* (New York: W.W. Norton, 1979), 85–6 and A.H. Conrad and J.R. Meyer, "Income Growth and Structural Change: The United States in the Nineteenth Century," in *Studies in Econometric History* (London: Chapman and Hall, 1965), 115–82.

2 Michael Zakim, "The Reinvention of Tailoring" in *Ready-Made Democracy* (Chicago: University of Chicago Press, 2003), 71. Zakim identifies the economic importance of published pattern drafting systems for the ready-to-wear trade.

3 Joseph Couts, *Practical Guide for the Tailor's Cutting Room* (Glasgow: Blackie and Son, 1848), 64.

4 Gunther F. Hertzer, *Garment Cutting in the Twentieth Century* (Ohio: Self-published, 1892), 128.

5 Charles J. Stone, "Successful Cutters," in *International Custom Cutters' Association of America* proceedings (St. Louis, January 24–7, 1911), 87.

6 *American Gentleman* VI, no. 2 (September 1906), 18.

7 *American Gentleman* IX, no. 7 (September 1909), 22.

8 John West, *Revised Grand Edition* (New York: Self-published, 1890), 41; Charles Stone *Paramount Cutter* (Chicago: Meyer and Brother, 1887), 62.

9 William P. Field, tailor, Washington DC, personal communication with C. Roy, November 5, 1989. Mr. Field began his apprenticeship at Brinkman's in Hanover Square, London in 1946.

10 John Killey, *New System of Cutting* (Liverpool: Baldwin, Cradock, and Joy, 1821), 4.

11 Gabriel H. Chabot, *The Tailor's Compasses* (Baltimore: Self-published, 1829), v.

12 Ibid., viii.

13 Ibid., x.

14 B. Young and Simon S. Rathvon, *The Archetypal Consummation* (Columbia PA: J.L. Gossler and Company, 1845), 10.

15 Couts, *Practical Guide for the Tailor's Cutting Room*, 66.

16 Harry Simons, *Drafting Pants and Overalls* (New York: The Clothing Designer Co., 1915), 10–11.

17 Ibid., 18–19.

18 *The Popular Gentleman System* (Philadelphia: Popular Gentleman Service Company, 1917), 5.

19 Charles Hecklinger *The "Keystone" System* (New York: West Publishing Co., 1890), 102–4.

20 William D.F. Vincent, *Cutters' Practical Guide to the Cutting of all Kinds of Trousers* 8th edition (London: John Williamson Company, Limited, *c*. 1901), 69.

21 Frank A. Van Aarle, *Key Line System* (Toledo, OH: Self-published, 1892), 1–25.

22 William T. Crawford, *The Science and Art of Garment Cutting* (Providence, RI: Self-published, 1874), 3.

23 J.P. Thornton, *The Sectional System* (London: Minister & Co. Ltd., 1894) "Disproportion" 54–60.

24 Chabot, *The Tailor's Compasses*, ix.

25 George W. DuNah, "Block Patterns *vs.* Drafting," The Custom Cutter and Fashion *Review*. I, no. 9 (September 1890), 12.

26 T.H. Holding. *Block Patterns and How to Cut by Them* (London: The London Tailor Office, 1905), 9.

27 See Kevin Seligman "History of the Development of the Publication of Books, Professional Journals, and the Emergence of the Paper Pattern Industry" in *Cutting for All!* (Carbondale and Edwardsville: Southern Illinois University Press, 1996), 18–21.

Chapter 6

1 David E. Weisberg, *The Engineering Design Revolution: The People, Companies and Computer Systems that Changed Forever the Practice of Engineering.* http://www.cadhistory.net/, 2008: 9–14.

2 Ibid., 14–17.

3 Billie J. Collier and John R. Collier. "CAD/CAM in the Textile and Apparel Industry." *Clothing and Textiles Research Journal* 8, no. 3 (1990): 8–9.

4 He Yan and Susan S. Fiorito, "Communication: CAD/CAM Adoption in US Textile and Apparel Industries." *International Journal of Clothing Science and Technology* 14, no. 2 (2002): 135–9.

5 Daniel Cardoso Llach, *Builders of the Vision: Software and the Imagination of Design* (New York: Routledge, 2015), 31.

6 Ibid., 49–58.

7 Mike Barlow, *The State of CAD 2017: Reinventing Design and Manufacturing* (Sebastopol, CA: O'Reilly Media), 2017.

8 Cardoso Llach, *Builders of the Vision*, 49; Imre Horváth and Regine W. Vroom, "Ubiquitous Computer Aided Design: A Broken Promise or a Sleeping Beauty?" *Computer-Aided Design* 59, no. C (2015), 166–7.

9 Horváth and Vroom, "Ubiquitous Computer Aided Design," 167.

10 Ibid.,167–8.

11 Brian R. Johnson, *Design Computing: An Overview of an Emergent Field* (New York; London: Routledge, 2017), chapter 5.

12 Rimon Elias, *Digital Media A Problem-solving Approach for Computer Graphics* (Cham: Springer International Publishing, 2014), 9, 113; Johnson, *Design Computing*, chapter 5.

13 Barlow, *The State of CAD*.

14 Yong-Jin Liu, Dong-Liang Zhang, and Matthew Ming-Fai Yuen, "A Survey on CAD Methods in 3D Garment Design," *Computers in Industry* 61, no. 6 (2010), 576.

15 Anuj Desai, Nedal Nassar, and Marian Chertow, "American Seams: An Exploration of Hybrid Fast Fashion and Domestic Manufacturing Models in Relocalised Apparel Production," *The Journal of Corporate Citizenship*, no. 45 (2012): 54–5.

16 Ibid., 54.

17 Gwendolyn J. Sheldon, "The Impact of Technology on Apparel Designer Training," *Clothing and Textiles Research Journal* 6, no. 4 (1988), 20.

18 Mark Mittelhauser, "Employment Trends in Textiles and Apparel, 1973–2005," *Monthly Labor Review* 120, no. 8 (1997): 27.

19 Denise Lisette Bean, "Job Satisfaction among United States Textile and Apparel Designers Who Use Computer-Aided Design" (PhD dis., Texas Woman's University, 1997): 68.

20 US Bureau of Labor Statistics. Accessed May 20, 2018. https://data.bls.gov/pdq/SurveyOutputServlet

21 Mittelhauser, "Employment Trends," 26.

22 Bean, "Job Satisfaction," 72–3.

23 Frederic Segonds, Fabrice Mantelet, Nicolas Maranzana, and Stephane Gaillard, "Early Stages of Apparel Design: How to Define Collaborative Needs for PLM and Fashion?" *International Journal of Fashion Design, Technology and Education* 7, no. 2 (2014), 107.

24 Abu Sadat Muhammad Sayem, Richard Kennon, and Nick Clarke, "3D CAD Systems for the Clothing Industry," *International Journal of Fashion Design, Technology and Education* 3, no. 2 (2010), 51.

25 Desai, Nassar, and Chertow, "American Seams," 54–9.

26 Sayem, Kennon, and Clarke. "3D CAD Systems," 51.

27 Bean, "Job Satisfaction," 71–3.

28 Bean, "Job Satisfaction," 63–5; Cynthia Saylor Istook, "Computer-Aided-Design (CAD) in the Apparel Industry: An Exploration of Current Technology, Training, and Expectations for the Future" (PhD dis., Texas Woman's University, 1992), 7.

29 Paolo Barbieri, Francesco Ciabuschi, Luciano Fratocchi, and Matteo Vignoli, "Manufacturing Reshoring Explained: An Interpretative Framework of Ten Years of Research," in *Reshoring of Manufacturing: Drivers, Opportunities, and Challenges*, edited by Alessandra Vecchi (Cham: Springer, 2017), 31–3.

30 M. Stott, *Pattern Cutting for Clothing Using CAD; How to Use Lectra Modaris Pattern Cutting Software* (Cambridge: Woodhead Publishing Ltd., 2014), 1–6.

31 C.K. Chan, A. Luximon, J. Yang, and S.X. Peng. "Mannequin System of Interactive Smart Body Mapping for Real-Time CAD Pattern Design," *International Journal of Arts & Sciences* 6, no. 3 (2013), 501.

32 Stott, *Pattern Cutting*, 1.

33 Jaeil Lee and Camille Steen, *Technical Sourcebook for Designers* (New York: Fairchild Books, 2014), 35–42.

34 Stott, *Pattern Cutting*, 2–3.

35 Istook, "Computer-aided-design (CAD) in the Apparel Industry," 6.

36 Kathleen Fasanella, "CAD 101 part one." Fashion-Incubator, January 16, 2007. https://fashion-incubator.com/cad_101_part_one/

37 Sayem, Kennon, and Clarke. "3D CAD Systems," 45; G. Baciu and S. Liang "Human Interaction with Computers and Its Use in the Textile Apparel Industry," in *Computer Technology for Textiles and Apparel*, edited by Jinlian Hu (Cambridge: Woodhead Publishing Ltd., 2011), 208–9.

38 Tae J. Kang and Sung Min Kim, "Development of Three-dimensional Apparel CAD System: Part 1: Flat Garment Pattern Drafting System," *International Journal of Clothing Science and Technology* 12, no. 1 (2000), 26–9.

39 C.L. Istook, E. Newcomb, and H. Lim, "Three-Dimensional (3D) Technologies for Apparel and Textile Design," in *Computer Technology for Textiles and Apparel*, edited by Jinlian Hu (Cambridge: Woodhead Publishing Ltd., 2011), 296.

40 Ibid., 310–14.

41 Sayem, Kennon, and Clarke, "3D CAD Systems," 51–2.

42 Paul Clark and Walter Wilhelm, "3D in Apparel Design: A Revolution in the Industry," Lectra Media Center, https://www.drapersonline.com/Journals/1/Files/2011/6/15/Whitepaper_3D%20in%20apparel%20design_A%20revolution%20in%20the%20industry.pdf

43 Wilburn Newcomb, "AAMA Sees Savings from Technology (American Apparel Manufacturers Association)," *WWD* 156, no. 83 (1988), 8.

44 Collier and Collier, "CAD/CAM," 9.

45 D.X. Gong, B.K. Hinds, and J. McCartney, "Progress towards Effective Garment CAD," *International Journal of Clothing Science and Technology* 13, no. 1 (2001), 12–14.

46 H.Q. Huang, P.Y. Mok, Y.L. Kwok, and J.S. Au, "Block Pattern Generation: From Parameterizing Human Bodies to Fit Feature-aligned and Flattenable 3D Garments," *Computers in Industry* 63, no. 7 (2012), 680–2.

47 Kristina Shin, Sun Pui Ng, and Ma Liang, "A Geometrically Based Flattening Method for Three-dimensional to Two-dimensional Bra Pattern Conversion," *International Journal of Fashion Design, Technology and Education* 3, no. 1 (2010), 3–4.

48 Abtew et al., "Development of Comfortable and Well-Fitted Bra Pattern for Customized Female Soft Body Armor Through 3D Design Process of Adaptive Bust on Virtual Mannequin," *Computers in Industry*, 100 (2018), 7–9.

49 Charlie C.L. Wang, Shana S.-F. Smith, and Matthew M.F. Yuen, "Surface Flattening Based on Energy Model," *Computer-Aided Design* 34, no. 11 (2002), 824.

50 S. Thomassey and P. Bruniaux, "A Template of Ease Allowance for Garments Based on a 3D Reverse Methodology," *International Journal of Industrial Ergonomics* 43, no. 5 (2013), 409–15.

51 Yi Xiu, Zhen-Kai Wan, and Wen Cao, "A Constructive Approach toward a Parametric Pattern-making Model," *Textile Research Journal* 81, no. 10 (2011), 980.

52 Fasanella, "CAD 101 part one".

53 Sayem, Kennon, and Clarke. "3D CAD Systems," 49.

54 Yamini Jhanji, "Computer-Aided Design, Garment Designing and Patternmaking," in *Automation in Garment Manufacturing*, edited by Rajkishore Nayak (Cambridge: Woodhead Publishing Ltd., 2018), 262.

55 K. Kennedy, "Pattern Construction," in *Garment Manufacturing Technology*, edited by Rajkishore Nayak and Rajiv Padhye (Cambridge: Elsevier Science & Technology, 2015), 217.

56 Fasanella, "CAD 101 part one."

57 Bean, "Job Satisfaction," 70; Istook, "Computer-aided-design (CAD)," 11–12.

58 Sheldon, "The Impact of Technology." 22–3.

59 Bean, "Job Satisfaction," 76.

60 Fabiola Bertolotti, Diego Maria Macri, and Maria Rita Tagliaventi, "Social and Organisational Implications of CAD Usage: A Grounded Theory in a Fashion Company," *New Technology, Work and Employment* 19, no. 2 (2004), 111–14.

61 Istook, "Computer-aided-design (CAD)," 12–14.

62 Fasanella, "CAD 101 part one".

63 Ibid.

64 Yan and Fiorito, "CAD/CAM Adoption," 137.

65 Istook, "Computer-aided-design (CAD)," 20.

66 Daniel James Easters, "Global Communication Part 1: The Use of Apparel CAD Technology," *International Journal of Fashion Design, Technology and Education* 5, no. 1 (2012), 51–2.

67 Barrie Leonie, "Where Next for Walmart's 3D Apparel Design Pilot?" Just-style.com, July 13, 2016. https://www.just-style.com/analysis/where-next-for-walmarts-3d-apparel-design-pilot_id128315.aspx

68 Ibid.

69 Jessica Bain, "'Darn Right I'm a Feminist ... Sew What?' The Politics of Contemporary Home Dressmaking: Sewing, Slow Fashion and Feminism," *Women's Studies International Forum* 54 (2016), 63; Addie Martindale and Ellen McKinney,

"Sew or Purchase? Home Sewer Consumer Decision Process," *Journal of Fashion Marketing and Management: An International Journal* 22, no. 2 (2018), 181–4.

70 Karen Labat, Carol Salusso, and Jongeun Rhee, "Home Sewers' Satisfaction with Fit of Apparel Patterns," *Journal of Fashion Marketing and Management: An International Journal* 11, no. 3 (2007), 434.

71 Ibid., 435–8.

72 Ibid., 439.

73 Nicole Smith, "Pattern Drafting Software," *Threads*. March 5, 2009. https://www.threadsmagazine.com/2009/03/05/pattern-drafting-software

74 Pattern Review, "My Label 3D Fashion Software," forum started on October 11, 2009 in *Patterns and Notions*. Accessed May 5, 2018. http://sewing.patternreview.com/SewingDiscussions/topic/44525.2009

75 Elaine Polvinen, "OptiTex/Siemens#3: FIT Technology Bernina MyLabel," *Virtual Fashion Technology*, November 28, 2009. https://fashiontech.wordpress.com/2008/04/04/optitexsiemens3-fit-technology-bernina-mylabel/

76 Yan and Fiorito, "CAD/CAM Adoption," 140.

77 Janet R. Wimmer and Valerie L. Giddings, "Investigation of Factors Influencing CAD Selection and Use for Apparel Design," *Journal of Family and Consumer Sciences* 89, no. 3 (1997), 50.

78 Nirupama Pundir, *Fashion Technology: Today and Tomorrow* (New Delhi: Mittal Publications, 2007), 224.

79 Linda M. Breazeale, "Prof Dresses Up Apparel Software," Mississippi State University Extension Service, December 8, 1997. http://extension.msstate.edu/news/feature-story/1997/prof-dresses-apparel-software

80 Wimmer and Giddings, "Investigation of Factors Influencing CAD," 52.

81 Johnson, *Design Computing*, chapter 7.

82 Jane E. Workman, and Ling Zhang, "Relationship of General and Apparel Spatial Visualization Ability," *Clothing and Textiles Research Journal* 17, no. 4 (1999), 170.

83 Fatma Baytar, "Apparel CAD Patternmaking with 3D Simulations: Impact of Recurrent Use of Virtual Prototypes on Students' Skill Development," *International Journal of Fashion Design, Technology and Education* 11, no. 2 (2018), 194.

84 Liu, Zhang, and Yuen, "A Survey on CAD Methods," 591.

85 Thomassey and Bruniaux, "A Template of Ease Allowance," 406–7.

86 Harry Moser and Sandy Montalbano, "Why made-in-USA fashion is turning heads," *Industry Week*, 2018. http://www.industryweek.com/economy/why-made-usa-fashion-turning-heads

87 Istook, Newcomb, and H. Lim, "Three-dimensional (3D) technologies for apparel," 314.

88 Eundeok Kim and Kim K.P. Johnson, "Forecasting the US Fashion Industry with Industry Professionals – Part 1," *Journal of Fashion Marketing and Management: An International Journal* 13, no. 2 (2009), 265–6.

89 Istook, Newcomb, and H. Lim, "Three-dimensional (3D) technologies," 319.

90 Suuchi Ramesh, "5 Tech Trends Shaping the Future of Fashion Manufacturing," *GE Reports,* July 17, 2017. https://www.ge.com/reports/5-tech-trends-shaping-future-fashion-manufacturing/

Chapter 7

1 P. Gu, M. Hashemian, and A.Y.C. Nee, "Adaptable Design," *CIRP Annals – Manufacturing Technology* 53 no. 2 (2004), 539–57.

2 Gu, Hashemian, and A.Y.C. Nee, "Adaptable Design," 539–57.

3 Gu, Hashemian, and A.Y.C. Nee, "Adaptable Design," 539–57.

4 Meenal Mistry, "Fall 2010 Ready-To-Wear Rad Hourani," *Vogue* (February 14, 2010), https://www.vogue.com/fashion-shows/fall-2010-ready-to-wear/rad-hourani

5 Angela Belcastro, "The Convertible Dress Susanna Gioia For Lemuria," *Ganzo* (August 6, 2012), http://www.ganzomag.com/convertible-dress-lemuria.html

6 HipKnoTies, "Maternity," *Hipknoties,* https://hipknoties.com/pages/maternity

7 Karen L. LaBat, and Marilyn R. DeLong, "Body Cathexis and Satisfaction with Fit of Apparel," *Clothing and Textiles Research Journal* 8 no. 2 (1990), 43–8.

8 Huantian Cao, Rita Chang, Jo Kallal, Grace Manalo, Jennifer McCord, Jenna Shaw, and Heather Starner, "Adaptable Apparel: A Sustainable Design Solution for Excess Apparel Consumption Problem," *Journal of Fashion Marketing and Management: An International Journal* 18 no. 1 (2014), 52–69.

9 Be-Artha Petersen, "The Development and Construction of Sustainable Adjustable Clothing for Growing Children" (PhD diss., Cape Peninsula University of Technology, 2010).

10 Gu, Hashemian, and A.Y.C. Nee, "Adaptable Design," 539–57.

11 Cao, Chang, Kallal, Manalo, McCord, Shaw, and Starner, "Adaptable Apparel: A Sustainable Design Solution for Excess Apparel Consumption Problem," 52–69.

12 Petersen, "The Development and Construction of Sustainable Adjustable Clothing for Growing Children."

13 Gu, Hashemain, and A.Y.C. Nee, "Adaptable Design," 539–7.

14 Osmud Rahman, and Minjie Gong, "Sustainable Practices and Transformable Fashion Design – Chinese Professional and Consumer Perspectives," *International Journal of Fashion Design, Technology and Education* 9 no. 3 (2016), 233–47.

15 Addie Martindale and Ellen McKinney, "Self-Sewn Identity: How Female Home Sewers Use Garment Sewing To Control Self-Presentation," *Journal of Consumer Culture* (first published online March 2018), https://doi.org/10.1177/1469540518764238

16 Iowa State University, Textile and Clothing Museum, "About us," http://www.aeshm.hs.iastate.edu/tc-museum/about-us/

17 Snip-It Slip, 38, in Celanese Clairanese, Acetate Taffeta, *Slip*, 1950, Textile and Clothing Museum Ames, IA.

18 Elizabeth Henderson, "Athletic Garment," US Patent 4538,614, filed Jul 12, 1983, and issued Sep 3, 1985.

19 Warners, size 34/35 B, *Brassiere*, 1995, Textile and Clothing Museum, Ames, IA.

20 Jack Milton Michel, "Body Encircling Garments," US Patent 2970,597, filed May 5, 1959, and issued Feb 7, 1961.

21 Phyllis L. Sanchez, "Variable Length Apparatus for Hemmed Garments," US Patent 4149, 275, filed Dec 2, 1977, and issued Apr 17, 1979.

22 Thomas R. LeTourneau, "Adjustable Pant Leg System," US Patent 4200,938, filed Oct 25, 1977, and issued May 6, 1980.

23 Michael A. Howard, "Adjustable Length Garment," US Patent 5539,932, filed Jun 2, 1995, and issued Jul 30, 1996.

24 Howard, "Adjustable Length Garment".

25 Karima Ryan, "Modifying Garments to Provide an Adjustable Length Feature," US Patent 2008/0127398 A1, filed Dec 1, 2006, and issued Jun 5, 2008.

26 Joseph A. Lahnstein and Evelyn K. Lahnstein, "Adjustable Garment," US Patent 2705,326, filed Oct 25, 1951, and issued Apr 5, 1955.

27 Chin-Fu Chung, "Separtable Clothing Including Shirts", US Patent 5628,064, filed Sep 22, 1995, and issued May 13, 1997.

28 Dale D. McKee, "Adjustable Length Garment," US Patent 6408,438, filed Mar 30, 2001, and issued Jun 25, 2002.

29 Nathaniel Biern, "Length-Adjustable Ready-To-Wear Skirts," US Patent 2724,120, filed Jan 3, 1952, and issued Nov 22, 1955.

30 Eliot Peyser, "Garment Having Adjustable Sleeve Means," US Patent 4475,252, filed May 4, 1983, and issued Oct 9, 1984.

31 Gloria C. Kadison, "Adjustable Waist Band Arrangement," US Patent 3793,645, filed Oct 16, 1972, and issued Feb 26, 1974.

32 Diane Von Furstenberg, *Dress*, 1970, Textile and Clothing Museum, Ames IA.

33 Thomas R. Gaines, "Waistband for Garments," US Patent 1208,132, filed Jan 27, 1916, and issued Dec 12, 1916.

34 Claris Keller, "Adjustable Size Garments," US Patent 2777,130, filed Jun 14, 1954, and issued Jan 15, 1957.

35 George R. Cantil, "Adjustable Waist and Seat for Garments," US Patent 2755,481, filed Jun 28, 1954, and issued Jul 24, 1956.

36 Paul Lampkowitz, "Adjustable Elastic Waist for Trousers and Other Garments," US Patent 2749,556, filed Feb 12, 1954, and issued Jun 12, 1956.

37 Kleinert's, *Supporter*, 1972, Textile and Clothing Museum, Ames, IA.

38 John Reardon, "Expanded Waistband Structure for Garments," US Patent 5163,184, filed Oct 16, 1991, and issued Nov 17, 1992.

39 James H. Gardner, "Garment Having an Adjustable Waist," US Patent 7516,499 B2, filed Oct 11, 2006, and issued Apr 14, 2009.

40 The Hub, Henry C Lytton & Sons, Chicago, *Vest*, late 19th century, Textile and Clothing Museum, Ames, IA.

41 Madsen, *Coat, Laboratory*, 1919, Textile and Clothing Museum, Ames, IA.

42 June S. Erickson, "Adjustable Garments, Such as Adjustable Shirts and Pants," US Patent 2010/0306901 A1, filed Jun 3, 2010, and issued Dec 9, 2010.

43 Claris Keller, "Adjustable Size Garments," US Patent 2777,130, filed Jun 14, 1954, and issued Jan 15, 1957.

44 William Padernacht, "Adjustable Coat," US Patent 1010,679, filed Jul 7, 1910, and issued Dec 5, 1911.

45 Allan Stuart, Roslyn Heights, and Harold Drachman, "Adjustable Sleeping Garment," US Patent 2905,944, filed May 1, 1958, and issued Sep 29, 1959.

46 Gu, Hashemian, and A.Y.C. Nee, "Adaptable Design," 539–57.

47 Cao, Chang, Kallal, Manalo, McCord, Shaw, and Starner, "Adaptable Apparel: A Sustainable Design Solution for Excess Apparel Consumption Problem," 52–69.

48 Gu, Hashemian, and A.Y.C. Nee, "Adaptable Design," 539–57.

49 Jeong Yim Lee, Cynthia L. Istook, Yun Ja Nam, and Sun Mi Park, "Comparison of body shape between USA and Korean women," *International Journal of Clothing Science and Technology*, 19, no. 5 (2007), 374–91.

50 Suzanne Loker, Susan Ashdown, and Katherine Schoenfelder, "Size-specific Analysis of Body Scan Data to Improve Apparel Fit," *JTATM* 4, no. 3 (Spring 2005).

51 Marina Alexander, Gina R. Pisut, and Andrada Ivanescu, "Investigating Women's Plus-Size Body Measurements and Hip Shape Variation Based on SizeUSA Data," *International Journal of Fashion Design, Technology and Education* 5, no. 1 (2011), 3–12.

52 Rose Otieno, Chris Harrow, and Gaynor Lea-Greenwood, "The Unhappy Shopper, A Retail Experience: Exploring Fashion, Fit and Affordability," *International Journal of Retail & Distribution Management* 33 no. 4 (2005), 298–309.

53 LaBat and DeLong, "Body cathexis and satisfaction with fit of apparel," 43–8.

54 Adriana Petrova and Susan P. Ashdown, "Three-Dimensional Body Scan Data Analysis Body Size and Shape Dependence of Ease Values for Pants' Fit," *Clothing and Textiles Research Journal* 26 no. 3 (2008), 227–52.

55 Kelsey McKinney, "Why It's So Hard to Find a Bra That Fits" (February 3, 2017), https://www.racked.com/2017/2/3/14172482/bra-sizing-lingerie

56 Z. Hussain, N. Roberts, G.H. Whitehouse, M. García-Fiñana, and D. Percy, "Estimation of Breast Volume and Its Variation During the Menstrual Cycle Using MRI And Stereology," *The British Journal of Radiology* 72 no. 855 (1999), 236–45.

Chapter 8

1 Karen J. Chan, "The Relationship of Motivation for Sewing, Amount of Sewing, Perceived Depersonalization of the Job, and Creativity" (MA thesis, Oregon State University, Corvallis, OR, 1975), 7.

2 Joy Spanabel Emery, *A History of the Paper Pattern Industry: The Home Dressmaking Fashion Revolution* (New York: Bloomsbury, 2014), 33–4.

3 Zeeshan Haider, "All Sewn Up: The Popularity of Do-It-Yourself Fashion Will Strengthen Industry Growth," *IBISWorld Industry Report*, no. 45113 (2014), 13. Zeeshan Haider, "Loose thread: Competition from e-commerce and online auctions will stunt growth," *IBISWorld Industry Report*, no. 45113 (2015): 13. "Sewing, Needlework, and Piece Goods Stores," *Highbeam Business*, 2015, accessed May, 7, 2016, http://business.highbeam.com/industry-reports/retail/sewing-needlework-piece-goods-stores/

4 Mary Brooks Pickens, *A Dictionary of Costume and Fashion: Historic and Modern: With Over 950 Illustrations* (Mineola, NY: Dover, 1999), 244.

5 Emery, 33–4; 55–9.

6 Emery, 34.

7 Emery, 40–3.

8 Sarah Gordon, *"Make it Yourself:" Home Sewing, Gender, and Culture 1890–1930* (New York, NY: Columbia University Press, 2009), 7.

9 Emery, 178–9.

10 Joan Courtless, "Home Sewing Trends," *Family Economics Review*, 4 (1982), 19.

11 Addie Martindale, "Women's Motivations to Sew Clothing for Themselves," (PhD dissertation, Iowa State University, Iowa, 2017), 36.

12 Johnny Saldaña, *The Coding Manual for Qualitative Researchers* (London: SAGE, 2016), 55.

13 Robert Kozinets, *Netnography: Doing Ethnographic Research Online* (Thousand Oaks, CA: Sage Publications, 2010), 58.

14 "PDF Pattern Sales and Promotion." Facebook. Accessed April 5, 2018, https://www.facebook.com/groups/PDFPatternsalesandpromotion

15 Haider, 13.

16 Rica A. Chansky, "A Stitch in Time: Third-wave Feminist Reclamation of Needled Imagery," *Journal of Popular Culture,* 43 (2010), 695.

17 Sarah Hall and Mark Jayne, "Make, Mend and Befriend: Geographies of Austerity, Crafting and Friendship in Contemporary Cultures of Dressmaking in

the UK," *Gender, Place & Culture*, 23 no. 2 (2016), 216. Emily Matchar, *Homeward Bound: Why Women are Embracing the New* (New York: Simon and Schuster, 2013), 12.

18 Haider, 6.

19 Amy Twigger Holroyd, *Folk Fashion* (London: I.B. Tauris & Co. Ltd, 2017), 31.

20 Michelle Sidler, "Living in McJobdom," in *Third Wave Agenda: Being Feminist, Doing Feminist*, eds. Leslie Haywood and Jennifer Drake (Minneapolis: University of Minnesota, 1997), 25.

21 Chansky, 689.

22 Matchar, 161.

23 Jennifer Sabella, "Craftivism: Is Crafting the New Activism?" *Columbia Chronicle Online Edition* (May 1, 2006), accessed May 7, 2018. https://columbiachronicle.com

24 Colin Campbell, "The Craft Consumer: Culture, Craft, and Consumption in a Postmodern Society," *Journal of Consumer Culture*, 5 no.1 (2005), 33.

25 "Sewing, Needlework, and Piece Goods Stores."

26 Haider, 5.

27 "Sewing, Needlework, and Piece Goods Stores."

28 Sarah Lewis-Hammond, "The Rise of Mending," *The Guardian* (May 19, 2014), accessed May 2, 2018. https://www.theguardian.com/lifeandstyle/2014/may/19/ the-rise-of-mending-how-britain-learned-to-repair-clothes-again

29 Lewis-Hammond.

30 Sarah Jane, "24% of 18–30 Year Olds Have Taken up Sewing in the Last Year," *Craft Business* (July 27, 2016), accessed February 1, 2017. http://www.craftbusiness.com/ news/view/24-of-18-30-year-olds-have-taken-up-sewing-in-the-last-year

31 Laura M. Holson, "Dusting off the Sewing Machine," *New York Times* (July 4, 2012), accessed April 7, 2016. http://www.nytimes.com/2012/07/05/fashion/dusting-off- the-sewing-machine.html?_r=0. Lewis-Hammond, "The Rise of Mending." Janice Podsada, "Ministries, Classes at Stores Aim to Teach Students Sewing," *The Hartford Courant* (March 10, 2012), accessed May 4, 2018. https://www.questia.com/ newspaper/1P2-36560524/ministries-classes-at-stores-aim-to-teach-student

32 Lewis-Hammond.

33 Garth Johnson, "Down the Tubes: In Search of Internet Craft," in *Handmade Nation: The Rise of DIY, Art, Craft, and Design*, eds. Faith Levine and Cortney Heimerl (New York: Princeton Architectural Press, 2008), 31.

34 Twigger Holroyd, 33.

35 Hall and Jayne, 226.

36 Rachel Fry, "Craftivism: The Role of Feminism in Craft Activism," (MA thesis., Saint Mary's University, Nova Scotia, 2014), 113.

37 Twigger Holroyd, 44.

38 Martindale, 58.

39 Jennifer Russum, "Leveraging the Linky Party: Knowledge is Sharing in the Blogosphere," *Women, Work, and the Web*, ed. Carol Smallwood (Lanham: Rowman & Littlefield, 2015), 99.

40 "Sewing classes," Craftsy, accessed May 7, 2018. http://www.craftsy.com/classes/sewing

41 "Home page," Pattern Review, accessed, April 23, 2018, http://sewing.patternreview.com

42 "Home page," BurdaStyle, accessed April 1, 2017, http://www.burdastyle.com 43-BurdaStyle

43 "Home Page," Pattern Review.

44 "Home Page," Pattern Review.

45 "Home page," BurdaStyle.

46 "Home page," BurdaStyle.

47 "Media Kit 2," Sewing Rabbit, accessed May 5, 2018 http://www.mesewcrazy.com/media-kit-2

48 Holson.

49 "Sewing inspiration and tutorials," Facebook. Accessed May 5, 2017, https://www.facebook.com/groups/Sewinginspirationandtutorials/

50 Martindale, "Women's Motivations to Sew Clothing for Themselves," 58.

Chapter 9

1 Paul Khalil Sauicer, "Cape Verdean Youth Fashion: Identity in Clothing," *Fashion Theory*, 15, no. 1 (2011), 50–66.

2 Carolyn Cooper, "Dancehall Dress: Competing Codes of Decency in Jamaica," in *Black Style*, Carol Tulloch (London: V&A Publications, 2004), 68–83.

3 Tulloch, Carol, "Out of Many One People: The Relativity of Dress, Race and Ethnicity to Jamaica," 359–82 and Bibi Bakare-Yusuf, "Fabricating Identities: Survival and the Imagination in Jamaican Dancehall Culture," *Fashion Theory Journal of Dress, Body and Culture*, 10, no. 4 (2006), 461–83.

4 Steeve O. Buckridge, *The Language of Dress: Resistance and Accommodation in Jamaica, 1750–1890* (Kingston: University of West Indies Press, 2004), 1–15.

5 Carol Tulloch, "No Place Like Home. Home Dressmaking and Creativity in the Jamaican Community of the 1940s and 1960s," in *The Culture of Sewing, Gender, Consumption and Home Dressmaking*, edited by Barbara Burman (London: Berg, 1999), 111–25.

6 Davinia Gregory, "A Tale of Two Houses: Tracing Transitory Changes to Two Jamaican Social Classes through their Micro-cultures of Sewing in the Independence Period (1960–1970)," *TEXTILE*, 16, no. 2 (2018), 126–45.

7 Tulloch, 111–25.

8 Gregory, 126–45.

9 Tulloch, 111–25.

10 Gregory, 3–19.

11 Mrs. Lewinson, 'Miss Cherry'.

12 Ibid.

13 Tulloch, 111–25.

14 Mrs. Lewinson, 'Miss Cherry'.

15 Ibid.

16 Barrington Young (brother of patternmaker, Gloria West) in discussion with the author, July 2016.

17 Ibid.

18 Gregory, 3–19.

19 Andrea Graham (patternmaker) in discussion with the author, August 2017.

20 Ibid.

21 Ibid.

22 Ibid.

23 Ibid.

Chapter 10

1 Werner Meissner, "China's Search for Cultural and National Identity from the Nineteenth Century to the Present," *China Perspectives*, 68 (2006), 41–54.

2 Verity Wilson, *Chinese Dress* (London: V&A, 1990).

3 Yuan Zujie, *Dressing for Power: Rite, Costume, and State Authority in Ming Dynasty China* (New York: Springer-Verlag, 2007), 182–5.

4 Valerie Steele and John Major, *Decoding Dragons: Clothing and Chines Identity* (New Haven: Yale University Press, 1999), 28–34.

5 R.L. Thorp, *Son of Heaven, Imperial Arts of China* (Son of Heaven Press, 1988), 82–6.

6 Ibid.

7 Steele and Major, 28–34.

8 Margaret Medley, *The "Illustrated Regulations" for Ceremonial Paraphernalia of the Ch'ing [Qing] Dynasty* (London: Han-Shan Tan, 1982).

9 Verity Wilson, *Chinese Dress* (London: V&A, 1990),19.

10 The Victoria and Albert Museum in London has a collection of un-tailored dragon robes. These show the final lengths of fabrics, known as bolts, and the consistent width of the fabric in relation to the loom which wove the fabric.

11 Wilson, 20, 21.

12 Joy Spanabel Emery, *A History of the Paper Pattern Industry* (New York: Bloomsbury, 2014), 5.

13 Ibid., 6–8.

14 Rock-of-eye is the freehand method of mentally calculating a drafting formula using a measure and chalk. It relies on experience with pattern shapes and dimensions.

15 A.C. Scott, *Chinese Costume in Transition* (Singapore: Donald Moore, 1958), 7, 21, 22.

16 Identified in a copperplate engraving of a European Pavilion at the Garden of Perfect Clarity in Yuanmingyuan, Beijing, China, after drawings by Yi Lantai, 1781–6. Victoria and Albert Museum, Museum no. 29452.

17 Catherine Ladds, "China and Treaty-port Imperialism," in *The Encyclopedia of Empire* (New York: Wiley Publications, 2016), 1–6.

18 Ibid.

19 Antonio Finnane, *Changing Clothes in China, Fashion, History, Nation* (London: Hurst, 2007), 64.

20 Wen-hui Tsai, *From Tradition to Modernity: A Socio-historical Interpretation on China's Struggle Toward Modernization Since the Mid 19th Century* (Occasional Papers/Reprint Series in Contemporary Asian Studies, 1986), 19–21.

21 Bryna Goodman and David Goodman, *Twentieth Century Colonialism and China: Localities, the Everyday and the World* (Abingdon, UK: Routledge, 2012), 3–9.

22 Christine Tsui, *China Fashions: Conversations with Designers* (London: Berg, 2009), 3.

23 The term Hong Bang tailors is thought to be derived from foreign customers, mainly Dutch, who had a reddish-colored hair. Hong is Chinese for red. Bang refers to a group—tailors in this case.

24 Darts allow fit into garments based on pattern pieces which accommodate and reflect body shapes. These are modeled as today on stands or dress forms.

25 Tsai, 19–21.

26 Finnane, 71–93.

27 Ibid.

28 Ibid.

29 Liao Jun, Xu Xing, *Zhong Guo Fu Shi Bai Nian* (Shanghai: Shanghai Cultural Publishing, 2009), 80–5.

30 Zhao Li, Liu Rui Pu, *Min Guo Chu Nian Ban Bu De Fu Zhi Kao Lun* (Academic Fashion Guide, 2016), 25–31.

31 The *Qipao* is the Mandarin Chinese translation whilst the *Cheongsam* is the Cantonese pronunciation.

32 Wessie Ling, "Chinese Modernity, Identity and Nationalism: The Qipao in Republican China," in *Fashions: Exploring Fashion through Cultures* (Oxford: Inter-Disciplinary Press, 2012), 79–89.

33 Ladds, 5.

34 The decade of 1919–28 saw mass protests beginning with the May Fourth movement as a reaction against the government's weak response to China's treatment in the treaty of Versailles which allowed Germany and Japan to retain control of land in Shandong.

35 Jonathan Fenby, *The History of Modern China, The Fall and Rise of a Great Power 1850–2008* (New York: Penguin, 2008), 351.

36 Ibid., 383–6.

37 David Kidd, *Peking Story: The Last Days of Old China* (New York: Review Books Classics, 2003). The book recalls the story of the family pictured. David Kidd married the woman fifth from the left on the back row. The grandmother of this author's wife is pictured on the back row fourth from the left.

38 Verity Wilson, "Dress and the Cultural Revolution," in *China Chic: East Meets West,* (New Haven: Yale University Press 1999), 172–8.

39 A.C. Scott, *Chinese Costume in Transition* (Singapore, Donald Moore Publications, 1958), 94–7.

40 Yuming Lu interviewed by the author about his early recollections of life in Shanghai in the 1950s and 1960s, December 2017.

41 Zhao Yan interviewed by the author about his early recollections of life in Beijing in the 1950s and 1960s, January 2018.

42 Sang Ye, "*From Rags to Revolution: Behind the Seams of Social Change,*" in *Evolution and Revolution, Chinese Dress, 1700s–1900s* (New York: Powerhouse Publishing, 1997), 46–7.

43 Antonio Finnane provides an excellent investigation of the Dress Reform campaign. The Dress Reform campaign was a government initiative supporting the development of new fashions and the textile industry to modernize clothing in China. This included fashion shows and the development of products to develop sartorial change.

44 *The People's Daily* (March 31, 1956) announced the exhibition saying, "Fashion Exhibition opens today, there will be 535 pieces of clothing exhibited for men, women's and children and for Spring, Summer and Autumn seasons. There will also be a variety of new design of flower (printed) cotton fabric, silk and wool. Already 83,000 people have registered to visit the show."

45 "Let a hundred flowers bloom" and "Let a hundred schools of thought contend" were the declarations from Chairman Mao in May 1956. The Hundred Flowers movement as it became known, was initially intended to give the population both an opinion and a voice in the development of China, however it was later seen as a trap to ensnare so-called rightist dissidents who in reality did not fully agree with Mao's doctrine.

46 The Great Leap Forward was a campaign to develop industrialization and agriculture in China by labor-intensive methods including communes and small-scale

production units through mass mobilisation between 1958 and 1960. Poor management, lack of expertise and drought led to 20 million people dying of starvation.

47 Interview between Shuzhen Zhang and the author on the topics of clothing and community in Shanghai. January 2018.

Chapter 11

1 Halil Inalcik and Donald Quataert, *An Economic and Social History of the Ottoman Empire: 1300–1914* (Cambridge: Cambridge University Press, 1994).

2 Walter B. Denny, "Ottoman Turkish Textiles," *Textile Museum Journal*, no. 3–2 (1972), 55–66.

3 Patricia L. Baker, *Islamic Textiles* (London: British Museum Press, 1995).

4 Jennifer Wearden and Marianne Ellis, *Ottoman Embroidery* (London: Victoria and Albert Museum, 2001).

5 Donald Quataert, "Clothing Laws, State, and Society in the Ottoman Empire, 1720–1829," *International Journal of Middle East Studies,* no. 29–03 (1997): 403–25.

6 Michael Humphreys and Andrew D. Brown, "Dress and Identity: A Turkish case study," *Journal of Management Studies*, no. 39–7 (2002): 927–52.

7 Matthew Elliot, "Dress Codes in the Ottoman Empire: The Case of the Franks," in *Ottoman Costumes: From Textile to Identity*, 103–23. Edited by S. Fraoqhi and C.K. Neumann (Istanbul: Eren, 2004).

8 Charlotte Jirousek, "Ottoman Influences in Western Dress," in *Ottoman Costumes: From Textile to Identity*, 231–51. Edited by S. Fraoqhi and C.K. Neumann (Istanbul: Eren, 2004).

9 Emine Koca and Fatma Koc, "Kiyafetnameler Ve Ralamb'in Kiyafet Albümün'deki 17. Yüzyil Osmanli Toplumu Giysi Özelliklerinin Incelenmesi," *Electronic Turkish Studies*, no. 9–11 (2014): 371–94.

10 Bahattin Yaman, "Fit for The Court: Ottoman Royal Costumes and Their Tailors, From the Sixteenth to Eighteenth Century," *Ars Orientalis*, no. 42 (2012), 89–101.

11 Yaman, "Fit for The Court," 89.

12 Fikret Altay, *Kaftanlar* (Istanbul: Yapi ve Kredi Bankasi Yayinlari, 1979).

13 Charlotte Jirousek, "The Kaftan and Its Origins," in *Berg Encyclopedia of World Dress and Fashion: Central and Southwest Asia*, 134–138. Edited by G. Vogelsang-Eastwood (Oxford: Berg Publishers, 2010).

14 Fatma Koc and Emine Koca, "The Clothing Culture of the Turks and the Entari (Part 1: History)," *Folk Life*, no 49–1 (2011), 10–29.

15 Lale Gorunur, and Semra Ogel, "Osmanli kaftanlari ile entarilerinin farklari ve kullanilislari," *İTÜDERGİSİ/b*, no 3–1 (2006), 59–68.

16 Jirousek, "Ottoman Influences in Western Dress," 233.

17 Gorunur and Ogel, "Osmanli kaftanlari ile entarilerinin farklari ve kullanilislari," 59.

18 Hatice Tezcan, "16.–17. Yüzyıllarda Osmanlı Sarayında Kadın Modası," *P Dergisi*, 12 (1999), 54–69.

19 Filiz O. Gunduz and Serife Gulcu, *"Osmanli Donemi Kaftanlaıına Yeni Yorumlar"* (Konya: Selcuk Universitesi, 2003).

20 Doreen Yarwood, *The Encyclopedia of World Costume,"* 321 (New York: Bonanza Books, 1986).

21 Yuksel Sahin, "Topkapı Sarayı Müzesinde Bulunan Bir Grup Kaftanın Dikiş Kalıpları Ve Anadolu Giysileriyle Benzerlikleri," *Folklor/Edebiyat Dergisi*, no. 10–37 (2004), 197–225.

22 Sabahattin Türkoglu, *Tarih Boyunca Anadolu'da Giyim-Kuşam* (Istanbul: Garanti Bankası, 2002).

23 Yaman, "Fit for The Court" 95.

24 Nurhan Atasoy, Walter B. Denny, Louise. W. Mackie, Serife Atlihan, and Hulya Tezcan, *Ipek, the Crescent and the Rose: Imperial Ottoman Silks and Velvets* (London: Azimuth Editions, 2001).

25 Fatma Koc and Emine Koca, "The Clothing Culture of the Turks and the Entari (Part 1: History)," 12.

26 A general name given to craftsmen and artists of numerous types.

27 Ozden Suslu, "Topkapı Sarayı ve Türk İslam Eserleri Müzelerinde Bulunan XVI. Yüzyıla ait Osmanlı Minyatürlerindeki Kumaş Desenlerinin İncelenmesi," *Sanat Tarihi Yıllığı/Journal of Art History*, 6 (1976), 215–78.

28 Sidika Bilgen, "Osmanli Donemi Turk Kadin Giyimi," PhD dissertation, Sosyal Bilimler Enstitusu Gazi Universitesi, 24, 1999.

29 Atelier that produced silver and gold strings.

30 Hulya Tezcan, "16. Yüzyıldan 20. Yüzyıla Türk Kumaş Sanatı," *Türkiye'miz Kültür ve Sanat Dergisi*, no. 58 (1989), 2837.

31 Tezcan, "16. Yüzyıldan 20. Yüzyıla Türk Kumaş Sanatı," 31.

32 Selin Ipek, "Ottoman Fabrics During the 18th and 19th Centuries," in *Textiles and Politics: Textile Society of America 13th Biennial Symposium Proceedings*, 18–22 September: Washington DC (2012).

33 Ipek, "Ottoman Fabrics During the 18th and 19th Centuries," 2.

34 Silk (of atlas silk moth) satin fabric.

35 A triangular motif consisting of two wavy lines and three circles, two of which are under the third. The three circles resembled the spots on a leopard and the two wavy lines resembled the tiger skin. This motif was considered to be a symbol of strength,

power and sovereignty and extensively used in decorating the Kaftan of the Ottoman Sultans and their sons.

36 Tulay Gumuser, "Contemporary Usage of Turkish Traditional Motifs in Product Designs," *Idil Sanat ve Dil Dergisi*, no. 5–13 (2012), 218–30.

37 Sumiyo Okumura, "Garments of the Ottoman Sultans," 2018, http://www. turkishculture.org/textile-arts-159.htm

38 Godets inserted on the center front and/or to sides to add volume to kaftan hem.

39 Koc and Koca, "The Clothing Culture of the Turks and the Entari (Part 1: History)," 29.

40 Edward Seymour Forster, *The Turkish letters of Ogier Ghiselin de Busbecq, Imperial Ambassador at Constantinople, 1554–1562: translated from the Latin of the Elzevir edition of 1663* (Baton Rouge: Louisiana State University Press, 2013).

41 Lale and Ogel "Osmanli kaftanlari ile entarilerinin farklari ve kullanilislari," 62.

42 Hülya Tezcan, *Osmanlı Sarayının Çocukları: Şehzadeler Ve Hanım Sultanların Yaşamları Giysileri* (Istanbul: Aygaz, 2006).

43 Amanda Phillips, "Ottoman Hil'at: Between Commodity and Charisma," in *Frontiers of the Ottoman Imagination: Studies in Honour of Rhoads*, 111–138. Edited by M. Hadjianastasis (Leiden: Brill, 2015).

44 Jirousek, "Ottoman Influences in Western Dress," 239.

45 Fur-lined kaftan.

46 Lale and Ogel, "Osmanli kaftanlari ile entarilerinin farklari ve kullanilislari," 62.

47 Altay, *Kaftanlar*.

48 Mouradgea D'Ohsson, *18. Yuzyıl Turkiye'sinde Orf ve Adetler* (Istanbul: Kervan, 1977).

49 Jirousek, "Ottoman Influences in Western Dress," 239.

50 A motif developed by the Seljuks from Central Asian Turkic cave paintings of animals and birds by stylizing the wings and beaks. The motif was replicated and developed around the Islamic world.

51 Adam Williamson, "Biomorphic Art: The Art of Arabesque," 2018, http:// artofislamicpattern.com/resources/introduction-to-islimi/

52 Atasoy, Denny, Mackie, Atlihan, and Tezcan, *Ipek, the Crescent and the Rose*, 200.

53 Jirousek, "Ottoman Influences in Western Dress," 247.

54 Gorunur and Ogel, "Osmanli kaftanlari ile entarilerinin farklari ve kullanilislari," 63.

55 Atasoy and others define *çarpana* as 5–8 cm high and 2–3 mm thin square, triangle, hexagon, or octagon card made of wood, leather, or ivory with holes on each corner used to weave the narrow width *çaprast* in *Ipek, the Crescent and the Rose: Imperial Ottoman Silks and Velvets*.

56 Jirousek, "Ottoman Influences in Western Dress," 240.

Bibliography

Chapter 1

Barich, Katherine and Marion McNealy. *Drei Schnittbücher: Three Austrian Master Tailor Books of the 16th Century.* Kennewick, WA: Nadel and Faden Press, 2015.

Burnham, Dorothy K. *Cut My Cote.* Toronto: Royal Ontario Museum, 1973.

Chase, Johanna. *Sew and Save.* Glasgow: The Literary Press Ltd., n.d.

Dior, Christian. *Dior by Dior: The Autobiography of Christian Dior.* 1957. Trans Antonia Fraser. London: V&A Publications, 2007.

Emery, Joy S. *A History of the Paper Pattern Industry.* New York: Bloomsbury Academic, 2014.

Giles, Edward B. *The History of the Art of Cutting in England.* 1887. Facsimile of the first edition. New Delhi, India: Isha Books, 2013.

Hawes, Elizabeth. *Fashion is Spinach.* 1938. Facsimile of the first edition. London: Forgotten Books, 2012.

Kidwell, Claudia B. *Cutting a Fashionable Fit.* Washington, DC: Smithsonian Institution Press, 1979.

The Pictorial Guide to Modern Home Needlecraft. London: Odhams Press Limited, 1946.

Seligman, Kevin L. *Cutting For All: The Sartorial Arts, Related Crafts and the Commercial Paper Pattern.* Carbondale, IL: Southern Illinois University Press, 1996.

Van Buren, Anne H. *Illuminating Fashion: Dress in the Art of Medieval France and the Netherlands, 1325–1515.* New York: The Morgan Library and Museum, 2011.

Wood, Maggie. "We Wore What We Got." *Women's Clothes in World War II.* Warwickshire, England: Warwickshire Books, 1989.

Chapter 2

Ashwin, Clive. *A History of Century of Art Education.* London: Middlesex University, 1998.

Breward, Christopher. *Fashion.* Oxford: Oxford University Press, 2003.

Breward, Christopher. "Fashion's Front and Back: 'Rag Trade' Cultures and Cultures of Consumption in Post-War London *c.* 1945–1970." *The London Journal* 31, no. 1 (2006), 15–40.

Buckley, Cheryl. *Designing Modern Britain.* London: Reaktion Books, 1990.

Clark, Hazel. "SLOW + FASHION—an Oxymoron—or a Promise for the Future . . .?" *Fashion Theory* 12, no. 4 (2008), 427–46.

Davenport, Elsie. *Your Handweaving*. London: The Sylvan Press Ltd., 1948.

Efland, Arthur. *A History of Art Education*. New York: Teachers College Press, 1990.

Emery, Joy Spanabel. *A History of the Paper Pattern Industry: The Home Dressmaking Revolution*. New York: Bloomsbury, 2014.

de la Haye, Amy. "Court Dressmaking in Mayfair from the 1890s to the 1920s." In *London Couture 1923–1975: British Luxury*, edited by Amy de la Haye and Edwina Ehrman, 9–30. London: V&A Publishing, 2015.

Dougherty, Betty. *Your Leatherwork*. London: The Sylvan Press Ltd., 1947.

Dougherty, Betty. *Your Linocraft*. London: The Sylvan Press Ltd., 1949.

Flanders, Amy. "'Our Ambassadors': British Books, American Competition and the Great Book Export Drive 1940–60." *The English History Review* 125, no. 515 (2010): 875–911.

Fletcher, Kate. "Slow Fashion: An Invitation for Systems Change." *Fashion Practice* 2, no. 2 (2010), 259–65.

Garland, Marge. "Artifices, Confections, and Manufactures." In *The Anatomy of Design: A Series of Inaugural Lectures by Professors of the Royal College of Art*, edited by R. Moynihan, 81–9. London: The Royal College of Art, 1951.

Green, Peter, "Obituary Miss Sheila McEwan: Artist and Teacher." *Hornsey Journal* (London), June, 1982.

Greenhalgh, Paul. "A History of Craft." In *The Craft of Culture*, edited by Peter Dormer, 20–52. Manchester: Manchester University Press, 1997.

Holman, Valarie. *Print for Victory: Book Publishing in England 1939–1945*. London: The British Library, 2008.

Hornsey School of Art Prospectus 1955/6, Box HCA/5/7/20, Hornsey School of Art Archive, Middlesex University, London.

Hulme, W.H. *The Practice of Garment-Pattern Making*. London: The National Trade Press, 1946.

MacEwan, E. Sheila. *Your Pattern Cutting*. London: The Sylvan Press Ltd, 1950.

MacEwan, E. Sheila. Interviewed by Peter Green transcripts, August 4, 1981, Box HCA/3/2/4, MacEwan Papers, Hornsey College of Art Archive, Middlesex University, London.

McKenzie, D.F. *Bibliography and the Sociology of Texts*. Cambridge: Cambridge University Press, 1999.

Morris, F.R. *Ladies' Garment Cutting and Making*. London: New Era Publishing Co. Ltd., 1950.

Owen, Margaret. Foreword to *Your Leatherwork*, by Betty Dougherty, 7. London: The Sylvan Press, 1947.

Palmer, Alexander. "Virtual Home Dressmaking: Dressmakers and Seamstresses in Post-War Toronto." In *The Culture of Sewing: Gender, Consumption and Home Dressmaking*, edited by Barbara Burman, 207–22. Oxford: Berg, 1999.

Parker, Rozsika. *The Subversive Stitch: Embroidery and the Making of the Feminine*. London: I.B. Tauris & Co. Ltd., 2010.

Reynolds, Helen. *Couture or Trade: An Early Pictorial Record of the London College of Fashion*. London: Phillimore & Co., 1997.

Seligman, Kevin L. *Cutting for All!: The Sartorial Arts, Related Crafts, and the Commercial Pattern Industry: A Bibliographic Reference Guide for Designers, Technicians, and Historians*. Carbondale: Southern Illinois University Press, 1996.

Squires, Claire. "Britain from 1914." In *The Book: A Global History*, edited by Michael F. Suarez S.J. and H.R. Woudhuysen, 311–19. Oxford: Oxford University Press, 2013.

Chapter 3

Archival Sources

American National Red Cross. Northern Division, Red Cross Northern Division Records. Minnesota Historical Society, St. Paul, Minnesota.

Records of the American National Red Cross, 1881–2008, Record Group 200, Central Decimal Files, 1881–1982, Series 2 1917–34, Series 3 1935–46, Series 4 1947–64, National Archives College Park, Maryland.

Bibliography

American National Red Cross. *The Work of the American Red Cross During the War: A Statement of Finances and Accomplishments for the Period July 1, 1917, to February 28, 1919*. Washington, DC: Washington DC, 1919.

American Red Cross Annual Report for the Year Ended June 30, 1918. Washington DC, 1918.

American Red Cross Annual Report for the Year Ended June 30, 1919. Washington DC, 1919.

American Red Cross Annual Report for the Year Ended June 30, 1920. Washington DC, 1920.

American Red Cross Annual Report for the Year Ended June 30, 1965. Washington DC, 1965.

"Art Needlework." *Dry Goods Economist*, August 11, 1917.

Clark, Ida C. *American Women and The World War*. New York and London: D. Appleton and Company, 1918.

Homer, Joy. "Present Arms." *The Red Cross Courier*, November 1941.

"Hurry Up Knitting for Our Soldiers." *The Touchstone*, October 1917.

Irwin, Julia F. *Making the World Safe: The American Red Cross and a Nation's Humanitarian Awakening*. New York, Oxford University Press, 2013.

"Instructions for Knitting." *Alaska Railroad Record*, 1918.

Johnson, Burges. "Mars Invades the Campus." *Red Cross Magazine*, December 1917.

Jones, Marian Moser. *The American Red Cross from Clara Barton to the New Deal*. Baltimore: Johns Hopkins University Press, 2012.

Lynch, Reah Jeannette. *"Win the War" Cook Book*. St. Louis County Unit, Woman's Committee, Council of National Defense, Missouri Division, 1918.

MacDonald, Anne L. *No Idle Hands: The Social History of American Knitting*. New York: Random House Publishing Group, 1990.

The Pittsburgh Chapter, American Red Cross: A History of the Activities of the American Red Cross. Pittsburgh Chapter. Pittsburgh, PA: Pittsburgh Printing Company, 1922.

Chapter 4

"AWVS Sewing Classes: Remaking of Clothes Will Be Taught Twice a Week." *The New York Times* (June 1, 1944), 12. www.timesmachine.com

A Bag of Tricks for Home Sewing. Memphis, TN: National Cotton Council, 1945.

"Bank for Savings Promotes Sewing." *The New York Times* (December 6, 1945), 29. www.timesmachine.com

Bubolz, Margaret M. "Home Economics and Home Sewing in the United States, 1870–1940." In *The Culture of Sewing*, edited by Barbara Burman, 303–25. New York: Berg, 1999.

Chase, Joanna. *Sew and Save*. Glasgow: The Literary Press Limited, n.d.

"The Complete Book of Sewing. By Constance Talbot." *The New York Times* (July 11, 1943), 58. www.timesmachine.com

Daniell, Raymond. "British People Demand Greater War Effort." *The New York Times* (September 27, 1943), 3. www.timesmachine.com

Franks, Catherine. *The Pictorial Guide to Modern Home Dressmaking*. London: Odhams Press, Ltd., 1940.

"Home Sewing Gain Blamed on Prices." *The New York Times* (August 3, 1948), 34. www.timesmachine.com

Laboissonniere, Wade. *Blueprints of Fashion: Home Sewing Patterns of the 1940s*, 2nd Edition. Atglen, PA: Schiffer Publishing, 2009.

"Leaflet Gives Aid on Remaking Suits." *The New York Times* (November 30, 1942), 16. www.timesmachine.com

Make and Mend for Victory. Spool Cotton Company, 1942.

Make Do and Mend. United Kingdom: Ministry of Information, 1943.

"More Home Sewing Urged." *The New York Times* (April 7, 1942), 25. www.timesmachine.com

"Pattern Industry Gains as Home Sewing, Through WPB Order, Has Renaissance." *The New York Times* (July 16, 1942), 14. www.timesmachine.com

"Patterns to Save Fabric." *The New York Times* (May 27, 1943), 22. www.timesmachine.com

The Pictorial Guide to Modern Home Needlecraft. London: Odhams Press, Ltd., reprinted 1946.

"Push Cotton Bags for Home Sewing." *The New York Times* (September 22, 1946), 105. www.timesmachine.com

"Relief Recipients Trained for Jobs: Welfare Department School Teaches Household Skills to 100 Women All over 50." *The New York Times* (September 27, 1943), 16. www.timesmachine.com

"Remodeling of Cast-Off Clothes to Conserve Material is Taught." *The New York Times* (March 9, 1942), 11. www.timesmachine.com

"Revival of Home Sewing Brings a 40% Rise in Yard Goods Sale." *The New York Times* (February 20, 1943), 16. www.timesmachine.com

Reynolds, Helen. "'Your Clothes are Materials of War.' The British Government's Promotion of Home Sewing During the Second World War." In *The Culture of Sewing,* edited by Barbara Burman, 327–38. New York: Berg, 1999.

"Salvage Fair Planned: Garments Made From Odds and Ends to Be Shown Next Month." *The New York Times* (May 26, 1942), 18. www.timesmachine.com

"Salvage Sewing Unit of America Bundles Will Open 2-Day Fashion Fair Tuesday." *The New York Times* (June 14, 1942), 78. www.timesmachine.com

"Sewing Kit's Value in War Stressed: Woman's Outfit Made From Man's Old Suit Among Raiment on Display." *The New York Times* (June 11, 1942), 22. www.timesmachine.com

Singer Make-Over Guide: Ideas and Instructions for Renewing-Altering and Restyling Clothing and Fabric Furnishings. New York: Singer Sewing Machine Company, 1943.

"Thrift Shops are Short of Goods Due to Mounting Demands of War." *The New York Times* (March 28, 1942), 28. www.timesmachine.com

Veillon, Dominique. *Fashion Under the Occupation.* Trans. Miriam Kochan. New York: Berg, 2002.

Vogue Pattern Service. *Vogue's Book of Smart Dressmaking.* London: Vogue Pattern Service, n.d.

Walford, Jonathan. *Forties Fashion: From Siren Suits to the New Look.* New York: Thames and Hudson, 2005.

Wood, Maggie. *"We Wore What We Got." Women's Clothes in World War II.* Warwickshire, England: Warwickshire Books, 1989.

"WPB Fixes Rules for Women's Wear." *The New York Times* (April 9, 1942), 22. www.timesmachine.com

Chapter 5

Brundage, W.W. *Complete System of Cutting.* New York: Self-published, 1867.

Chabot, G.H. *The Tailor's Compasses.* Baltimore: Self-published, 1829.

Conrad, A.H. and J.R. Meyer. "Income Growth and Structural Change: The United States in the Nineteenth Century." In *Studies in Econometric History*. London: Chapman and Hall, 1965.

Couts, Joseph. *Practical Guide for the Tailor's Cutting Room*. Glasgow: Blackie and Son, 1848.

Crawford, William T. *The Science and Art of Garment Cutting*. Providence, RI: Self-published, 1874.

DuNah, George W. "Block Patterns *vs*. Drafting." *The Custom Cutter and Fashion Review* I, no. 9 (September 1890): 12.

Hansen, H.J. *Seamless and Artistic Frock Coat System*. Self-published, Goshen, IN: 1889.

Hecklinger, Charles. *The "Keystone" System*. New York: West Publishing Co., 1890.

Hertzer, Gunther F. *Garment Cutting in the Twentieth Century*. Self-published, Tiffen, OH: 1892.

Holding, T.H. *Block Patterns and How to Cut by Them*. London: The London Tailor Office, 1905.

Kidwell, Claudia and M. Christman. *Suiting Everyone*. Washington, DC: The Smithsonian Institution, 1974.

Killey, John. *New System of Cutting*. Liverpool: Baldwin, Cradock, and Joy, 1821.

Lee, Susan and Peter Passell. "Economic Growth Before 1860." In *New Economic View of American History*. New York: W.W. Norton, 1979.

Moxley, John. *Every One His Own Tailor*. Danville, VT: Self-published, 1823.

The Popular Gentleman System. Philadelphia: Popular Gentleman Service Company, 1917

Roy, Catherine. *The Tailoring Trade 1800–1920; Including an Analysis of Pattern Drafting Systems and an Examination of the Trade in Canada*. MSc thesis, University of Alberta, 1990.

Seligman, Kevin. *Cutting for All!* Carbondale and Edwardsville: Southern Illinois University Press, 1996.

Simons, Harry. *Drafting Pants and Overalls*. New York: The Clothing Designer Co., 1915.

Stone, Charles J. *Stone's Paramount Cutter*. Chicago: Meyer and Brother, 1887.

Stone, Charles J. *Stone's Superlative Coat and Vest System*. Chicago: The Chas. J. Stone Co. Cutting School, *c*.1892.

Stone, Charles J. *Stone's New Superlative Coat and Vest System*. Chicago: C.J. Stone Cutting School, 1900.

Stone, Charles J. *Stone's Advanced Superlative Coat and Vest System*. Chicago: The Chas. J. Stone Company, 1910.

Stone, Charles J. "Successful Cutters." In *International Custom Cutters' Association of America* proceedings. St. Louis: 1911.

Trautmann, Patricia A. *Clothing America*. The Costume Society of America, Region II, 1987.

Thornton, J.P. *The Sectional System*. London: Minister & Co. Ltd., 1894.

Van Aarle, Frank A. *Key Line System*. Toledo, OH: Self-published, 1892.

Vincent, William D.F. *The Cutters' Practical Guide to the Cutting of all Kinds of Trousers.* 8th edition. London: John Williamson Company, Limited, *c.* 1901.

West, John. *Revised Grand Edition.* New York: Self-published, 1890.

Young, B. and Simon S. Rathvon. *The Archetypal Consummation.* Columbia PA: J.L. Gossler and Company, 1845.

Zakim, Michael. "The Reinvention of Tailoring." In *Ready-Made Democracy* Chicago: University of Chicago Press, 2003.

Chapter 6

Abtew, Mulat Alubel, Pascal Bruniaux, François Boussu, Carmen Loghin, Irina Cristian, and Yan Chen. "Development of Comfortable and Well-Fitted Bra Pattern for Customized Female Soft Body Armor Through 3D Design Process of Adaptive Bust on Virtual Mannequin." *Computers in Industry,* 100 (2018): 7–20.

Baciu, G. and S. Liang. "Human Interaction with Computers and Its Use in the Textile Apparel Industry." In *Computer Technology for Textiles and Apparel,* edited by Jinlian Hu, 203–18. Cambridge: Woodhead Publishing Ltd. 2011.

Bain, Jessica. "'Darn Right I'm a Feminist . . . Sew What?' The Politics of Contemporary Home Dressmaking: Sewing, Slow Fashion and Feminism." *Women's Studies International Forum,* 54 (2016), 57–66.

Barbieri, Paolo, Francesco Ciabuschi, Luciano Fratocchi, and Matteo Vignoli. "Manufacturing Reshoring Explained: An Interpretative Framework of Ten Years of Research." In *Reshoring of Manufacturing: Drivers, Opportunities, and Challenges,* edited by Alessandra Vecchi, 3–37. Cham: Springer, 2017.

Barlow, Mike. *The State of CAD 2017: Reinventing Design and Manufacturing.* Sebastopol, CA: O'Reilly Media, 2017.

Barrie Leonie. "Where Next for Walmart's 3D Apparel Design Pilot?" *Just-style.com,* July 13, 2016. https://www.just-style.com/analysis/where-next-for-walmarts-3d-apparel-design-pilot_id128315.aspx

Baytar, Fatma. "Apparel CAD Patternmaking with 3D Simulations: Impact of Recurrent Use of Virtual Prototypes on Students' Skill Development." *International Journal of Fashion Design, Technology and Education* 11, no. 2 (2018), 187–95.

Bean, Denise Lisette. "Job Satisfaction among United States Textile and Apparel Designers Who Use Computer-Aided Design." PhD dis., Texas Woman's University, 1997.

Bertolotti, Fabiola, Diego Maria Macri, and Maria Rita Tagliaventi. "Social and Organisational Implications of CAD Usage: A Grounded Theory in a Fashion Company." *New Technology, Work and Employment* 19, no. 2 (2004), 110–27.

Breazeale, Linda M. "Prof Dresses Up Apparel Software," Mississippi State University Extension Service, December 8, 1997. http://extension.msstate.edu/news/feature-story/1997/prof-dresses-apparel-software

Cardoso Llach, Daniel. *Builders of the Vision: Software and the Imagination of Design.* New York: Routledge, 2015.

Chan C.K., A. Luximon, J. Yang, and S.X. Peng. "Mannequin System of Interactive Smart Body Mapping for Real-Time CAD Pattern Design." *International Journal of Arts & Sciences* 6, no. 3 (2013): 501–7.

Clark, Paul and Walter Wilhelm. "3D in Apparel Design: A Revolution in the Industry." Lectra Media Center. https://www.drapersonline.com/Journals/1/Files/2011/6/15/ Whitepaper_3D%20in%20apparel%20design_A%20revolution%20in%20the%20 industry.pdf

Collier, Billie J. and John R. Collier. "CAD/CAM in the Textile and Apparel Industry." *Clothing and Textiles Research Journal* 8, no. 3 (1990): 7–13.

Desai, Anuj, Nedal Nassar, and Marian Chertow. "American Seams: An Exploration of Hybrid Fast Fashion and Domestic Manufacturing Models in Relocalised Apparel Production." *The Journal of Corporate Citizenship*, no. 45 (2012): 53–78.

Easters, Daniel James. "Global Communication Part 1: The Use of Apparel CAD Technology." *International Journal of Fashion Design, Technology and Education* 5, no. 1 (2012), 45–54.

Elias, Rimon. *Digital Media A Problem-solving Approach for Computer Graphics.* Cham: Springer International Publishing, 2014.

Fasanella, Kathleen. "CAD 101 part one." Fashion-Incubator, January 16, 2007. https://fashion-incubator.com/cad_101_part_one/

Gong, D.X, B.K. Hinds, and J. McCartney. "Progress towards Effective Garment CAD." *International Journal of Clothing Science and Technology* 13, no. 1 (2001), 12–23.

Huang, H.Q, P.Y. Mok, Y.L. Kwok, and J.S. Au. "Block Pattern Generation: From Parameterizing Human Bodies to Fit Feature-aligned and Flattenable 3D Garments." *Computers in Industry* 63, no. 7 (2012), 680–91.

Horváth, Imre and Regine W. Vroom. "Ubiquitous Computer Aided Design: A Broken Promise or a Sleeping Beauty?" *Computer-Aided Design* 59, no. C (2015), 161–75.

Istook, Cynthia Saylor. "Computer-Aided-Design (CAD) in the Apparel Industry: An Exploration of Current Technology, Training, and Expectations for the Future." PhD dis., Texas Woman's University, 1992.

Istook, Cynthia, E. Newcomb, and H. Lim. "Three-Dimensional (3D) Technologies for Apparel and Textile Design." In *Computer Technology for Textiles and Apparel*, edited by Jinlian Hu, 296–320. Cambridge: Woodhead Publishing Ltd., 2011.

Jhanji, Yamini. "Computer-Aided Design, Garment Designing and Patternmaking." In *Automation in Garment Manufacturing*, edited by Rajkishore Nayak, 253–90. Cambridge: Woodhead Publishing Ltd., 2018.

Johnson, Brian R. *Design Computing: An Overview of an Emergent Field.* New York; London: Routledge, 2017.

Kang, Tae J. and Sung Min Kim. "Development of Three-dimensional Apparel CAD System: Part 1: Flat Garment Pattern Drafting System." *International Journal of Clothing Science and Technology* 12, no. 1 (2000), 26–38.

Kennedy, K. "Pattern Construction." In *Garment Manufacturing Technology*, edited by Rajkishore Nayak and Rajiv Padhye, 205–20. Cambridge: Elsevier Science & Technology, 2015.

Kim, Eundeok and Kim K.P. Johnson. "Forecasting the US Fashion Industry with Industry Professionals—Part 1." *Journal of Fashion Marketing and Management: An International Journal* 13, no. 2 (2009), 256–67.

Labat, Karen, Carol Salusso, and Jongeun Rhee. "Home Sewers' Satisfaction with Fit of Apparel Patterns." *Journal of Fashion Marketing and Management: An International Journal* 11, no. 3 (2007), 429–40.

Lee, Jaeil and Camille Steen. *Technical Sourcebook for Designers*. New York: Fairchild Books, 2014.

Leonie Barrie. "Leveraging the Business Benefits of 3D Virtual Design." *Just-style.com*, July 8, 2015. https://www.just-style.com/analysis/leveraging-the-business-benefits-of-3d-virtual-design_id125630.aspx

Liu, Yong-Jin, Dong-Liang Zhang, and Matthew Ming-Fai Yuen. "A Survey on CAD Methods in 3D Garment Design." *Computers in Industry* 61, no. 6 (2010), 576–93.

Martindale, Addie and Ellen McKinney. "Sew or Purchase? Home Sewer Consumer Decision Process." *Journal of Fashion Marketing and Management: An International Journal* 22, no. 2 (2018), 176–88.

Mittelhauser, Mark. "Employment Trends in Textiles and Apparel, 1973–2005." *Monthly Labor Review* 120, no. 8 (1997), 24–35.

Moser, Harry and Sandy Montalbano. "Why Made-in-USA Fashion is Turning Heads." *Industry Week*, January 18, 2018. http://www.industryweek.com/economy/why-made-usa-fashion-turning-heads

Newcomb, Wilburn. "AAMA Sees Savings from Technology (American Apparel Manufacturers Association)." *WWD* 156, no. 83 (1988), 8.

Pattern Review. "My Label 3D Fashion Software." Forum started on October 11, 2009 in *Patterns and Notions*. Accessed May 5, 2018. http://sewing.patternreview.com/SewingDiscussions/topic/44525.2009

Polvinen, Elaine. "OptiTex/Siemens#3: FIT Technology Bernina MyLabel." *Virtual Fashion Technology*, November 28, 2009. https://fashiontech.wordpress.com/2008/04/04/optitexsiemens3-fit-technology-bernina-mylabel/

Pundir, Nirupama. *Fashion Technology: Today and Tomorrow*. New Delhi: Mittal Publications, 2007.

Ramesh, Suuchi. "5 Tech Trends Shaping the Future of Fashion Manufacturing." *GE Reports*, July 17, 2017. https://www.ge.com/reports/5-tech-trends-shaping-future-fashion-manufacturing/

Sayem, Abu Sadat Muhammad, Richard Kennon, and Nick Clarke. "3D CAD Systems for the Clothing Industry." *International Journal of Fashion Design, Technology and Education* 3, no. 2 (2010), 45–53.

Segonds, Frederic, Fabrice Mantelet, Nicolas Maranzana, and Stephane Gaillard. "Early Stages of Apparel Design: How to Define Collaborative Needs for PLM and

Fashion?" *International Journal of Fashion Design, Technology and Education* 7, no. 2 (2014), 107.

Sheldon, Gwendolyn J. "The Impact of Technology on Apparel Designer Training." *Clothing and Textiles Research Journal* 6, no. 4 (1988), 20–5.

Shin, Kristina, Sun Pui Ng, and Ma Liang. "A Geometrically Based Flattening Method for Three-dimensional to Two-dimensional Bra Pattern Conversion." *International Journal of Fashion Design, Technology and Education* 3, no. 1 (2010), 3–14.

Smith, Nicole. "Pattern Drafting Software." *Threads.* March 5, 2009. https://www.threadsmagazine.com/2009/03/05/pattern-drafting-software

Stott, M. *Pattern Cutting for Clothing Using CAD; How to Use Lectra Modaris Pattern Cutting Software.* Cambridge: Woodhead Publishing Series in Textiles: No. 137, 2014.

Thomassey, S. and P. Bruniaux. "A Template of Ease Allowance for Garments Based on a 3D Reverse Methodology." *International Journal of Industrial Ergonomics* 43, no. 5 (2013): 406–16.

U.S. Bureau of Labor Statistics. Accessed May 20, 2018. https://data.bls.gov/pdq/SurveyOutputServlet

Yan, He and Susan S. Fiorito. "Communication: CAD/CAM Adoption in US Textile and Apparel Industries." *International Journal of Clothing Science and Technology* 14, no. 2 (2002), 132–40.

Yi Xiu, Zhen-Kai Wan and Wen Cao. "A Constructive Approach toward a Parametric Pattern-making Model." *Textile Research Journal* 81, no. 10 (2011), 979–91.

Wang, Charlie C.L, Shana S.-F. Smith, and Matthew M.F. Yuen. "Surface Flattening Based on Energy Model." *Computer-Aided Design* 34, no. 11 (2002), 823–33.

Weisberg, David E. *The Engineering Design Revolution: The People, Companies and Computer Systems that Changed Forever the Practice of Engineering.* 2008. http://www.cadhistory.net/

Wimmer, Janet R. and Valerie L. Giddings, "Investigation of Factors Influencing CAD Selection and Use for Apparel Design." *Journal of Family and Consumer Sciences* 89, no. 3 (1997), 48.

Workman, Jane E. and Ling Zhang. "Relationship of General and Apparel Spatial Visualization Ability." *Clothing and Textiles Research Journal* 17, no. 4 (1999), 169–75.

Chapter 7

Alexander, Marina, Gina R. Pisut, and Andrada Ivanescu. "Investigating Women's Plus-Size Body Measurements and Hip Shape Variation Based on SizeUSA Data," *International Journal of Fashion Design, Technology and Education* 5, no. 1 (2011), 3–12.

Belcastro, Angela. "The Convertible Dress, Susanna Gioia for Lemuria," *Ganzo,* August 6, 2012, http://www.ganzomag.com/convertible-dress-lemuria.html

Biern, Nathaniel. "Length-Adjustable Ready-To-Wear Skirts," US Patent 2724,120, filed
    Jan 3, 1952, and issued Nov 22, 1955.

Cantil, George R. "Adjustable Waist and Seat for Garments," US Patent 2755,481, filed
    Jun 28, 1954, and issued Jul 24, 1956.

Cao, Huantian, Rita Chang, Jo Kallal, Grace Manalo, Jennifer McCord, Jenna Shaw,
    and Heather Starner. "Adaptable Apparel: A Sustainable Design Solution for
    Excess Apparel Consumption Problem." *Journal of Fashion Marketing and
    Management: An International Journal* 18 (1), 2014: 52–69. doi:10.1108/JFMM-08-
    2012-0046.

Chung, Chin-Fu. "Separtable Clothing Including Shirts," US Patent 5628,064, filed
    Sep 22, 1995, and issued May 13, 1997.

Diane Von Furstenberg. *Dress*, Textile and Clothing Museum, Ames, IA, 1970.

Erickson, June S. "Adjustable Garments, Such as Adjustable Shirts and Pants," US Patent
    2010/0306901 A1, filed Jun 3, 2010, and issued Dec 9, 2010.

Gaines, Thomas R. "Waistband for Garments," US Patent 1208,132, filed Jan 27, 1916,
    and issued Dec 12, 1916.

Gardner, James H. "Garment Having an Adjustable Waist," US Patent 7516,499 B2, filed
    Oct 11, 2006, and issued Apr 14, 2009.

Gu, P., M. Hashemian, and A.Y.C. Nee. "Adaptable Design." *CIRP Annals—
    Manufacturing Technology* 53 (2) 2004: 539–57. doi:10.1016/S0007-8506(07)60028-6.

Henderson, Elizabeth. "Athletic Garment," US Patent 4538,614, filed Jul 12, 1983, and
    issued Sep 3, 1985.

HipKnoTies. "Maternity," *Hipknoties*. https://hipknoties.com/pages/maternity

Howard, Michael A. "Adjustable Length Garment," US Patent 5539,932, filed Jun 2, 1995,
    and issued Jul 30, 1996.

Hussain, Z., N. Roberts, G.H. Whitehouse, M. García-Fiñana, and D. Percy. "Estimation
    of Breast Volume and Its Variation During the Menstrual Cycle Using MRI And
    Stereology," *The British Journal of Radiology* 72 no. 855 (1999), 236–45.

Kadison, Gloria C. "Adjustable Waist Band Arrangement," US Patent 3793,645, filed
    Oct 16, 1972, and issued Feb 26, 1974.

Keller, Claris. "Adjustable Size Garments," US Patent 2777,130, filed Jun 14, 1954, and
    issued Jan 15, 1957.

Kent, Jacqueline C., Leon Mitoulas, David B. Cox, Robyn A. Owens, and Peter E.
    Hartmann. "Breast Volume and Milk Production during Extended Lactation in
    Women." *Experimental Physiology* 84, no. 2 (1999), 435–47.

Kleinert's, *Supporter.* Textile and Clothing Museum, Ames, IA, 1972.

LaBat, Karen L., and Marilyn R. DeLong. "Body cathexis and satisfaction with fit of
    apparel." *Clothing and Textiles Research Journal* 8 (2) 1990, 43–8.

Lahnstein, Joseph A. and Evelyn K. Lahnstein. "Adjustable Garment," US Patent
    2705,326, filed Oct 25, 1951, and issued Apr 5, 1955.

Lampkowitz, Paul. "Adjustable Elastic Waist for Trousers and Other Garments," US
    Patent 2749,556, filed Feb 12, 1954, and issued Jun 12, 1956.

Lee, Jeong Yim, Cynthia L. Istook, Yun Ja Nam, and Sun Mi Park, "Comparison of body shape between USA and Korean women," *International Journal of Clothing Science and Technology*, 19, no. 5 (2007), 374–91.

LeTourneau, Thomas R. "Adjustable Pant Leg System," US Patent 4200,938, filed Oct 25, 1977, and issued May 6, 1980.

Loker, Suzanne, Susan Ashdown, and Katherine Schoenfelder. "Size-specific Analysis of Body Scan Data to Improve Apparel Fit," *JTATM* 4, no.3 (Spring 2005).

Madsen. *Coat, Laboratory*. Textile and Clothing Museum, Ames, IA, 1919.

Martindale, Addie and Ellen McKinney. "Self-Sewn Identity: How Female Home Sewers Use Garment Sewing To Control Self-Presentation," Journal of Consumer Culture (first published online March 2018), https://doi.org/10.1177/1469540518764238

McKee, Dale D. "Adjustable Length Garment," US Patent 6408,438, filed Mar 30, 2001 and issued Jun 25, 2002.

McKinney, Kelsey. "Why It's So Hard to Find a Bra That Fits", February 3, 2017, https://www.racked.com/2017/2/3/14172482/bra-sizing-lingerie

Michel, Jack Milton. "Body Encircling Garments," US Patent 2970,597, filed May 5, 1959, and issued Feb 7, 1961.

Mistry, Meenal. "Fall 2010 Ready-To-Wear Rad Hourani," *Vogue*. February 14, 2010, https://www.vogue.com/fashion-shows/fall-2010-ready-to-wear/rad-hourani

Naccash, Edmund P. "Adjustable Waistbands," US Patent 2854,670, filed Jan 27, 1956, and issued Oct 7, 1958.

Otieno, Rose, Chris Harrow, and Gaynor Lea-Greenwood, "The Unhappy Shopper, A Retail Experience: Exploring Fashion, Fit and Affordability", *International Journal of Retail & Distribution Management* 33 no. 4 (2005), 298–309.

Padernacht, William. "Adjustable Coat," US Patent 1010,679, filed Jul 7, 1910, and issued Dec 5, 1911.

Petersen, Be-Artha. "The Development and Construction of Sustainable Adjustable Clothing For Growing Children" (PhD diss., Cape Peninsula University of Technology, 2010).

Petrova, Adriana and Susan P. Ashdown. "Three-Dimensional Body Scan Data Analysis Body Size and Shape Dependence of Ease Values for Pants' Fit." *Clothing and Textiles Research Journal* 26 no. 3 (2008), 227–52.

Peyser, Eliot. "Garment Having Adjustable Sleeve Means," US Patent 4475,252, filed May 4, 1983, and issued Oct 9, 1984.

Rahman, Osmud, and Minjie Gong. "Sustainable Practices and Transformable Fashion Design—Chinese Professional and Consumer Perspectives." *International Journal of Fashion Design, Technology and Education* 9 no. 3 (2016): 233–47. doi:10.1080/17543 266.2016.1167256.

Reardon, John. "Expanded Waistband Structure for Garments," US Patent 5163,184, filed Oct 16, 1991, and issued Nov 17, 1992.

Ryan, Karima. "Modifying Garments to Provide an Adjustable Length Feature," US Patent 2008/0127398 A1, filed Dec 1, 2006, and issued Jun 5, 2008.

Sanchez, Phyllis L. "Variable Length Apparatus for Hemmed Garments," US Patent 4149, 275, filed Dec 2, 1977, and issued Apr 17, 1979.

Snip-It Slip, 38, In Celanese Clairanese, Acetate Taffeta, *Slip*. Textile and Clothing Museum, Ames, IA, 1950.

Stuart, Allan, Roslyn Heights, and Harold Drachman. "Adjustable Sleeping Garment," US Patent 2905,944, filed May 1, 1958, and issued Sep 29, 1959.

The Hub, Henry C. Lytton & Sons, Chicago, *Vest*, late 19th, Textile and Clothing Museum, Ames, IA.

Warners, size 34/35 B, *Brassiere*, 1995, Textile and Clothing Museum, Ames, IA.

Chapter 8

Campbell, Colin. "The Craft Consumer: Culture, Craft, and Consumption in a Postmodern Society." *Journal of Consumer Culture,* 5 no.1 (2005): 23–42.

Chan, Karen. "The Relationship of Motivation for Sewing, Amount of Sewing, Perceived Depersonalization of the Job, and Creativity." Master's thesis, Oregon State University, 1975.

Chansky, Rica A. "A Stitch in Time: Third-wave Feminist Reclamation of Needled Imagery." *Journal of Popular Culture,* 43 (2010), 681–700.

Courtless, Joan C. "Home Sewing Trends." *Family Economics Review,* 4 (1982), 19–22.

"Craftsy." Sewing classes (2018). http://www.craftsy.com/classes/sewing

Emery, Joy Spanabel. *A History of the Paper Pattern Industry: The Home Dressmaking Fashion Revolution.* New York, Bloomsbury, 2014.

Fry, Rita. "Craftivism: The Role of Feminism in Craft Activism." Master's thesis, Saint Mary's University, 2014.

Gordon, Sarah. *"Make it Yourself": Home Sewing, Gender, and Culture 1890–1930.* New York, NY: Columbia University Press, 2009.

Haider, Zeeshan. All Sewn Up: The popularity of do-it-yourself fashion will strengthen industry growth. *IBISWorld Industry Report, No. 45113,* 2014.

Haider, Zeeshan. Loose Thread: Competition from e-commerce and online auctions will stunt growth. *IBISWorld Industry Report,* No. 45113, July 2015.

Hall, Sarah and Mark Jayne. "Make, Mend and Befriend: Geographies of austerity, crafting and friendship in contemporary cultures of dressmaking in the UK." *Gender, Place & Culture,* 23 no. 2 (2016), 216–34.

Holson, Laura M. "Dusting off the Sewing Machine." *New York Times,* July 4, 2012. http://www.nytimes.com/2012/07/05/fashion/dusting-off-the-sewing-machine.html?_r=0

"Home page," *BurdaStyle,* April 1, 2017, http://www.burdastyle.com 43- BurdaStyle

Jane, S. "24% of 18–30 Year Olds Have Taken up Sewing in the Last Year." *Craft Business,* July 27, 2016. http://www.craftbusiness.com/news/view/24-of-18-30-year-olds-have-taken-up-sewing-in-the-last-year

Johnson, Garth. "Down the tubes: In search of internet craft." In *Handmade Nation: The rise of DIY, Art, Craft, and Design,* edited by Faith Levine and Cortney Heimerl, 30. New York: Princeton Architectural Press, 2002.

Kozinets, Robert. *Netnography: Doing ethnographic research online.* Thousand Oaks, CA: Sage Publications, 2010.

Lewis-Hammond, Sarah. "The Rise of Mending: How Britain Learned to Repair Clothes Again." *The Guardian*, May 19, 2014. http://www.theguardian.com/lifeandstyle /2014/may/19/the-rise-of-mending-how-britain-learned-to-repair-clothes-again

Matchar, Emily. *Homeward Bound: Why Women are Embracing the New.* New York: Simon and Schuster, 2013.

Martindale, Addie. "Women's Motivations to Sew Clothing for Themselves." PhD dissertation, Iowa State University, 2017.

"*Media Kit 2*." Sewing Rabbit. http://www.mesewcrazy.com/media-kit-2

"PDF Pattern Sales and Promotion." Facebook. https://www.facebook.com/groups/PDF Patternsalesandpromotion/

Pickens, Mary Brooks. *A Dictionary of Costume and Fashion: Historic and modern: With over 950 illustrations.* Mineola, NY: Dover, 1999.

Podsada, Janice. "Ministries, Classes at Stores Aim to Teach Students." *The Hartford Courant,* March 10, 2012. https://www.questia.com/newspaper/1P2-36560524/ ministries-classes-at-stores-aim-to-teach-student

Russum, Jennifer. "Leveraging the linky party: Knowledge is sharing in the blogosphere." In *Women, Work, and the Web,* edited by Carol Smallwood, 91, Lanham: Rowman & Littlefield, 2015.

Sabella, Jennifer. "Craftivism: Is Crafting the New Activism?" *Columbia Chronicle Online Edition*, May 1, 2006. https://columbiachronicle.com

Saldaña, Johnny. *The Coding Manual for Qualitative Researchers.* London: SAGE, 2016.

"Sewing inspiration and tutorials." Facebook. https://www.facebook.com/groups/ Sewinginspirationandtutorials/

Sewing, Needlework, and Piece Goods Stores, *Highbeam Business*, 2015, http://business. highbeam.com/industry-reports/retail/sewing-needlework-piece-goods-stores/

Sidler, Michelle. "Living in McJobdom." In *Third Wave Agenda: Being Feminist, doing Feminist*, edited by Leslie Haywood and Jennifer Drake, 25, Minneapolis: University of Minnesota, 1997.

Twigger Holroyd, Amy. *Folk Fashion,* London: I.B. Tauris & Co. Ltd., 2017.

Chapter 9

Barkare-Yusuf, Bibi. "Fabricating Identities: Survival and the Imagination in Jamaican Dancehall Culture." *Fashion Theory Journal of Dress, Body and Culture*, 10, no. 4 (2006), 461–83.

Buckridge, Steeve O. *The Language of Dress: Resistance and Accommodation in Jamaica, 1750–1890*. Kingston: University of West Indies Press, 2004.

Cooper, Carolyn. "Dancehall Dress: Competing Codes of Decency in Jamaica." In *Black Style*, Carol Tulloch. London: V&A Publications, 2004, 68–83.

Gregory, Davinia. *"A Tale of Two Houses: Tracing Transitory Changes to Two Jamaican Social Classes through their Micro-cultures of Sewing in the Independence Period (1960–1970)." TEXTILE*, 16, no. 2 (2018), 126–45.

Saucier, Paul Khalil. "Cape Verdean Youth Fashion: Identity in Clothing," *Fashion Theory*, 15, no.1 (2011): 50–66.

Tulloch, Carol. "Out of Many One People: The Relativity of Dress, Race and Ethnicity to Jamaica." *Fashion Theory*, 2, no. 4 (1998), 359–82.

Tulloch, Carol. "No Place Like Home. Home Dressmaking and Creativity in the Jamaican Community of the 1940s and 1960s." In *The Culture of Sewing, Gender, Consumption and Home Dressmaking*. Edited by Barbara Burman, 111–25. London: Berg, 1999.

Chapter 10

Emery, Joy Spanabel. *A History of the Paper Pattern Industry*. New York: Bloomsbury, 2014.

Fenby, Jonathan. *The History of Modern China, The Fall and Rise of a Great Power 1850–2008*. New York: Penguin, 2008.

Finnane, Antonio. *Changing Clothes in China, Fashion, History, Nation*. London, Hurst, 2007.

Goodman, Byrna and David Goodman. *Twentieth Century Colonialism and China: Localities, the Everyday and the World*. Abingdon, UK: Routledge, 2012.

Jun, Liao and Xu Xing, *Zhong Guo Fu Shi Bai Nian*. Shanghai: Shanghai Cultural Publishing, 2009.

Kidd, David. *Peking Story: The Last Days of Old China*. New York: Review Books Classics, 2003.

Ladds, Catherine. "China and Treaty-port Imperialism." In *The Encyclopedia of Empire* 1–6. New York: Wiley Publications, 2016.

Li, Zhao and Liu RuiPu, *Min Guo Chu Nian Ban Bu De Fu Zhi Kao Lun*, 25–31. Academic Fashion Guide, 2016.

Ling, Wessie. "Chinese Modernity, Identity and Nationalism: The Qipao in Republican China." In *Fashions: Exploring Fashion through Cultures,* 79–89. Oxford: Inter-Disciplinary Press, 2012.

Medley, Margaret. *The "Illustrated Regulations" for Ceremonial Paraphernalia of the Ch'ing [Qing] Dynasty*. London, Han-Shan Tan, 1982.

Meissner, Werner. "China's Search for Cultural and National Identity from the Nineteenth Century to the Present." *China Perspectives*, 68 (2006): 41–54.

Scott, A.C. *Chinese Costume in Transition*. Singapore: Donald Moore, 1958.

Steele, Valerie and John Major. *Decoding Dragons: Clothing and Chines Identity*. New Haven, Yale University Press, 1999.

Thorp, R.L. *Son of Heaven, Imperial Arts of China*. Son of Heaven Press, 1988.

Tsai, Wen-hui. *From Tradition to Modernity: A Socio-historical Interpretation on China's Struggle Toward Modernization Since the Mid 19th Century*. Occasional Papers/ Reprint Series in Contemporary Asian Studies, 1986.

Tsui, Christine. *China Fashions: Conversations with Designers*, 3. London: Berg, 2009.

Wilson, Verity. *Chinese Dress*. London: V&A, 1990.

Wilson, Verity. "Dress and the Cultural Revolution." In *China Chic: East Meets West*, 172–8. New Haven, Yale University Press, 1999.

Ye, Sang. "From Rags to Revolution: Behind the Seams of Social Change." In *Evolution and Revolution, Chinese Dress, 1700s–1900s*, 46–7. New York: Powerhouse Publishing, 1997.

Zujie, Yuan. *Dressing for Power: Rite, Costume, and State Authority in Ming Dynasty China*. New York, Springer-Verlag, 2007.

Chapter 11

Altay, Fikret. *Kaftanlar*. Istanbul: Yapi ve Kredi Bankasi Yayinlari, 1979.

Argit, Betul Ipsirli. "Clothing Habits, Regulations and Non-Muslims in the Ottoman Empire." *Journal of Academic Studies*, no. 6–24 (2005), 79–96.

Atasoy, Nurhan, Walter B. Denny, Louise W. Mackie, Serife Atlihan, and Hulya Tezcan. *Ipek, the Crescent and the Rose: Imperial Ottoman Silks and Velvets*. London: Azimuth Editions, 2001.

Baker, Patricia L. *Islamic Textiles*. London: British Museum Press, 1995.

Bilgen, Sidika. "Osmanli Donemi Turk Kadin Giyimi." PhD dissertation, Sosyal Bilimler Enstitusu Gazi Universitesi, 24, 1999.

Denny, Walter B. "Ottoman Turkish Textiles." *Textile Museum Journal*, no. 3–2 (1972), 55–66.

D'Ohsson, Mouradgea. *18. Yuzyıl Turkiye'sinde Orf ve Adetler*. Istanbul: Kervan, 1977.

Elliot, Matthew. "Dress Codes in the Ottoman Empire: The Case of the Franks." In *Ottoman Costumes: From Textile to Identity*, 103–23. Edited by S. Fraoqhi and C.K. Neumann. Istanbul: Eren, 2004.

Ersoy, Ahmet. "A Sartorial Tribute to Late Tanzimat Ottomanism: The Elbise-i Osmaniyye Album." *Muqarnas-New Haven*, no. 20 (2003): 187–207.

Fletcher, Ben, Mehlika Orakcioglu, and Ismail Orakcioglu. "Enclothed Cognition and Hidden Meanings in Important Ottoman Textiles." *Textile: Journal of Cloth and Culture*, no. 14–3 (2016), 360–75.

Forster, Edward Seymour. *The Turkish Letters of Ogier Ghiselin de Busbecq, Imperial Ambassador at Constantinople, 1554–1562: translated from the Latin of the Elzevir edition of 1663.* Baton Rouge: Louisiana State University Press, 2013.

Gorunur, Lale and Semra Ogel. "Osmanli kaftanlari ile entarilerinin farklari ve kullanilislari." *İTÜDERGİSİ/b*, no. 3–1 (2006), 59–68.

Gunduz, Filiz O. and Serife Gulcu. *"Osmanli Donemi Kaftanlaiına Yeni Yorumlar."* Konya: Selcuk Universitesi, 2003.

Gumuser, Tulay. "Contemporary Usage of Turkish Traditional Motifs in Product Designs." *Idil Sanat ve Dil Dergisi*, no. 5–13 (2012), 218–30.

Humphreys, Michael and Andrew D. Brown. "Dress and Identity: A Turkish case study." *Journal of Management Studies*, no. 39–7 (2002), 927–52.

Inalcik, Halil. *The Ottoman Empire: 1300–1600.* London: Hachette, 2013.

Inalcik, Halil and Donald Quataert. *An Economic and Social History of the Ottoman Empire: 1300–1914.* Cambridge: Cambridge University Press, 1994.

Ipek, Selin. "Ottoman Fabrics During the 18th and 19th Centuries." In *Textiles and Politics: Textile Society of America 13th Biennial Symposium Proceedings*, 18–22 September: Washington DC. 2012.

Jirousek, Charlotte. "More than Oriental Splendor: European and Ottoman Headgear, 1380–1580." *Dress*, no. 22 (1995).

Jirousek, Charlotte. "Ottoman Influences in Western Dress." In *Ottoman Costumes: From Textile to Identity*, edited by S. Fraoqhi and C.K. Neumann, 231–51. Istanbul: Eren, 2004.

Jirousek, Charlotte. "The Kaftan and Its Origins," In *Berg Encyclopedia of World Dress and Fashion: Central and Southwest Asia*, edited by G. Vogelsang-Eastwood, 134–8. Oxford: Berg Publishers, 2010.

Koc, Fatma and Koca Emine. "The Westernization Process in Ottoman Women's Garments: 18th Century–20th Century." *Asian Journal of Women's Studies*, no. 13–4 (2007), 57–84.

Koc, Fatma and Emine Koca. "The Clothing Culture of the Turks and the Entari (Part 1: History)," *Folk Life,* no. 49–1 (2011), 10–29.

Koca, Emine and Fatma Koc. "Kiyafetnameler Ve Ralamb'in Kiyafet Albümün'deki 17. Yüzyil Osmanli Toplumu Giysi Özelliklerinin Incelenmesi." *Electronic Turkish Studies.* no. 9–11 (2014), 371–94.

Micklewright, Nancy. "Ottoman Dress." In *Berg Encyclopedia of World Dress and Fashion: Central and Southwest Asia,* edited by Gillian Vogelsang-Eastwood, 126–33. Oxford: Berg Publishers, 2010.

Okumura, Sumiyo. "Garments of the Ottoman Sultans," 2018. http://www.turkishculture.org/textile-arts-159.htm

Phillips, Amanda. "Ottoman Hil'at: Between Commodity and Charisma." In *Frontiers of the Ottoman Imagination: Studies in Honour of Rhoads*, edited by M. Hadjianastasis, 111–138. Leiden: Brill, 2015.

Quataert, Donald. "Clothing Laws, State, and Society in the Ottoman Empire, 1720–1829." *International Journal of Middle East Studies*, no. 29–03 (1997), 403–25.

Quataert, Donald (ed). *Consumption Studies and the History of the Ottoman Empire, 1550–1922: An introduction.* Albany: SUNY Press, 2000.

Quataert, Donald. *The Ottoman Empire, 1700–1922.* Cambridge University Press, 2005.

Sahin, Yuksel. "Topkapı Sarayı Müzesinde Bulunan Bir Grup Kaftanın Dikiş Kalıpları Ve Anadolu Giysileriyle Benzerlikleri." *Folklor/Edebiyat Dergisi*, no. 10–37 (2004), 197–225.

Scarce, Jennifer. "Principles of Ottoman Turkish Costume." *Costume*, no. 22–1 (1988), 13–31.

Smith, Charlotte Colding. "Depicted with Extraordinary Skill: Ottoman Dress in Sixteenth-Century German Printed Costume Books." *Textile History*, no: 44–1 (2013), 25–50.

Suslu, Ozden. "Topkapı Sarayı ve Türk İslam Eserleri Müzelerinde Bulunan XVI. Yüzyıla ait Osmanlı Minyatürlerindeki Kumaş Desenlerinin İncelenmesi." *Sanat Tarihi Yıllığı/Journal of Art History*, 6 (1976), 215–78.

Tezcan, Hatice. "16.–17. Yüzyıllarda Osmanlı Sarayında Kadın Modası." *P Dergisi*, 12 (1999), 54–69.

Tezcan, Hülya. "16. Yüzyıldan 20. Yüzyıla Türk Kumaş Sanatı." *Türkiye'miz Kültür ve Sanat Dergisi*, no. 58 (1989), 28–37.

Tezcan, Hülya. *Osmanlı Sarayının Çocukları: Şehzadeler Ve Hanım Sultanların Yaşamları Giysileri.* Istanbul: Aygaz, 2006.

Türkoglu, Sabahattin. *Tarih Boyunca Anadolu'da Giyim-Kuşam.* Istanbul: Garanti Bankası, 2002.

Wearden, Jennifer and Marianne Ellis. *Ottoman Embroidery.* London: Victoria and Albert Museum, 2001.

Williamson, Adam. "Biomorphic Art: The Art of Arabesque," 2018. http://artofislamicpattern.com/resources/introduction-to-islimi/

Yaman, Bahattin. "Fit for The Court: Ottoman Royal Costumes and Their Tailors, From the Sixteenth to Eighteenth Century." *Ars Orientalis*, no. 42 (2012), 89–101.

Yarwood, Doreen. *The Encyclopedia of World Costume*, 321. New York: Bonanza Books, 1986.

Index